Visions of En

Talking Images Series

edited by Yann Perreau

Series ISSN 1744-9901

Visions of England: class & culture in contemporary cinema Paul Dave

Film Fables Jacques Rancière

Cinema: *the archaeology of film & the memory of a century* Jean-Luc Godard & Youssef Ishaghpour

Forthcoming:

The Hollywood Interviews: *the return of the directors* Nicholas Saada

Film World: *the directors' interviews* Michel Ciment

Visions of England
Class and Culture in Contemporary Cinema

PAUL DAVE

Oxford • New York

First published in 2006 by
Berg
Editorial offices:
1st Floor, Angel Court, 81 St Clements Street, Oxford, OX4 1AW, UK
175 Fifth Avenue, New York, NY 10010, USA

Berg is the imprint of Oxford International Publishers Ltd.

Library of Congress Cataloguing-in-Publication Data

Dave, Paul.
  Visions of England : class and culture in contemporary cinema / Paul Dave.
    p. cm. — (Talking images series)
  Includes bibliographical references and index.
  ISBN-13: 978-1-84520-293-4 (pbk. : alk. paper)
  ISBN-10: 1-84520-293-7 (pbk. : alk. paper)
  ISBN-13: 978-1-84520-292-7 (hardback : alk. paper)
  ISBN-10: 1-84520-292-9 (hardback : alk. paper)
  1. Motion pictures—Great Britain. 2. England—In motion pictures. 3. Social
classes in motion pictures. I. Title. II. Series.

  PN1993.5.G7D38 2006
  791.43'6552—dc22
                                                                    2005034776

British Library Cataloguing-in-Publication Data

A catalogue record for this book is available from the British Library.

ISBN-13 978 1 84520 292 7 (Cloth)
ISBN-10 1 84520 292 9 (Cloth)

ISBN-13 978 1 84520 293 4 (Paper)
ISBN-10 1 84520 293 7 (Paper)

Typeset by JS Typesetting Ltd, Porthcawl, Mid Glamorgan
Printed in the United Kingdom by Biddles Ltd, King's Lynn

www.bergpublishers.com

In memory of my son Thomas.

Contents

Acknowledgements

This book has its origins in the mid 1990s when I was working as a part-time teacher in London. I owe a lot to the students I was fortunate enough to have in my adult education classes at Birkbeck College, Morley College, City Literary Institute, City University and Merton College. At the same time I began teaching at the University of East London where most of the book was written and where I was lucky to benefit from the friendship and learning of Michael O'Pray. I would also like to thank my other colleagues and friends at UEL over the years, including Gill Addison, David A. Bailey, Guy Barefoot, Hugh Bowman, Emma Burchfield, David Ellis Butler, Andrew Branch, Andrew Calcutt, Christine Clegg, Pauline De Souza, Maxine Duggan, Ray Durgnat, Nadine Edwards, Frida Eriksson, Paul Gormley, Russell Hedges, Jeanette Ioannou, Ray Kiely, Ulysses Lyons, Iain MacRury, Robert Miller, Mark Nash, Jill Nelmes, Biddy Peppin, Aaron Petten, Judith Preece, Sara Preibsch, Susannah Radstone, Debbie Raymond, Kelly Robinson, Alka Seghal, Andrew Stephenson and Christine Sprengler. The Department of Social Sciences, Media and Cultural Studies at UEL granted me research leave in the autumn of 2004 which enabled me to finish the book.

Outside UEL I received encouragement from the editorial teams of the *New Left Review* and *Historical Materialism*. Robin Blackburn, Sebastian Budgen, Gareth Dale, Esther Leslie, Julian Stallabrass, Ben Watson, Ellen Wood and Andrew Wright offered help and advice and all of them, in different ways, represented for me models of engaged intellectual activity which I have found sustaining. Patrick Keiller generously responded to my many requests for information. For their advice and encouragement thanks to George Barber, Thomas Elsaesser, Andrew Higson, John Hill, Steve Neale, Chris Walker and Mike Wayne. My editor, Tristan Palmer, intervened at a decisive stage in this project and I am grateful to him for all his help. Thanks also to my parents, Brenda and Shivraj Dave, who have helped to shape my long fascination with Englishness.

This book took me away from Julia and our children – Anne, Gabriel and Jesse – for long hours and sometimes days. This is something I will always hold against it. Without Julia this book would never have been started or finished.

I would like to thank Routledge Press for permission to reproduce material from my essay 'Representations of Capitalism, History and Nation in the Work of

Patrick Keiller' in J. Ashby and A. Higson (eds), *British Cinema: Past and Present*, 2000, pp. 339–51. Also I would like to thank the editors of *Film International* for permission to reproduce material from my essay 'Apocalypse, Millennium, Jubilee', *Film International*, Issue 10 2004. Finally, I would like to thank the editors of *New Left Review* for permission to reproduce some material from my essay 'Heritage Cinema and the Bourgeois Paradigm', *New Left Review*, 224, 1997.

Figure 1 *Robinson in Space* (1997) – Reading Routemaster. Courtesy of the BFI

Preface

A few years ago I began making a film in which I hoped to explore the peculiarities of the renowned English culture of class. My research included the following: the children's fiction of C.S. Lewis and Philip Pullman; the history of Newgate Prison; the films of Michael Powell and Emeric Pressburger; the illuminated poems of William Blake; the writings of that group of post-war historians now collectively referred to as the British Marxist Historians; the film adaptations of the adventures of Baroness Emmuska Orczy's fictional, counter-revolutionary gentleman hero, Sir Percy Blakeney, codename: *The Scarlet Pimpernel*; the history of Marble Arch; the novels of Charles Dickens and their film adaptations, in particular *Great Expectations* (1946); the conflicts of the English Revolution, especially in the year of 1649; the early-eighteenth-century war between the Atlantic pirates and the English State; and the Gordon Riots of 1780. The film is not finished; however, its guiding ideas are the same as those which prompted the writing of this book. If you asked me to summarise those ideas then I might say something like this:

> *Englishness*, the historically hegemonic form of *Britishness*, provides a repertoire of class images – the infamous *English class system* – which strenuously seeks to contain the distorting pressures of Britain's 'peculiarly capitalist' past and present.[1] The idea of a national obsession with class needs, therefore, to be expanded upon – that obsession has less to do with some English national 'character' and more to do with the containment of class struggle. The enchantment of Englishness is the dissociation of class and class struggle or, what amounts to the same thing, class and capitalism.

The thesis that Britain is historically hypercapitalist or 'peculiarly capitalist' and that cultures of Englishness can be understood as an elaborate containment of the destabilising forces of this history is taken from the work of Ellen Meiksins Wood.[2] She argues that England is the birthplace of capitalism as a systemic social form and that its culture is indelibly marked by this fact.[3] In my own film I used an opposition between *teatime* and *bedtime* to capture the tensions within the English culture of class. The English vision of teatime – fetishistically displayed in countless British films – with its complex, class-coded rituals, sought to hold in place an exquisitely ordered, hierarchical 'imaginary community'.[4] It does not

take much to set this vision of Englishness spinning out of control into what
might be called the *turmoil beyond the teapot*. As the promotional blurb for the
high-English, class-anatomy of *Gosford Park* (2001) has it: *Tea at 4, murder at
Midnight!* [5] So much presses in around the national tea-table – the expropriations
of the commons; the Atlantic slave trade; the profits of the East India Company; the
dietary habits of the world's first mass proletariat; and a whole intercontinental
saga of struggle and historic upheaval.[6] These are stories that are rarely directly
addressed in the culture of Englishness – they may yet find a place for themselves
in future cultures of Britishness, as is suggested, for instance, by the films of the
black workshop movement of the 1980s, notably Black Audio Film Collective's
Handsworth Songs (1987).

   Again, in the context of my own film, I thought of these untold stories as bedtime ones whose attractiveness lay in their promise to break the enchantments of
teatime.[7] Indeed, it is precisely the 'disenchantment' of England that melancholic
conservatives like Roger Scruton lament.[8] For Scruton contemporary historical
accounts of a vigorous Britishness, such as that provided in Linda Colley's
influential book *Britons*, fail to register the true Englishness of the Britain of
the past, along with the ultimate Englishness of the British Empire.[9] Indeed, as
Scruton puts it:

   Only one group of Her Majesty's subjects saw itself as British – namely, those
   immigrants from the former Empire who seized on the idea of British nationality as a means of having no real nationality at all, certainly no nationality that
   would conflict with ethnic or religious loyalties, forged far away and years
   before. There were black British or Bangladeshis, but not black or Bangladeshi
   English; and there were few black British who saw themselves primarily as
   subjects of the English Crown.[10]

As David Cannadine argues, the British Empire and the English class system
worked symbiotically to strengthen one another, producing what he calls a
distinctive 'ornamentalism'.[11] When film historians point to the regressive
romances of empire to be found in 'heritage' films such as *A Passage to India*
(1984) they are identifying the residues of this same, historically tenacious
'ornamentalism'.[12] The post-war process of decolonisation has made its own
contribution to the weakening of these resources of the spectacle of class.
However, the 'containing' role of the English culture of class – its attempt to
direct our understanding of the national past and present in particular ways
– still requires contesting, especially in an era in which an ethnically diverse,
regionally specific, multinational, socially heterogeneous Britain is struggling to
assert itself. A Britain of complexly interwoven, hybrid identities such as those
evoked in films like *My Beautiful Laundrette* (1985), *Young Soul Rebels* (1991),
Bhaji on the Beach (1993) and *East is East* (1999), needs to be counterposed to

nostalgic representations of Englishness and class to be found in key examples of the stylish and brash *Brit* flicks of the late 1990s drawn from the gangster cycle or the so-called 'post-heritage' film.[13]

However, when we consign a certain kind of Englishness to the past it is important to remain vigilant about what goes along with it. It is one thing to celebrate the reinvention of the contemporary nation through its diverse cultures and experiences, but it is something altogether different if this hopeful, inclusive, 'convivial', multicultural Britain is posed against not just the backward-looking obsessions of Englishness but of 'class' itself.[14] That is to say, if the 'imagined community' of England is losing its grip, then for many 'class struggle' and even 'the working class' have an equally archaic ring to them. (I will address the theme of the 'disappearing' working class in *Brassed Off* (1996), *The Full Monty* (1997), *Among Giants* (1998), *Dockers* (1999), and *Billy Elliot* (2000), all of which are, to varying degrees, elegies for an older, industrial, northern working class.) Rather than endorsing notions of working-class disappearance or the perennially revived myths of a general classlessness, I will be concerned with exploring the ways in which changes in the experiences of class have worked their way into contemporary British films. For example, many since 1979 have imagined the working class as sucked into 'underclass' swamps or co-opted by 'Thatcherism'.[15] To what extent, however, are films like *Nil by Mouth* (1997) or *Trainspotting* (1996) best approached through such concepts as the working-class 'underclass'? In various places I examine representations of the 'underclass' and seek to show how they reveal more about a complex range of middle-class attitudes towards the working class than they do about any contemporary reappearance of the *lumpenproletariat* – a more venerable class categorisation that I explore in my discussion of *Performance* (1970) in Chapter 5.

Altering the angle of vision, how might the changes in middle-class cultural and political horizons in recent years have worked their way into what have been called 'fairy-tale' films centred on London – including *Sliding Doors* (1997), *Notting Hill* (1999), *Bridget Jones's Diary* (2001) and *Bridget Jones: The Edge of Reason* (2004)?[16] In the case of *Sliding Doors* I will seek to show how, in the peculiarity of its narrative form and generic patterning, instabilities and cracks in the category of the middle class open up – especially as the central character is placed within the force field of the neo-liberal labour market. This 'neo-liberal' capitalism, whose ideological traces I have sought out in the various films featured in the book, is to be understood as an 'advanced' form that has travelled back to its fundamentalist 'market' roots. 'Neo' signals the return of 'free' market after the post-war interlude of social democratic regulation. 'Liberal' signals that any such regulative, welfarist tampering with the market is to be viewed as an infraction of the 'liberty' of capital.[17] Again, as we will see in the analysis of *Sliding Doors* and in the discussion of representations of the working class in Chapter 3, this form of capitalism has a particularly invasive relationship to working-class lives and indeed to the very category of the 'worker'.

In the writing of this book I have found Wood's work on capitalism, class and Englishness crucial for a number of reasons. First, she has sought to give a historically specific account of the origin of capitalism that helps to conceptually clarify its systemic features.[18] (In this respect, I have drawn extensively on her discussion of what she calls the 'bourgeois paradigm'[19] and the 'commercialisation model' of capitalism.)[20] As we will see in Chapter 7, at a time when neo-liberal capitalism is in danger of becoming thoroughly naturalised and of appearing triumphantly illimitable, such historical and conceptual limiting is important. Second, she has systematised the theoretical underpinnings of a tradition of Marxist historiography in which class is understood in terms of the experience of struggle.[21] This takes class out of the classificatory, taxonomic realm that is so assiduously cultivated in the *English class system* and relocates it at the heart of the *capitalist system* where processes and relationships of exploitation and competition rule.

If, as Wood insists, class acquires its most fundamental characteristics because of its position at the heart of the capitalist system, then it follows that an attention to shifting representations of capitalism needs to be a central part of this study. Consequently, in different places in the book, I have attempted to track those contemporary metamorphoses of capitalism in which it appears as *millennial*, *occult, gentlemanly, peculiar* and *commercial*. I will argue that these different 'faces' of capitalism represent a process of evasion, an ideological process whereby the constraints of the capitalist system are mitigated, denied and even transformed into their opposites. Thus, imaged as *millennial*,[22] capitalism becomes a kind of achieved utopia – I will look in Chapter 2 at those 'fairy-tale' London films of the 1990s and beyond which depend on an *idyllic* denial of the logic of capitalism as a social form. Pictured as *occult*, capitalism becomes an irresistible force. In Chapter 7 I will look at how, in Iain Sinclair and Chris Petit's film *London Orbital* (2002), the occult functioning of neo-liberal capitalism is figured in terms of London's entrapment by dark forces. When presented as *gentlemanly*, social dilapidation and decay are understood as attributes of a *peculiar*, defectively English manifestation of capitalism's logic rather than as intrinsically unavoidable consequences of its systematic imperatives of profit maximisation, competition and exploitation. Again, in Chapter 6, I will look at these distinctions as they are presented in Patrick Keiller's *Robinson in Space* (1997). Finally, as an ahistorical image of the market, the *commercialisation* model of capitalism puts itself forward as the metabolism of human civilisation itself. I will examine this model of capitalism in Peter Ackroyd's writings in as much as they help to clarify the figurative structure of Sinclair and Petit's *London Orbital*. The commercialisation model of capitalism will also feature in my analysis of films as different as *South West 9* (2001) and *Snatch* (2000). Crucially, I argue that the representations of capitalism listed above intersect with and influence the representation of class in contemporary British film culture. Thus, to take the example of images of the working class as 'underclass', I suggest that what some have called the *millennial* image of neo-liberal capitalism enables and invigorates representations of working-class abjection, ruination and hopelessness. It does this by effecting a general shift in the location of social value – away from labour, and decisively towards capital.[23] To turn to the other end of the social scale, *gentlemanly* capitalism inflates the political significance of the aristocracy and diminishes that of bourgeoisie.

Finally, a note on the scope and structure of the book. Generally, the films discussed here fall into the period stretching between 1990 and the present. My choices are not intended to represent a survey of the national output during this time, but rather to help focus and develop the book's principles themes of class, capitalism and nation. (If I stray beyond this time frame – as I do in my chapter on *Performance* – then this is in response to a film which has acquired a pressing contemporary significance in the context of discussions of class and nation.) Just as the book is not exhaustive in terms of production trends, so it is also subject to an apparent narrowing of national focus, from British to English. (Again, this has been determined by the decision to focus on the ways in which images of Englishness affect our understanding of class.) I have, nevertheless, tried to offset this contraction with a countermovement. Thus, my interpretation of individual films regularly reinstates or seeks out a sense of the wider, supranational class contexts which Englishness has historically obscured. The 'Atlantic' perspective of the book – to be seen, for instance, in the readings of *South West 9*, *Performance* and *Jubilee* (1978) – emerges out of that attempt.

As for the book's structure, the Introduction seeks to give an explanation of the *relational* model of class I have adopted. It also provides a cursory account of the some of the shifts in the representation of class in British cinema since the 1930s – shifts which I present in terms of a metanarrative tracing the distance travelled from an emergent, social democratic national community in the early 1940s, to the neo-liberal fracturing of any such community in the 1980s and beyond. I have organised this material around a very particular view of the national cinema – that afforded by the critical concept of the 'pastoral' with its emphasis on *class relationships*. Finally, there is an extended discussion of an evolving British cinema of multicultural difference. Chapters 1, 2 and 3 trace representations of the classes in 'descending order', a concession to the deeply engrained, traditional metaphorics of class which is determined solely by reasons of presentational clarity. Chapter 1 looks at representations of the upper class found in 'heritage' films released since 1979. Chapters 2 and 3 concentrate on representations of the middle classes and the working class respectively. Chapters 4 and 5 look at class relationships. The latter analyses the countercultural bohemianism of *Performance*, and the former considers the peculiar class dynamic inscribed within *Trainspotting*, whose nominal class subject is the non-working-class 'underclass'. In Chapters 6 and 7 the focus is on capitalism and the ways in which its representation can affect our sense of class potential, history and politics.

Introduction
British Cinema and Class: Pastoral Visions

There is no universally agreed answer to the question – 'what is class?' However, we can, with some confidence, outline the theoretical crux of all thinking about class. As Wood puts it: 'There are really only two ways of thinking theoretically about class: either as a structural location or as a social relation'.[1] In broad terms, the model of class that will be used throughout this study is one which rejects the 'structural location' model with its Weberian emphases, in favour of a 'social relation' model associated with Marxism and historical materialism. In the former class is imagined in terms of social layers, strata, identities and groupings. This is what Wood calls the dominant 'geological' conception of class.[2] In the social relation model, class is understood as the force or relationship which shapes such identities and groupings. As Mike Wayne puts it in arguing for the priority of the historical materialist conception of class: 'Questions about the occupational or educational background [i.e. structural conceptions] of people do not begin to address how class is shaping these social phenomena'.[3]

To paraphrase Wood's account of this historical materialist approach to class, the shaping force or relationship referred to by Wayne is that which obtains between appropriators (the capitalist class) and producers (the working class) within the capitalist mode of production.[4] This relationship is exploitative because it obliges those who own nothing but their own labour power to sell it to those who dominate the capitalist marketplace through their ownership of the means of production. Or, to put it crudely, those who own the means by which life and livelihood can be secured enrich themselves at the expense of those whose socially essential labour sustains the system. Because this relationship is exploitative it necessarily induces contradictions, antagonisms and conflicts which cannot be contained in some restricted 'economic' realm and which spread ever outwards, affecting, in various subtle and not so subtle ways, all aspects of social life.[5]

Despite the clarity of this conceptual opposition between class understood as a *location* and class understood as a *determining relation*, there remains a tension which confuses things – a tension well described in Raymond Williams's analysis of the everyday vocabulary of class:

The middle class, with which the earners of salaries normally aligned themselves, is an expression of relative social position and thus of social distinction. The working class, specialised from the different notion of the *useful* or *productive classes*, is an expression of economic relationships. Thus the two common modern class terms rest on different models, and the position of those who are conscious of relative social position and thus of social distinction, and yet, within an economic relationship, sell and are dependent on their labour, is the point of critical overlap between the models and the terms.[6]

This 'overlap' then affects not just the middle class, whose very name suggests relative social position, but also the working class, which, despite its name, is also subject to considerations of relative social place or distinction. It needs to be added that as a descriptive category or as a marker of social distinction class appears to offer taxonomic assurances of social stability – metaphorically, the certainty of a *place* – whilst as an index of the fundamental terms of participation in the capitalist social system it works to undermine the illusion of social stability. The 'essential ambiguity' of class then is that its uses cover both the incitement to descriptive classification – what Williams refers to as the breaking down of class into 'smaller and smaller categories' – and social processes which cannot be meaningfully grasped in any such fashion.[7]

How do these definitions and troubled distinctions fit within a specific historical context such as that provided by what is called the 'English class system'? A good place to begin answering such questions is with Cannadine's synoptical account of the dominant perceptions of class in Britain from the early eighteenth century to the present.[8] Cannadine claims that these perceptions are rooted in three enduring, overlapping but nevertheless differently structured models of society – the hierarchical, the dichotomous and the triadic. The hierarchical model gives us society as a 'seamless web' of ascending distinction – differentiation is therefore most brilliant towards the social apex and most obscure towards the base.[9] The triadic model gives us three collective groups – upper, middle and lower. Finally, the dichotomous model provides an 'adversarial picture' of 'us' and 'them'.[10] All three models use the language of class. It is the hierarchical conception of class which, Cannandine argues, has 'had the widest, most powerful and most abiding appeal'.[11] As he explains:

In part this is because Britain retains intact an elaborate, formal system of rank and precedence, culminating in the monarchy itself ... But in addition, and more broadly, a Briton's place in this class hierarchy is also determined by such considerations as ancestry, accent, education, deportment, mode of dress, patterns of recreation, type of housing and style of life ... Taken together, it is these formal and informal hierarchies of prestige and status which people often have in mind when they speak of the 'British class system' ...[12]

This class system sustains, on a massive scale, Wood's 'geological' model of class. Cannadine provides a useful historical compendium of such class imagery, however, his conceptualisation of class confines it to matters of identity and consequently he is inclined to flatly reject Marxist approaches. Take the following justification he gives for the abandonment of Marxist approaches to British social history:

> Today, scholars are much more inclined to stress ... the general absence of clear-cut classes and of clear-cut class conflict, and the way in which different social groupings and identities merged easily and imperceptibly into one another in the seamless web of the social fabric ... With so many fluctuating and sometimes contradictory senses of identity, which constantly cut across each other, there no longer seems any justification for privileging class identity – or class analysis.[13]

Cannadine's argument takes us from a dismissal of Marxist-liberal metanarratives 'built around class formation, class conflict and political revolution' to the micropolitical complexities of a social world of multiple social identities evoked in this quote.[14] But whether we are talking of large, collective abstractions or small-scale groupings of individuals traversed by multiple lines of social affiliation, class is conceived of as identity. By contrast, for Wood, class cannot be adequately understood unless it is connected to capitalism. In turn, capitalism cannot be understood unless the social property relations it involves and the struggles that they entail are kept in sight. Therefore, Wood's conceptualisation of class starts with class struggle.[15]

That Cannadine is not unaware of the claims of this approach to class can be seen in his choice of the title for his book's second chapter, 'The Eighteenth Century: Class without Class Struggle'.[16] This is a jocular reworking of a famous E.P. Thompson essay entitled 'Eighteenth-Century English Society: Class Struggle without Class?'[17] Thompson, as Wood has argued, advocated a view of class in which the experiences of capitalist exploitation endured by diverse social groups establishes the basis upon which such groups might identify themselves in class terms.[18] However, as the title of his article suggests, it may sometimes be necessary to concentrate on class struggle in the absence of such class consciousness. Class struggle then is anterior to achieved class formation.[19] In inverting Thompson's formula, Cannadine actually offers a clear formulation of the ideological effect of the English class system. That is to say, when class and class struggle are separated the former loses its credibility as explanatory concept and becomes little more than a descriptive one. As such class can simultaneously be the central social fact or 'simply one element of social differentiation' amongst many others.[20] To view class in this way – as primarily a category of social differentiation – is to reduce it, as Colin Barker has argued, to 'merely one among a host of issues, of no greater significance than any other. Those who assert the especial importance of "class struggle" do, within this conception, seem to engage in the "economic reductionism" of which Marxism's critics regularly accuse them. Why "privilege" one form of "stratification" and "differentiation" over all others'.[21] But, as Wood's elucidation of Thompson makes clear, such accusations, in as much as they fail to engage with the idea of class as a relationship, misrecognise the significance of the 'Marxist' concept they are 'dismissing'.[22]

THE NAIRN–ANDERSON THESES

The English class system occupies center stage in the so-called Nairn–Anderson theses. Originally formulated in the early 1960s and added to since, a 'history of the classes' has been offered by Tom Nairn and Perry Anderson in response to what they perceive as a crisis caused by the long-term effects of the archaic British political system, its anachronistic class structure, and its inefficient economy.[23] In 1964 Anderson argued that the English revolution of the seventeenth century was 'the first, most mediated and least pure bourgeois revolution of any major European country'.[24] It occurred too soon for a fledgling bourgeoisie to fulfill its historic destiny as the agent of modernity, and although it resulted in the establishment of the economic conditions that would favour capitalism, unhappily it left intact an archaic social structure. Consequently, a rejuvenated, hegemonic *ancien régime* had no reason to modernise the social order and bourgeois subordination (economic, cultural and political) produced, in turn, a subordinate proletariat. This is a controversial account of national history, one in which the class system records the imprint of class *immobilism* and *compromise* rather than struggle and progress. Nairn has subsequently forcefully argued that Britain's pre-modern institutions, such as its monarchy, betray the persistence of an incomplete process of capitalist modernisation.[25] As Wood points out, for Nairn, class in Britain is not 'a recognizably modern, capitalist phenomenon'.[26] Instead it embodies a 'hierarchy of status and style' typical of pre-modern societies.[27] Nairn therefore puts 'class' into inverted commas to signify this difference – as such the 'class' system is to be understood as a pseudo-feudal *caste system*.[28]

As my brief summary reveals, there is a sliding in the Nairn–Anderson theses between English and British reference points. This is a result of their central argument that it is the impact of *England's* political history – its premature bourgeois revolution which nevertheless oversaw the successful transition to capitalism, and its enduring, unmodernised state – which determines the subsequent cast of *British* national identity. Wood is in agreement about the historical importance of England within the construction of Britishness, but she has a very different view of its significance. For her, Nairn and Anderson fail to pierce the surface archaism of Englishness.[29] She argues that there is a paradoxical relationship between the culture of Englishness, as it is transmitted through the class system, and the history of capitalism.[30] England is the birthplace of capitalism and English culture is the 'pristine' culture of capitalism – but it is a culture in which the convulsions that this historic rupture brought about have remained disguised. Oddly, this original culture of capitalism is the same one that is renowned for its self-conscious archaisms, of which the class system is the sustaining example.[31] That is to say, here we have a historically new social system (capitalism) that breaks down older methods of establishing hierarchies/inequalities (the 'extra-economic' distinctions of rank that accompany feudalism) but that nonetheless produces an ideologically effective afterimage of that older caste culture (the 'often ludicrous emphasis on matters of style, culture and language' or the 'pre-capitalist symbolism' that is at the heart of the class system as it mimics the old, inflexible distinctions of the feudal caste system).[32]

From Wood's perspective, Nairn's caste culture is an ideology of class which acquires its 'salience' in British culture and its priority over competing, typically modern ideologies (such as nationalism) because the conflicts that it was called upon to contain were those that were inherent in the social relations of the capitalist system.[33] It was not the unity of the 'body politic' (national unity) that was at stake in England, as it was elsewhere in Europe where, as a response to the historic parcellisation of sovereignties, *modern* nationalist ideologies developed and thrived.[34] In England such jurisdictional disputes were resolved through the agency of the Absolutist State prior to the Revolution of 1649. Here it was the disruption of social unity implicit in the competition and antagonism of the capitalist system that required a response – one provided by the hypertrophied imagery of class found in the English class system. Thus, to imagine England is to imagine a frozen unity of class differences. The most extreme polarisations of the class system – for instance the *patrician/plebeian* couple – often provide representations of essential Englishness rather than evidence of class struggle.

Furthermore, for Wood, Nairn and Anderson's approach to class history belongs to what she calls the 'bourgeois paradigm'.[35] This is her term for what she sees as the dominant model of historical change in Western culture.[36] It carries particular assumptions about the role of the classes and capitalism in those processes of change – she argues that it establishes inflexible links between capitalism, the bourgeoisie and modernity on the one hand, and the aristocracy, feudalism and pre-modernity on the other. The progressive movement of history involves the passage from the latter to the former, thus the aristocracy is to be understood as a strictly non-capitalist, agrarian, feudal class whilst the bourgeoisie is to be understood as a capitalist and urban class.[37] The problem with these assumptions, argues Wood, is that the actual development of capitalism in England contradicts such patterns of progression and class association.[38] Capitalist social relations developed first in agriculture and flourished with the involvement of aristocratic landowners. Indeed, when the data of the English class system is fed into the bourgeois paradigm what emerges is the illusion – perpetuated by Nairn and Anderson – that British capitalist modernity has somehow been forestalled by an aristocratic hegemony. As we will see in Chapter 6, Keiller's *Robinson in Space* destabilises such preconceptions about the historical roles of the aristocracy and bourgeoisie. It does so, in part, through a complex framing and scrutiny of English 'heritage spectacle' in which the latter ceases to offer support to Nairn–Anderson style judgments about national backwardness, and is instead seen to fit with the evidence of a thriving capitalist economy.[39]

THE PASTORAL

An important aspect of Keiller's *Robinson in Space* is its use of histories of oppression and exploitation to undermine traditional landscapes of English pastoralism. As Williams argues, the latter, with its projection of harmonious relations between the patrician and the rustic lower orders on the country estate, mystifies the social relations of agrarian capitalism – Wood's founding moment for the 'pristine culture of capitalism'.[40] Nevertheless, the pastoral remains a complex cultural form, producing a range of ambiguous political meanings, and it allows us to reflect on the changing representation of class relationships in British cinema. There are precedents for this – in his book on the construction of a national cinema in Britain from the 1920s to the 1990s, Andrew Higson places particular emphasis on the idea of the pastoral, which, following William Empson, he points out is not 'necessarily a question of subject-matter, but is an attitude, a perspective on social relations'.[41] That is to say, as the 'dominant mobilising myth of the British people' the pastoral cannot be restricted to classical rural idylls, such as those so often celebrated in the English heritage film from Cecil Hepworth's *Comin' Thro' The Rye* (1923) to Merchant and Ivory's *A Room with a View* (1985) and *Howards End* (1991).[42] It can just as easily be applied to the urban scene – Higson's case-study examples include the Gracie Fields vehicle *Sing As We Go* (1934) and the wartime story-documentaries *Millions Like Us* (1943) and *This Happy Breed* (1944). In both rural and urban contexts, the pastoral provides an image of the national 'community' as 'one large family whose common concerns ride above any sectional interests'.[43] The pastoral vision then offers a simplification and harmonising of the complexity of class and social relations that is common to heritage and documentary-realist films, two genres which for Higson have been central in the construction of a 'national' cinema since the 1910s and 1920s respectively. The range encompassed by these films – from the elevated milieu of the upper classes to the sphere of 'ordinary' people and 'everyday life' – is itself indicative of the pastoral's ability to bring into one frame of reference social extremes. Defined as a form which establishes self-conscious alliances across the social scale, the pastoral lies at the intersection of ideologies of class and nation and is a good example of Wood's argument, alluded to earlier, in which she insists on the historically specific importance of class ideologies in the English national mythos.

This pastoral myth of nationalism contains significant variations of emphasis. Nostalgic, conservative inflections as well as forward-looking and democratic ones are to be found in the history of British cinema, as Higson recognises. In the case of the heritage film, he sees evidence of a nostalgic ruralism which is posed against industrial democracy and the experiences of modernity. For instance, the heritage pastoral of a film like *Comin' Thro' The Rye* projects an image of social stability based on an 'upstairs–downstairs sense of class relations' within an 'organic community' in which 'social relations, always potentially antagonistic and exploitative, are presented as natural, even splendid'.[44] Higson aligns this aspect of the pastoral myth to Nairn's comments about English nationalism lacking authentic democratic roots – as he comments: 'Nairn suggests that the English mythology is ... dominated by patrician benevolence and popular deference to authority.'[45] From one point of view then, heritage pastoral seems to offer support for the Nairn–Anderson theses and the bourgeois paradigm underpinning them.

This debilitating patrician/plebeian mythology of Englishness that Nairn finds at the heart of British nationalism fits with what Terry Eagleton refers to as pastoral 'class collaborationism'.[46] We can pursue signs of this phenomenon not only in the heritage film but also in the history of popular film genres. A good place to start is with Sue Harper's work on costume film from the 1930s to the 1950s.[47] Within this genre Harper identifies an image of class which embodies an 'aristocratic/proletarian alliance' – she discusses its appearance in the films made by a number of directors and studios, including Alexander Korda's *The Private Life of Henry VIII* (1933), *The Scarlet Pimpernel* (1935) and *Lady Hamilton* (1941); Herbert Wilcox's *Nell Gwyn* (1934) and *Peg of Old Drury* (1935), and various Gainsborough Studios productions such as *The Man in Grey* (1943), *Fanny by Gaslight* (1944) and *Jassy* (1947).[48] One of the distinctive features unifying these films is the suggestion of a special relationship spanning the extremes of the class system. Furthermore, Harper argues that the images of the aristocracy they contain function according to the principles of what she calls *symbolic substitutionism*.[49] That is to say, the work of Korda and Gainsborough resonated with working-class and female audiences because their images of aristocratic style foregrounded issues of sexual pleasure, licence and political populism that tapped into the repressed desires and fears of such marginal social groups. Images of the aristocratic milieu figured the past as a place of potential liberation and offered a vision of social confidence and dexterity, a populist vision which, as Harper says, suggested that such gifts might be 'the property of all classes'.[50]

One imagines that Nairn and Anderson would see the celebration of patrician glamour in these films as consonant with the ideologies of Englishness that have accompanied their stalled history of the classes. Take the opposition which Harper establishes between Korda and Michael Balcon. The films whose production both men presided over pointed towards different ethics of leadership. Korda was entranced by the aristocratic figurehead, the *Scarlet Pimpernel*, as a source of 'symbolic power'.[51] Balcon's historical films at Gaumont-British – including *The*

Iron Duke (1935), *Tudor Rose* (1936) and *Rhodes of Africa* (1936) – 'focused on the middle classes' and supported a 'puritan ethic'.[52] In Harper's own prose then, the distinction between the two men suggests an analogy with the English Revolution – Balcon is the puritan and Korda, the cavalier. This historical short-hand, in which middle-class struggle and pain is contrasted with aristocratic success and pleasure, echoes Anderson's arguments about the centrality of the failures of the English 'bourgeois' revolution. As Harper says of Wilcox's film *Nell Gwyn*, 'The film ... presents the argument that the crucial class alignment is between the aristocracy and the lower classes; this negotiated alliance effectively excludes the middle class'.[53] Furthermore, Korda's obsession with the Scarlet Pimpernel might remind us of the significance of the French Revolution for Anderson – the English counter-revolutionary response to France marks that moment in which the aristocratic hegemony over the bourgeoisie is sealed.

Harper's reading of the films' 'social function' – their subtle handling of class and gender issues – certainly points to aspects of popular film that Nairn and Anderson's jaundiced view of the backward culture of Englishness would be unable to pick up.[54] Nevertheless, even if we resist reading the pastoral converg-ences of patrician/plebeian class polarities in terms of the Nairn–Anderson theses, Harper's insistence on these films' use of 'deeply-rooted' and resonant 'cultural topoi', encourages us to approach them from a longer historical view of English-ness and class.[55] In this respect, Wood's explanation of the role of class imagery as a means of screening-off class struggle might help us to address the *resonance* of cultural topoi such as those associated with the counter-revolutionary Scarlet Pimpernel. The Pimpernel myth seems structured around that fundamental image of ruling-class fear, a revolutionary 'mob' manipulated by its malcontented social superiors. It is from a French mob that the Pimpernel, in his disguise as a foppish Regency aristocrat, rescues aristocratic victims of a brutal revolutionary elite. It could be argued, however, that this image of the French mob has roots in an English one. Discourses of English nationalism draw a strong distinction between the bestial, revolutionary French lower orders and the anti-revolutionary 'maturity' of the English ones – it is precisely this maturity that forms one key aspect of the 'aristocratic/proletarian alliance'.[56] However, English history and culture are marked by the persisting anticipation and actuality of upheaval from below. As Eagleton has argued in his reconstruction of the origins of the 'aesthetic' in English culture, it needs to be remembered that ruling-class poise balances on the traumatic encounter with the lower classes in the revolutionary 1640s.[57] Post-revolutionary equilibrium was borrowed from an aristocratic style and did not represent the calm, organic evolution of the class's superiority and leadership but rather the active repression of the 'apocalyptic debate' of the mid seventeenth century.[58] Thus, if we take *The Return of the Scarlet Pimpernel* (1937), the cautionary relevance of the history of English class struggle is clear. In one scene the Pimpernel (Barry K. Barnes) likens the tyranny of Robespierre (Francis Lister) to that attributed to Cromwell – at the Pimpernel's prompting the

French remove Robespierre. Implicitly then the political wisdom of the English ruling classes is derived from uncomfortable experience.

Furthermore, it is not just the English and French revolutions that Sir Percy's complex persona responds to – the American Revolution has left its mark on him too. As Linda Colley points out, the traumatic loss of the American colonies triggered a 'patrician renaissance'[59] in which the ruling elite were obliged to demonstrate their 'patriotic utility'.[60] A central part of this cultural reshaping involved a rejection of patrician cosmopolitanism and particularly French fashion and styles in favour of, amongst other things, a new cult of martial heroism and state service, and a new regulation of sexuality in which a greater emphasis was placed on domesticity and even 'ostentatious uxoriousness'.[61] This shift from 'peacock male to sombre man of action' is clearly central to any understanding of the Pimpernel/Sir Percy opposition.[62] Thus, in *The Scarlet Pimpernel*, in public, Sir Percy (Leslie Howard) plays the role of an extravagantly fashionable, 'lazy nincompoop' who seems to have little interest in his wife, Marguerite (Merle Oberon), whilst in private he remains a courageous leader of men and a heartbroken husband. (He suspects the bourgeois Marguerite of involvement in the Terror.) It is as if the Pimpernel's domestic contortions act out the troubled history of his class.

Finally, we can relate the patrician bravura of the Pimpernel's class poly-morphism to the problem of class struggle. As Harper rightly observes, Baroness Orczy's original novel does not place the 'same degree of intensity' on this aspect of the Pimpernel's power.[63] The 1930s films revel in the class masquerades and impersonations in which Sir Percy demonstrates a class confidence that literally pretends to know the lower classes 'inside out'. Such performances necessarily imply a careful process of class-watching and cross-class scrutiny. It is interesting to note that, according to Thompson, spectacular, late-eighteenth-century, early-nineteenth-century ruling-class self-fashioning took place with an eye on internal, class-based threats as well as on external, national 'others'.[64] The Pimpernel myth's evocation of this historic moment of ruling class anxiety, along with its emphatic assertion of national unity over class conflict, was likely to resonate in the troubled decade of the 1930s. Whether or not this period deserved the nickname of the 'Devil's Decade', the social dislocation of the Depression certainly raised the issue of public order and the 'politics of the street' – precisely the domain in which the Pimpernel's most charismatic class impersonations take place.[65]

We can now return to Higson's second main component in the construction of a national cinema based on images of social unity – the documentary-realist film. Here he argues that in the documentary movement that gathered around John Grierson in the 1930s, and in the 'melodramas of everyday life' of the war years such as *This Happy Breed* and *Millions Like Us*, there was an attempt made to 'modernise and democratise the idea of heritage, by representing the mundane cultural traditions of the "ordinary people"'.[66] However, in the case of *This Happy*

Breed the representation of the nation clearly fits Nairn's disparaging remarks about the pre-modern forms of English nationalism – the film's 'conservative populism' is one in which 'traditional forms of political and social power' are ultimately re-affirmed.[67] *Millions Like Us*, on the other hand, with its stronger links to the documentary film movement and the 'broader field of social democratic cultural practice' that this movement drew on, does not just reproduce a pastoral vision of the nation in which class discord is harmonised, but also manages to convey the tense expectation that class conflict might, in the uncertain post-war future, crack open such communions.[68] As Higson remarks, the improbability of the film's romance between a northern, working-class foreman of a munitions factory and a southern, upper-class 'society' girl is directly addressed in a scene in which, ironically, the couple are placed in an 'idyllic rural setting'.[69] Despite this, as Higson also notes, the scene takes seriously the possibilities of social reform based on an appreciation of the common interests shared by these two representatives of the extremes of the class system in the conditions of wartime emergency. Expressing the hopes for and likely difficulties facing an egalitarian post-war future, this scene is a good example of the complex, ambivalent political effects generated by the pastoral. The humanism of this emergent social democratic culture, quickened by wartime collectivity, was perhaps most strikingly captured by Humphrey Jennings in films such as *Heart of Britain* (1941), *Listen to Britain* (1942), *Fires Were Started* (1943) and *A Diary for Timothy* (1946). In these films Jennings gave form to a national pastoral embodying what he elsewhere called the 'prismatic radiance of humanity'.[70]

Film historians agree that between the 1940s and the 1980s there was a progressive dislocation of the unity of the national community as imaged in wartime films. With propaganda necessities in abeyance, the very credibility of a 'secure social cohesion or moral and political consensus' built on the foundation of a knowable, 'family-community-nation' was stretched thin.[71] Thus, Ealing comedies such as *Passport to Pimlico* (1949) and *Whisky Galore* (1949) are only able to hang onto the idea of community through ingenious narrative devices that re-invoke wartime conditions of 'siege and insularity'.[72] In what Robert Murphy refers to as the 'riff-raff realist' films produced between 1945 and 1950 – roughly the period of the first post-war Labour government – that community is already being challenged by the figure of the 'spiv' or black-marketeer. Amongst the notable films in this cycle Murphy includes *Waterloo Road* (1945), *They Made Me a Fugitive* (1947), *It Always Rains on Sunday* (1947), *Brighton Rock* (1947), *The Third Man* (1949) and *Night and the City* (1950).[73] As Peter Wollen points out, spivs were viewed ambivalently in these films.[74] They were seen as parasites on the community's moral economy and at the same time as attractively reckless libertarians who managed to bring some relief from the oppressive, bureaucratic controls of post-war austerity and rationing.[75] Behind such complex films, with their ambivalence and stylistic exaggerations, one senses the struggle of post-war austerity and the difficulties involved in sustaining the Labour government's proposed 'new Jerusalem' in which there would be 'fair shares for all'.[76] The spiv stood for a market that was *black* and *free* rather than for the *regulated* one which was required to sustain social democratic 'community'. It is not surprising that discontent with post-war rationing and regulation expressed itself in terms of a fascination for those social figures whose lives suggested alternatives and in-between states of existence.

Challenges to that older, wartime idealisation of consensus and community are clear in the 'social problem' films of the early 1950s, and in the Northern 'New Wave' of the late 1950s and early 1960s. Thus, in the latter, individualised, male, working-class protagonists act out their personal dramas against a community which is little more than an inert or threatening 'backdrop'.[77] Later, with the collapse of the social democratic moment in the 1970s, and in the context of the deindustrialisation of the 1980s, the representation of the older working-class communities – especially northern ones – effectively disappears from British film.[78] However, by the mid 1990s, at a point when the period of Tory rule that had begun in 1979 was clearly struggling to maintain the earlier energy of New Right political and economic neo-liberalism, films expressing desires for cross-class solidarity and pastoral, 'national wholeness' began to re-appear.[79] *Brassed Off*, *The Full Monty* and *Up 'n' Under* (1997) are marked, to varying degrees, by such desires. For Julia Hallam such films represented a 'hankering' for 'Ealing ghosts' – that is to say for 'an idealised image of a nation united by adversity'.[80] However, despite this brief return of the imagery of northern working-class community, what marks the representation of class in the 1990s, when viewed from a wider perspective, is a split between a 'fairy-tale' world of privilege and an 'underclass' world of working-class origins. In Chapter 2, with the help of the work of Mikhail Bakhtin, I will be looking at a number of these contemporary 'fairy-tale' films in terms of a specific declension of the pastoral – the metropolitan *idyll*. *Notting Hill* provides a good example of the unruffled exclusivity and social segregation of these idylls. When such romantic comedies are placed against the social realist 'underclass films' of the same era the abiding impression created is of the unsurpassable social distance between the classes.

However, such distances do not lessen the compulsive desire to imaginatively explore class relationships. In this respect it is interesting to note that observers on contemporary British culture such as Julian Stallabrass[81] have identified a re-emergence of the tradition of urban pastoral which he traces back to William Hogarth and to what historians have called the vision of a 'chaotic and un-harmonious' London of the early eighteenth century.[82] The immediate context for Stallabrass's references to the urban pastoral is the work of those British fine artists of the 1990s that has been referred to collectively as *Britart*. Renaming this cultural formation 'high art lite', he describes it as a type of class voyeurism in which the middle classes wallow in the spectacle of abjection provided by a fractured and defeated working class – the latter being viewed as a 'lumpen', picturesque residue of its heroic past, often metonymically reduced to the

dilapidation of it own urban environment.[83] Avoiding the respectful sentimental-
ism for a national pastoral grounded in an industrial working-class of the past – the
elegiacs of *Brassed Off* and *The Full Monty* for instance – *Britart's* urban pastoral
apes the 'grossest and most clichéd outlines'[84] of the culture that it imagines
this marooned, 'unreconstructed working class' subsists on.[85] As Stallabrass puts
it, 'simple rural folk enjoying rustic pleasures have become replaced by the
characters of the inner city, similarly devoted in middle-class fantasy to the joys of
politically incorrect humour, the circulation of obscenities, the joys of violence,
crime and vandalism, carefree sexual encounters and drug-taking'.[86]

These obsessions are not restricted to the British artists and critics that
Stallabrass discusses; they are also prevalent in many contemporary British films,
particularly those associated with the 1990s revival of the gangster cycle.[87] In
films such as *Lock, Stock and Two Smoking Barrels* (1998) and *Snatch*, for instance, we are offered, as Steve Chibnall puts it, a 'Dickensian vision of a city
gone to seed, surviving as a grown-up playground for hustlers adept at "picking
peanuts out of poo"'.[88] The combination of an excremental vision of the city
and nostalgic images of 'unreconstructed' forms of working-class masculinity
found in Guy Ritchie's films fits closely with Stallabrass's account of the urban
pastoral in contemporary *Britart*. (I will return to Ritchie's films later in this
introduction.)

In sum, it is clear that the humanism of the wartime pastoral tradition has been
subject to a considerable deformation to produce a contemporary urban pastoral
which carries little sense of hope or even loss. Pastoral humanism of the type
expressed in Jennings's work is replaced by a voyeuristic feeling for the distance
between the middle-class connoisseurs of popular, demotic cultural forms and
the *underclass naturals* that embody them. Another way of putting this would
be to say that the ruins of the post-war 'new Jerusalem' – now the subject matter
for much of the urban pastoral – are no longer recognised as the disappointed
dreams supposedly once common to the middle class and the working class. To
an extent these ruins become an enigma for the middle class and they are viewed
'from a distance' in the manner that one might view 'the archaeological remains
of some disaster or the passing of an era'.[89]

Despite these differences between the present and the past, it is perhaps
important to note that the class voyeurism of the contemporary urban pastoral
is not entirely absent from the earlier national pastoral associated with the social
realist film of the 1930s and 1940s. Higson notes that the origins of this tradition
of film-making lie partly in the nineteenth-century bourgeois anthropological
literary genre of 'Unknown' or 'Darkest' England – a genre that can be seen
ironised in Iain Sinclair's gothic visions of Thatcherite London.[90] Sinclair's work
– the films and writings – has a complex relationship to this contemporary urban
pastoral. Rather than taking advantage of the spectacle of urban degradation
and neglect in the manner of a tourist 'of the inner city', Sinclair makes clear
his contempt for the culture of middle-class gentrification to which such a view

can be connected.[91] His London requires the uncomfortably close-up view of the obsessive.[92] That is to say, he generally locates himself in the scene rather than maintaining the necessary distance of the voyeur and consequently his visions, unlike those to be found in the contemporary urban pastoral, do not provide spectacles of debased simplicity for detached sophisticates. London and its inhabitants appear as bewilderingly complex as their erudite explorer.

Fundamentally, Sinclair, like Keiller, gives no credence to the idea that urban degradation is to be taken at face value. Instead, London and its surrounding territories are 'read' in the manner of a hieratic script that is saturated with the energies of an unappeased past or 'dark heritage'.[93] In *London Orbital* that past is represented by the ruined dreams of progressive civic metropolitanism. To an extent then, there is a faint afterimage of the pastoral's common humanity in Sinclair's work. However, it needs to be noted that there are those who argue that Sinclair fails 'to break out of the eroticising and colonising gaze of flaneurie' that is clearly a feature of the contemporary urban pastoral.[94] Indeed, as we shall see in Chapter 7, there is a distanced and problematically jaundiced view of the working class to be found in *London Orbital*.

BEYOND THE NATIONAL PASTORAL

For Higson, writing in the mid 1990s, the post-war collapse and disappearance of the social realist 'myth' of a 'consensual national community' culminates in a film such as *My Beautiful Laundrette* in which it is the multiplication of other, previously excluded 'local communities' that is critical.[95] This relatively recent emergence of a more inclusive British cinema whose representation of the national collective contains distinctively black, Asian and Celtic dimensions, is described by John Hill as providing a 'new sense of difference and even conflict'.[96] That is to say, this is a British cinema in which essentialised identities of ethnicity, gender, nation and sexuality have been deconstructed so that their internal contradictions, conflicts and differences become visible and significant. If *Trainspotting* and *Human Traffic* (1999) are 'Scottish' and 'Welsh', they are just as much films which undermine romanticised notions of their own cultural 'roots'. Similarly, the multiculturalism of *My Beautiful Laundrette* or *Young Soul Rebels* (1991) cannot be mistaken for an uncritical liberal pluralism in which social heterogeneity is understood as the unproblematic mixing of distinct and self-coherent identities. On the contrary, such films display the complexity of their characters' allegiances and relationships as well as their dispersed, often conflicted sense of cultural belonging. Thus, identity in *East is East* and the Hanif Kureishi scripted *My Son the Fanatic* (1997) is strung out between the forces of 'tradition' and 'translation'.[97] The desire for pure, unitary, cultural identities based on traditional certainties is pitted, in both films, against the wishes of those for whom identity is irretrievably caught up in the 'cultures of hybridity' which have arisen as a result of diasporas created through post-war, post-colonial migration.[98]

The lives of such characters are 'translated' in the sense that they must work across boundaries, exchanging and transforming cultural signs and identities in the process.[99] In films like these, the cardinal points of 'self' and 'other' are unstable – *east is no longer east and west is no longer west.*

But do such images of culturally hybridised identity screen-off other, more fundamentally divisive forces? For Slavoj Žižek, the struggles against racism, sexism and homophobia that are associated with the promotion of such images need to be distinguished, theoretically and politically, from class struggle.[100] He argues that liberal left multiculturalism seeks to transform 'antagonism into difference' and thereby produce a 'peaceful coexistence of sexes, religions, ethnic groups'.[101] In this way, social conflict is conceptualised as merely an obstacle for the 'recognition of differences'.[102] It is of course true that sexism, racism and homophobia prevent the recognition of the particular, human qualities of women, gay people and ethnic minorities, and that the defusing of such antagonisms through the moral obligations of respect and tolerance is an urgent task. However, for Žižek, the divisions of class demand to be 'aggravated' in order to sustain a process of struggle whose objective is not the tolerant recognition of the 'difference' between the working class and the capitalist class, but its abolition.[103]

How might such arguments affect our sense of a British, multicultural cinema? In a film like *Bend It Like Beckham* (2002) the project of multiculturalism as a social emollient is clear. The story revolves around the difficulties endured by Jess (Parminder Nagra), a Sikh teenager who is discouraged by her parents from pursuing her ambitions as a professional football player. Here Gurinder Chadha is dealing with issues common to her earlier film *Bhaji on the Beach*, issues concerning the conflict between tradition and contemporary forms of diasporic, cultural hybridity. However, the predominantly festive, comic tone of *Bend It Like Beckham* defuses the unresolved tensions of the earlier film and a suburban *mise en scène* enfolds all the characters and most of the action within its protective limits. *Suburbia* here represents a diffusion of cultural difference into a general atmosphere of gentle, unthreatening eccentricity which leaves the film's multicultural novelties, emblematised by a mixing of signs ('Beckham' and 'Aloo Gobi' in the promotional material), tinged with overtones of a familiar Englishness. A repeated wide-angle crane shot moves back from Jess's parents' house, dressed with fairy lights to celebrate a Sikh wedding, and locates it in an English suburban landscape. On one level this shot exposes and amplifies cultural and ethnic difference; however, equally, it suggests that Jess's family belongs precisely where it is. The effect is achieved by a careful use of space – the camera movement, on each occasion, presents a view of sky above the houses and grass in front of them. The scale of the shot is thus calibrated to convey a difference whose magnitude is just right – Jess's 'exotically' dressed house is neither hidden in an enlarged space nor looming in a cramped one. Indeed this particular shot, a wide-angle view of grass and skies, most often in saturated colour, within which

Figure 2 *Bend It Like Beckham* – Jess in her garden. Courtesy of Redbus Distribution and The Works TSC Ltd and Christine Parry

the characters are securely contained, forms a motif running throughout the film. Through such means, the drama of transgressed inter-ethnic taboo is dissolved in an expansive, colourful spectacle, one in which the environmental preconditions for peaceful co-existence are never in doubt. The symbolic location – the western suburban approaches to Heathrow – also helps to create this impression of freedom. Racism is located almost exclusively in the past – it is the function of Jess's father to carry the burden of racial misery as a memory. The scars of his exclusion from an English cricket club – an echo of Norman Tebbit's 'cricket test' – are, however, healed by playing cricket with his daughter's Irish boyfriend on what looks like another nostalgic benchmark of Englishness, the village green celebrated in John Major's empty Orwellianisms.[104] The sunny suburbanism of *Bend It Like Beckham* then offers a kind of *multicultural pastoral* which supports a vision of *difference and harmony* rather than Hill's expanded British cinema of *difference and conflict*.

To return to Žižek, if class difference represents a structural, systemic social antagonism that needs, from the perspective of Marxism, to be exacerbated and overcome, then it is by definition excluded from this 'feel-good' multicultural party. However, there is a brief moment during the girls' farewell scene at Heathrow when the difference of class, if not the antagonism of class struggle, does intrude. Victoria Beckham and David Beckham – the former, through her Spice Girls past, a participant in what Moya Luckett calls a 'superficial multiculturalism' – miraculously materialise in the transnational space of the airport.[105] Eerily impersonated by body doubles on an elevated walkway, their celebrity silhouettes offer a vision of updated national success, along with a beatific endorsement of the two girls who refuse to conform to the prejudices of tradition. (David Beckham operates as a kind of 'trademark' throughout the film as a whole.) The presence of these tutelary figures who – as members of an international elite – are beyond the material constraints impinging on the majority, cannot but help point to Žižek's *different kind of difference*, *class*.

For Wayne, it is the exclusion of this materialist dynamic that weakens other British Asian films and the cultural politics of difference generally.[106] He argues that the images of social solidarity that films such as Chadha's *Bhaji on the Beach* reach out to, neglect the problem of 'social being' – that is to say, they evade those manifold aspects of material existence structured by the determining power of class relationships which put such unity in doubt.[107] As he puts it, 'We need to recognise that cultural similarities and continuities may be fissured by material differences (such as between the Black middle and working class), while the culturally different (the Moslem from a Turkish family and the white Catholic from Irish descent) may well share the same material interests as they work on the supermarket checkout tills'.[108] Material differences/interests will undermine the most promising multicultural rainbows as well as, potentially, bind together those whose distance from one another, measured in the complex discriminations of cultural difference, seem unsurpassable.

At a glance, it might seem that the gangster films of Ritchie have no place in a discussion of the politics of multiculturalism. However, *Snatch* appears to operate, in part, as a parody of British multiculturalism and it thus provides an interesting comparison to *Bend It Like Beckham*, which, despite its weaknesses, has clearly embraced a vision of multicultural heterogeneity and mixing. *Snatch*'s cast of characters is nationally and ethnically diverse – pretend Jews, Scots, Greeks, Americans, Russians, Irish travellers and black British all feature. As well as providing diverse characters, both *Snatch* and *Lock, Stock and Two Smoking Barrels* present identity as 'performed'. There is an overlap here with the non-essentialist approaches to identity that became an aspect of black and Asian film-making from the 1980s.[109] In what Chibnall refers to as the 'gangster light' cycle, which, along with Ritchie's work, includes films such as *Love, Honour and Obey* (1999), *Honest* (2000), *Rancid Aluminium* (2000) and *Circus* (2000), identity is improvised, in process, and to be viewed as complex.[110] These films share a quality of 'faux-ness' by which Chibnall means they are characterised by 'a knowing theatrical distortion of real life, a mutually condoned simulacrum, that, by a typically postmodern conceit, is something better than the real thing'.[111] In *Love, Honour and Obey* performance becomes identified as part of the 'ontology' of crime; as Johnny (Johnny Lee Miller), the character making the most extreme identification with this position, says: 'All gangsters are performers.'[112]

Of course any similarity between these films and the theoretical project informing the cultural politics of difference is superficial and misleading. The masquerades and performances in Ritchie's films are wearily familiar ones which produce stereotypes of Englishness and masculinity rather than new, unforeseen 'libertarian, pluralistic, hybrid' identities and alliances.[113] Indeed, Pamela Church Gibson argues that these films constitute a 'gangsta heritage' in which *mockney* 'geezers' are moved around a London 'stage-set' which provides a 'nostalgic vision of unreconstructed working-class man'.[114] Identity may then be a performance, but what is performed is already well known – a combination of Englishness and the 'class system' which in *Lock, Stock and Two Smoking Barrels* involves cheeky cockney 'chaps' along with 'squires in their manor houses and gypsies in the woods'.[115] Cora Kaplan seems right to identify this cultural phenomenon, which is so prominent in Ritchie's work, with the Blairite repression of class in any form other than a 'retro-social performance'.[116]

The multi-character, multicultural breadth of *Snatch* is as misleading as its treatment of identity. That is to say, whilst the diverse characters interact without engaging in overt and familiar forms of racism, the film appears to want the spectator to adopt a certain knowing self-consciousness about this. At various points, Ritchie has different white, English characters express what is comically signaled to be an unnegotiable prejudice for 'pikeys' or travellers. (In *Lock, Stock and Two Smoking Barrels* the group which fills this hate-role is occupational – traffic wardens). In slyly referencing the kind of reflex illiberalism that seeks to challenge a multiculturalism it sees as fake and sentimental, Ritchie distances himself from what is called 'political correctness'. A related example in which metropolitan multiculturalism is looked at askance can be found in the Samoan pub scene in *Lock, Stock and Two Smoking Barrels*. Here, four white 'chaps' find it impossible to order a 'proper' drink! In contrast to the witty, hopeful combinations of quintessential Englishness and foreign 'otherness' to be found in films like *Bhaji on the Beach*, in this scene we are given what is represented as absurdly gratuitous foreign messing with a no-nonsense, un-improvable English cultural institution – the 'pub'. The sarcastic, self-cancelling cultural difference of the name of *Snatch*'s main character, 'Turkish' (Jason Statham), creates a similar effect. Turkish may carry an 'exotic' name but as a character he is prosaically English. Ritchie's films provide then a kind of paradoxical *politically incorrect multiculturalism*.

SW9: 'NOTTING HILL IT AIN'T!'

South West 9 includes a scene which unmasks Ritchie's combination of traditional Englishness and empty British multiculturalism. Sal (Nicola Stapleton), a racist 'Essex girl', brandishing a gun – which in *faux* style turns out to be a replica – and talking cod gangster-speak derided by her own brother as 'Neanderthal', is faced down by a young black girl, Rafaela (Zebida Gardener-Sharper), who places a flower in the barrel of the pistol. Taking the flower out Sal remarks: 'I hate hippies.' Conventionally this 'hate-speech' formula precedes violent action and given the 'race' of the girl one might expect the gun to be fired at this point. In putting the line in the mouth of an explicit racist, the film makes clear the implications of the kind of humour that Ritchie alludes to. Sal's act of self-censorship – 'hippy' replacing the racist demotic she uses with her brother – indicates how, for the 'politically incorrect', the protocols of multicultural tolerance merely euphemise other, more 'real', deeply embedded prejudicies. Political incorrectness, from this perspective, is revealed as a form of nostalgia for more forthright, unencumbered expressions of abuse which are nevertheless simultaneously recognised to be unavailable or 'Neanderthal' as Douser (Frank Harper) puts it.

   South West 9 also has difficulties with multiculturalism; however, as we will see, these problems are less to do with the authenticity of its embrace of a newly emerging Britain, and more a result of the awkward interaction of its multicultural themes with the problem of 'social being'. The name of the film's production company Fruit Salad Films, also the co-producers of *Human Traffic*, is itself indicative of the film's multicultural political ambitions. With its connotations of sexual and racial *mixing-it-up*, this name might more appropriately gloss the 1980s work of Stephen Frears and Hanif Kureishi. Indeed one of the metaphors organising the narrative in *South West 9* – 'the great south London wash' or the process whereby 'everything circulates' – appears to be an intertextual echo of *My Beautiful Laundrette*'s titular conceit. In both *My Beautiful Laundrette* and *Sammy and Rosie Get Laid* (1987) the idea of circulation focuses on the passage of sexual partners and 'races' as a means for moving towards the world as *fruit salad*. Both films are reliant on an idea of sexuality as a way of representing the specificities of individual difference and desire as they cut across established cultural boundaries. They also present sexuality as a force for progressive change – as Omar (Gordon Warnecke) says in *My Beautiful Laundrette* 'much good can come from fucking'. Thus, even if sex is to be understood as involving social and cultural contexts – rather than being a simple, 'humanist triumph over social obstacles' – the films do, nevertheless, create the impression that the mutuality of good sex represents the principal means of dissolving the divisions and antagonisms of 'race', gender, sexual preference.[117] This impression of the importance of sexuality is reinforced by the films' representation of the political negligibility, or worse, of the working class. As Hill points out, 'it is striking how absent the working class are from Kureishi and Frears's work' and how in both films the 'social network' explored is 'largely that of the professional classes and an urban "underclass"'.[118] This elision – working class into 'underclass' – not only reflects a sense of the changes wrought by deindustrialisation, it also carries overtones of a specific political judgment on the working class which was becoming commonplace by the late 1980s. As the disillusioned socialist Papa (Roshan Seth) puts it in *My Beautiful Laundrette*: 'The working class are such a great disappointment.'

We will see that, despite itself, *South West 9* is also inclined to reject the working class in its fantasies of political action. The film picks up on established, utopian multicultural tropes, in particular the image of intercultural mixing and circulation. It is structured around the interconnecting lives of six characters in Brixton (postcode: SW9), an area of London which the promotional blurb describes as unique in Britain for its 'diversity of characters' and its 'true street culture'.[119] These characters are presented in terms of cultural identities – 'crustie', 'trustafarian', ex-'yuppy', 'buppy', 'scammer', 'Essex' boy and girl – which are revealed to be misleading and partial. For instance, Helen (Orlessa Edwards) is a black City banker – hence buppy – who, sickened by her bank's involvement in facilitating arms trading to Sierra Leone, has become a secret anti-capitalist anarchist. It is around Helen's stolen briefcase and through the party organised by Essex boys Jake (Stuart Laing) and Mitch (Mark Letheren) in an abandoned Brixton church, that the characters are brought together.

The film's narration is presented figuratively as a form of musical mixing. The narrator – black, Brixton-born Freddy (Wil Johnson) – is repeatedly shown in a studio assembling the soundtracks that accompany his voice-over. The associated figure for this activity – what Freddy calls 'robbing sounds' and 'plaigarising the everyday' – is the church/dancefloor where, along with the hybridising musical genres and sub-genres of techno/acid/psychedelic trance, it is the diversity of people in motion that expresses the kind of multicultural optimism that is also to be found in Fruit Salad's earlier production, *Human Traffic*. Another key, socially convergent space in which music has an important presence is the Dog Bar – formerly a famous Brixton pub, The Atlantic. This is a space where the area's diverse inhabitants are shown, happy together.

However, the optimism in *South West 9* is counterbalanced in various ways. Mitch, for instance, demystifies ex-City trader Jake's party in the church as a form of entrepreneurial cynicism couched in the language of love and community.

(The party's buzzword is 'Faith'.) Later on Mitch is 'wasted' when he accidentally absorbs a large amount of LSD. His subsequent hallucinations are presented as both drug-induced paranoia and as a form of truth-telling. Of particular importance is the scene in the Dog Bar during which a slow-dancing, shamanic Mitch scopes the room. His judgment – 'many lines, but none of them connect' – draws attention to the possible failures of solidarity that lie concealed beneath the contingent criss-crossing of those in the bar. The clichéd pathos of his expression of a traditional kind of liberalism – as he helplessly puts it, the lack of *connection* is 'sad' – points to a problem such political aspirations share with more contemporary and energetically robust forms of the 'politics of difference'. This is the problem of establishing social solidarities upon 'temporary, transient', and contingent alliances.[120]

From a position similar to that of Žižek's, the political challenge of solidarity is not to make all lines converge but to clarify which lines belong to enduring, structural antagonisms (the divergent interests of class) and which need to be recognised as vectors of potential unity amongst those who are materially aligned but may not necessarily be culturally similar. Mitch's expression then of the problem of solidarity at the heart of the politics of cultural difference may be a weak one; however, the film does not leave this problem undeveloped. Freddy's narration insistently brings the multi-character narrative into a tightly plotted and linear configuration which leads to a confrontation, one in which diverse trajectories or, as Freddy puts it, cultures, 'collide'. This is the moment outside the church when all the characters find themselves facing one another and Mitch who is brandishing a gun. This event is anticipated at the beginning of the film through the use of a flash-forward and its significance is emphasised by a question posed by Freddy which hangs over the entire film: 'How the fuck did we end up like this, all of us?' On one level, the question is simply a narrative lure whose reference is to the process of viewing the film, following its plot twists and unravelling its enigmas. However, on another level this question is the prototypical form of all authentic political thought – which is to say, it seeks a collective consciousness of historically unfolding, socially determining, encompassing processes.

How then is this fundamental question explored in the film? The first thing to note is that Freddy's narration is characterised by a concern for historical contextualisation. Indeed the remarks he makes immediately preceding his critical question place his own narrative within the historical framework provided by Christian millennialism. Observing that we are entering the third millennium, he sarcastically compares Christ's 'message of love' with our present 'peak of evolution' as evidenced in 'micro-chips, mobile phones, satellites, jets, lasers and star wars'. These comments frame a contradiction between promise/hope/potential – whether spiritual or technological – and grim actuality that is developed throughout the film in further historical frameworks. Thus, English colonialism is cited – Walter Raleigh 'scoring tobacco for the western world' is presented in terms of the pleasures of the international/intercultural exchange of commodities and 'the culture of hedonism'. At the same time, this culture is associated with the wasted lives of those who now inhabit Raleigh's derelict former banqueting halls (the Smokehouse – a 'crack den'). In the scene in which Helen takes cocaine in the toilets of the Dog Bar, a montage of documentary footage links global traffic in drugs and arms with African wars – a process which we are informed later is directly overseen by the forces of global capitalism represented by her own City bank. Finally, within this history of international exploitation and devastation, Freddy's narration directs us, in the form of documentary interpolations, to the Atlantic, diasporic history of the post-war period. Footage of Brixton in the 1950s, a destination which Freddy tells us his migrant parents' generation viewed as the 'land of milk and honey', demands to be contrasted with footage of the Brixton riots of 1981. The film brings this history up to date with its images of the animated, 'convivial', syncretic culture seen for instance in the Dog Bar – images which are in turn counterposed to its analysis of the gentrification of contemporary Brixton.[121] Kat's (Amelia Curtis) anarchist squat is in the process of being forcibly reclaimed by the police. Here, post-1981 inner-city 'regeneration' is associated with the socially polarising effects of the market – 'regeneration', in the form of reclaimed property, is little more than the good fortune of those who can afford it.

In sum then, in answering Freddy's question, *South West 9* creates historical continuities which suggest a systemic logic in which processes of change whilst benefiting some, *waste* others. (From this perspective the 'all of us' referred to in the question begins to register the stresses of material forces.) As the film's narrating consciousness, Freddy is intimately aware of how these forces circumscribe individual fates and how they set the conditions in which collectives might emerge and might be split apart. For instance, in his concern for Mitch there is evidence of a wider identification with those who are being *wasted* in the Smokehouse which he supplies as a runner. However, at the same time, the film is conscious of the ways that material interests might also produce antagonisms which can undermine hopeful alliances. The insecurity of his material situation as a drug-runner not only pulls Freddy towards those suffering from the drugs economy – whether they are black or white, from 'Essex' or Brixton, from Britain or Africa – but also towards the 'ultra-cushy ride' enjoyed by his boss. In a scene that is presented as a flash-forward, alternative future, we see Freddy assuming his boss's controlling position in the Smokehouse. In this scene he is wearing the same t-shirt that we will see him wearing at the end of the film when his boss demands to know whether he is 'in or out' of the business. It is possible then that the earlier, imaginary 'bad-ending' is an actualised one.

Overall, however, the film seems deeply uncertain about the relationships between material interests, cultural identity and the development of forms of political consciousness. This can be seen if we take the keyword 'roots'. In the case of Kat, the 'trustafarian' or rich girl/white rasta, 'roots' represent the pre-eminence of the material interests of class. Freddy describes her as 'slumming it' in the squat scene, and as she returns to a middle-class home, he ironically observes: 'never forget your roots girl'. In Helen's case, however, what might have been thought the most overriding set of class interests – her position in a City bank – prove to be chimerical and are substituted by an identification with the black African victims of global capitalism. This is not to suggest that 'roots' in the film represent the absolute priority of the claims of ethnic or racial belonging. Generally, it is the malleability of such allegiances that the film plumps for. In this respect it is 'routes' not 'roots' that are significant – which is to say, it is the mixing of peoples in Brixton, the 'great south London wash' in which, as Jake puts it, 'everything circulates', that enables the forging of progressive, cross-cultural solidarities.[122] 'Roots' can be cut – Douser rejects his fascist, 'nationalist' background. His name – a nickname that is not a culturally identified category – signifies his involvement in the Brixton riots of 1981. His sister Sal rejects him precisely because of his betrayal of his 'roots'.

But to return to Helen, her case is troubling because her political allegiances are so flagrantly inconsistent with her position within the black middle class. The plausibility of the way she operates in defiance of the logic of 'social being' can, nevertheless, find an explanation in the conception of capitalism which is at work in the film. Here we can return to the motif of circulation which not only does service in theories of cultural hybridisation ('the great south London wash') but also has a significant role to play in ideologies of neo-liberal capitalism. Recall that the phrase belongs to ex-City trader and 'budding' entrepreneur Jake – a character who carries the image of a banknote on his t-shirt as he restlessly roves around the streets of Brixton, on the make, hustling. What then are the dominant contemporary ideologies of capitalism and how might they be related to this film and the idea of circulation? For Paul Smith, the 'millennial dream' of neo-liberal capitalism is closely related to the idea that capitalism has broken with its 'productivist past' in a cyber-assisted world.[123] Finance capital is the essential form for this magical, frictionless image of a capitalist system freed from human labour. Likewise, for Jean Comaroff and John L. Comaroff 'millennial capitalism' is to be understood as '*both* capitalism at the millennium and capitalism in its messianic, salvific, even magical manifestations'.[124] Again, a 'magical' capitalism is related to the feeling that there has been an eclipse in the importance of production. Wealth is now believed to be created by the market itself and by 'speculation' – in particular through the 'flow of finance capital'.[125] In neo-liberal ideologies, it is as if capitalism has successfully emancipated itself from the working class whose disappearance as the source of value is matched by the disappearance of capitalism itself as a system which is inherently conflictual and competitive.[126] Wood's description of the 'commercialisation model' of capitalism seems relevant here.[127] The latter conceals the historically specific, exploitative social relations of production which have grounded capitalism, and instead lays emphasis on commerce and the circulation, in trade, of peoples and commodities. Such emphases give the impression that capitalism is the assertion of fundamental, 'universal' human activities which have existed in all societies, to varying degrees, and that contemporary capitalism is simply the apotheosis of the trans-cultural, trans-historical market principles of neo-liberal mythology.[128] In this way, the neo-liberal 'free' market is relieved of what for Wood is its 'dominant characteristic' – *compulsion* – which is in turn replaced by the principle of *opportunity*.[129] When the neo-liberal marketplace is understood as a space of energetic and fulfilling freedom, what disappears is the pressure of its universal and thus unavoidable grip on all aspects of material life.

Ritchie's 'gangster light' films are a good place to observe the subtle influence of this ideology of capitalism. It is in the narrative devices of *Lock, Stock and Two Smoking Barrels* and *Snatch* that its informing presence is evident. Both films use the convention of a circulating totemic object around which the multiple plot-lines converge – in *Lock, Stock and Two Smoking Barrels* it is the pair of antique shotguns and in *Snatch*, the eighty-six-carat diamond. The complex narratives constructed around these elusive objects implicate the characters in a maximalist logic of success or failure. One needs to be in the right place at the right time – but ultimate success is dependent on an inscrutable good fortune which manifests itself through the intricacies of the plotting itself. Furthermore, the intervention of this 'salvific' force demands a division between those who 'work' and those who are beyond working. In Ritchie's films characters do not 'work' they 'hustle' and as they do, they chase the blessing of a winning 'score'. Crucially, Ritchie's 'lads' need to learn not to work for someone else, or, as Turkish puts it, be in someone else's 'pocket'. In *Snatch*, such relationships lead to another cycle – the nitrogen cycle in which murdered competitors are fed to Brick Top's (Alan Ford) pigs. In both films the gambler's lucky streak is ghosted by a ruthless logic of elimination as the convoluted narratives bring competitors together and stage grand purges. The identification is with capital. The absent 'working' class is, by definition, a class of lost souls.

The issues raised by ideologies of neo-liberal capitalism will be returned to at various points during this book. What is of particular interest in the case of *South West 9* is the way in which its 'anti-capitalist' anarchism is captured by neo-liberal myths. Whilst the film wants to save those wasted by neo-liberal capital and to bring about a true, 'fruit salad' millennium – ambitions which distinguish it from the empty multiculturalism of Ritchie's films – it nevertheless seeks to do this, on one level, by means of the same neo-liberal, 'millennial' capitalism. That is to say, the profile of the 'magical' capitalism sketched above, helps to explain the peculiarities of a character like Helen. If capitalism is severed from class struggle and reconceived as a global system of circulating flows, then its points of weakness/opportunity – for individual enrichment or political attack – are only open to those who throw the switches on that traffic. Helen's suitcase, the film's totemic, circulating object, contains a polymorphic computer virus – a Trojan horse – which is 'sweet and innocent' on the surface, but a lot more 'cunning' underneath. Furthermore, it is a weapon whose use she describes as being limited to those who are in a 'privileged position'. According to this logic, the most challenging forms of politics emerge, unpredictably, from where they are least expected. But more than this, effective political action is the property of the already empowered. Helen and Jake then are doubles. The small entrepreneur's dream of being in the right place at the right time, poised to take advantage of the market, is a permanent possibility for the City banker. In this topsy-turvy world, the revolutionary is the capitalist, the rest are what Helen refers to contemptuously as 'nobodies'.

'BRITONS' AND THE ATLANTIC

South West 9 is a film which wants to escape from the Englishness it associates with the evils of global capitalism. The film ends with an animated computer-graphic in which an oversized anarchist baby runs amok in the City. This is preceded by documentary footage of the anti-capitalist riots in London which resulted in the defacement of the statue of Winston Churchill. The two locations clearly recognisable in this footage – the City and Westminster – represent the financial/monarchical duopoly which for many has represented the historical heart of the English national hegemony.[130]

Figure 3 *South West 9* – Anti-capitalist riot. © Fruit Salad Productions

A very different movement to replace the 'narrow nationalism' of an English-ness associated with the Tories has also been part of the New Labour project.[131] This movement finds parallels in the field of contemporary social history, particularly in the influential work of Colley, who has sought to address the 'present crisis' of Great British nationalism by which she means to refer to the passing of that older mixture of Protestantism, imperial conquest and commercial success.[132] Colley's book *Britons* anticipated a key component in the presentation of New Labour's project. That is to say, there is a common perception, shared by Colley and New Labour, that the nineteenth century produced a form of English nationalism in which the diversity of Britishness was erased by a fantasy of 'unity and singularity'.[133] By contrast, for Colley, the eighteenth century offers images of national belonging that appear more appropriate for our present moment – a moment in which the multicultural and multinational dimensions of the British archipelago have come to the fore.[134] She gives us an eighteenth-century Britain which was not nationalist in the sense of endorsing the mythic homogeneity of an 'ethno-cultural nation' but which was capacious enough to be able to contain a diverse range of people.[135] Quoting Defoe's famous lines on that 'heterogeneous thing, an Englishman' Colley draws attention to an eighteenth-century self-consciousness concerning the 'infinitely diverse' culture of the inhabitants of Great Britain.[136]

However, Colley's recovery of an earlier, 'creative' patriotism as a rational means for those lying outside the political nation to claim 'access to citizenship' is maintained at the cost of a detailed sense of the struggle between the classes as a dynamic, formative process within eighteenth-century civil society.[137] In a review of Colley's book, Thompson accepted that the evidence indicating national consensus rather than conflict in the period of the late eighteenth, early nineteenth centuries may have been scanted in his own work and received a just and elegant counterbalance in her study.[138] Nevertheless, he went on to suggest that *Britons* might be seen as 'top down' history, and that although Colley had produced a compelling account of the 'making of the British ruling class', she was less persuasive in her 'incorporation of the common people into the same thesis'.[139] Thompson also mentioned the evidence provided by the 'American Marxist' Peter Linebaugh in *The London Hanged*, published the year before Colley's book, as opening up a picture of 'different "Britons"' – a picture she 'hurries past with averted eyes'.[140]

South West 9 shows itself aware of these 'different Britons' mentioned by Thompson, and described by Linebaugh and his fellow historian Marcus Rediker as an *Atlantic proletariat*.[141] As Linebaugh and Rediker put it, the experiences of this proletariat – not a 'unified cultural class' or a 'race', but a collective which was male, female, of all ages, motley, 'multiethnic in appearance', planetary, '*self-active*' and '*creative*' – have been 'hidden' by a historically frozen image of the working class as a 'white, male, skilled, waged, nationalist, propertied artisan/citizen or industrial worker'.[142] *South West 9* also reaches back beyond this image.

We have seen how it establishes a historical narrative which brings together global capitalism and the colonialism of the early modern period, and how it structures this narrative around symbolic locations within Brixton – the Smokehouse and The Atlantic/Dog Bar. We are given the history of the latter in Freddy's introductory voice-over. Originally a Jamaican pub – Keiller makes reference to it in *London* (1994) in the context of the Tilbury arrival in 1948 of the *SS Windrush* – it was burnt down twice in the riots of the 1980s and rebuilt. Freddy's insistence on recording its original name must be considered a significant detail. Its role in the narrative is to provide a space in which paths intersect just as, in the work of historians Linebaugh and Rediker, the Atlantic is the space of the intercontinental exchanges and struggles that linked a heterogeneous, mobile, working class of many nations – what they call the 'many-headed hydra'.[143] Linebaugh and Rediker also mention the 'imperialist adventurer' Walter Raleigh – whose legacy the film figures through the Smokehouse – as one of the originators of the Hercules cult which flourished amongst the English ruling-class elite in the seventeenth century.[144] In mythology it was Hercules's role to tame the 'many-headed monster'.[145] Here is Žižek's irresolvable antagonism of class struggle. On the one hand, what Wood calls the 'empire of capitalism' and, on the other, a richly diverse planetary proletariat operating in the intercontinental space of the Atlantic.[146] Even if *South West 9* is prone to slip into fantasies of political omnipotence that are based on ideologies of neo-liberal capital, it nevertheless ends with insurrectionary images rather than with images of premature, peaceful co-existence.

CHAPTER 1

The Upper Classes: The Heritage Film

The upper reaches of the English class system seem to fascinate film-makers. In particular the monarchy, the aristocracy and the upper middle classes have featured prominently in what some critics have referred to as the British 'heritage film'.[1] This is a genre which has mainly been discussed in terms of the period after 1980, although for some its reach extends further back in British film history.[2] The range of films covered in early attempts to define the genre was relatively restricted, concentrating for instance on examples such as *Chariots of Fire* (1981), *Another Country* (1984) and the E.M. Forster adaptations of the 1980s, particularly those from James Ivory, Ismail Merchant and Ruth Prawer Jhabvala; however, more recent attempts to 'map the field' have produced a much wider view.[3] Thus, in his book-length study of the subject, Andrew Higson compiles a filmography of over a hundred costume dramas made or first released in the 1980s and 1990s with 'some British connection'.[4] Higson's early essays on the heritage film have been vigorously contested, and it will be the objective of this chapter to give a brief account of the ensuing 'debate' and to suggest new ways to approach its core concerns.

What is a heritage film? Sheldon Hall provides a useful taxonomy of the generic sub-categories and cycles most commonly identified by critics. First, adaptations of canonical literary texts, such as Forster's *Maurice* (1987), Dickens's *Little Dorrit* (1987), Austen's *Emma* (1996) and James's *The Golden Bowl* (2000); second, costume dramas adapted from modern literary or theatrical texts such as Julian Mitchell's *Another Country* and Kazuo Ishiguro's *The Remains of the Day* (1993); third, the 'Raj' revival films such as David Lean's *A Passage to India* (1984) along with television series such as *The Jewel in the Crown* (1985); and finally Shakespeare adaptations such as *Henry V* (1989) and *Much Ado About Nothing* (1993).[5] For his part, Higson recognises that the heritage label covers a 'diverse set of films and television programmes'; however, unlike Hall, who is sceptical that such a wide selection of texts can be usefully lumped together, he does see benefits in such a classification.[6] There are four reasons he gives for this – first, many of the films share a 'reputation for quality in British moving-image media'.[7] Second, many of the films stage an unresolved conflict between a secure, traditional, elite Englishness and a more unstable sense of national identity which is presented to us through the experiences of those whose lives lie on the social margins and who are traditionally mere 'footnotes' to the national past.[8] Thus, a privileged, elegant and alluring insiders' view of a 'core English identity' – bolstered by discourses of historical 'authenticity' and focusing on a limited period from 1880 to 1940 that has been seen as crucial in the formation of still influential conceptions of Englishness – faces off against the forces of flux and the perspective of the outsider.[9] This structural cleavage is echoed in the production history of the films. Many of the directors, producers, writers and actors – including, for instance, Ang Lee, Shekhar Kapur, Robert Altman, Cate Blanchett, Gwyneth Paltrow, Ismail Merchant, James Ivory and Ruth Prawer Jhabvala – are not English. The heritage film then is a promising place in which to examine the intersection between 'national representation' and 'international mythology'.[10] Higson's third justification of the usefulness of the heritage label can be related to the second. There are, he claims, formal and stylistic similarities running across the films – including a characteristically sumptuous *mise en scène* showcasing *heritage properties* (landscape, interiors, architecture, costumes).[11] Shot in a cinematographic style designed to display this spectacle, the films give the impression of celebrating a social order that their own narratives are preoccupied with questioning, particularly through the attention given to characters' attempts to transgress established boundaries of class, race, sex and gender. The final reason given by Higson in support of his classification is that heritage films intersect in numerous ways with the larger 'heritage industries' that have become such an important economic presence in the era of post-industrialisation. These films are, he argues, often linked to tourism and other commodifications of the past through their marketing and critical reception.[12]

Critics of Higson have felt that his original formulation of the genre over-states its conservative complexion.[13] As he himself later put it, such critics were objecting to his argument that the films are ideologically and aesthetically primed to articulate a 'nostalgic and conservative celebration of the values and lifestyles of the privileged classes' which turns its back on issues facing a contemporary, post-imperial Britain.[14] This is an argument that Higson calls the 'leftist cultural critique'[15] and it is one he has now distanced himself from by conceding that it remains only 'an interpretation'.[16] Furthermore, he has recognised the validity of arguments which maintain that the films' 'aesthetics of display'[17] can be seen in terms of the expressive *mise en scène* typical of the 'woman's film' rather than as a support for visions of a conservative, elite Englishness.[18] In making such arguments critics like Claire Monk have put issues of sexuality and gender onto the agenda, issues which she argues have been repressed by anti-heritage critics' focus on ideologies of nation and class.[19] In a related critique, Pam Cook argues that Higson's suspicion of the conservative ideology of the films reduplicates that long-standing antipathy in British film criticism for non-realist genres, and in particular for the costume dramas traditionally associated with female audiences.[20] Higson's most recent work, however, takes greater account of reception studies and he is certainly willing to admit that his earlier formulations at least implied a 'passive consumerist spectator'.[21] Finally, like Monk and Cook, Hall seeks to redeem the pleasures of particular audiences slighted in anti-heritage film criticism, and to insist on the specificity of a heterogeneous body of film in the face of what he sees as weak textual analysis, unconvincing contextualisation and spurious generic generalisation.[22]

It is in the spirit of a careful circumscription of the grand claims of heritage criticism that Monk provides a useful 'historicisation' of the heritage film idea.[23] First, she points out that the critique of the heritage film emerged in the early 1990s and was not immediately contemporaneous with the films cited.[24] It had gestated in the context of 1980s Thatcherite political and cultural policies – policies which had produced seminal anti-heritage texts by Patrick Wright and Robert Hewison.[25] Its trigger was Norman Stone's provocative right-wing criticisms of British cinema at the end of the 1980s.[26] In a *Sunday Times* article, Stone singled out for dispraise the work of Stephen Frears and Derek Jarman – his examples included the 'depressing' and 'revolting' *My Beautiful Laundrette*, *Sammy and Rosie Get Laid* and *The Last of England*.[27] By way of contrast he offered his congratulations to films such as *A Room with a View*, *Passage to India* and *Hope and Glory* (1987) – the first two were to become key targets for anti-heritage criticism.[28] The response from the academic left was, according to Monk, 'defensive' and 'reactively replicated' the 'reductive terms of debate' set by the New Right.[29] In this way, anti-heritage criticism fell victim to the distorting influence that the 'vicious polarisation and combativeness' of the period was having on cultural and political debate.[30] This situation produced a tendency towards a simple reversal of critical binaries which is illustrated for Monk by the argument in Higson's first essay that films featuring working-class subjects and a contemporary, post-imperial Britain – for instance, *Letter to Brezhnev* (1985) and *The Passion of Remembrance* (1986) – were of more value than heritage film nostalgia for Old England.[31]

Despite the importance of Monk's detailed contextualisation of the emergence of the heritage film idea, there is a problematic assumption in this account that the polarising currents of politically inspired cultural commentary are unnecessary *nastiness* – she talks of the cultural debate being 'infected' by the political strife of the time.[32] The impression given is that the leftist cultural critique of the heritage film was a wild, reflex response to New Right provocation, one which simply reversed the terms set by Stone, lacked any significant grip on the films themselves and fell into hopelessly elitist, masculinist positions. It might be possible, however, to combine the political and the aesthetic in readings of these films that take a wider view of the leftist cultural critique – without necessarily fully endorsing it – whilst at the same time avoiding the kind of *impoverished* critical analysis objected to by Monk and Hall.[33]

The general heritage culture criticism of the 1980s which influenced early formulations of the heritage film idea can be linked to the Nairn–Anderson theses of the 1960s and to what W.D. Rubinstein has called the 'cultural critique' of British economic decline.[34] For an example of this 'cultural critique' one might take Hewison's book on heritage culture. Hewison reproduces the outline of an argument common to Anthony Sampson, Martin J. Wiener, Corelli Barnett, Tom Nairn and Perry Anderson in which national decline is attributed to a regressive patrician ruling class with the institutional resources and cultural influence to block the long overdue moment of 'modern bourgeois civilisation'.[35] What needs to be stressed is that this long-standing belief in the potent and malign influence of the English past intensified in the 1980s as a result of what was perceived to be the Tory abuse of the autocratic, unmodernised and undemocratic powers of the State. The appearance of movements such as Charter 88 which lobbied for a 'written constitution' that it was felt would transform vulnerable British *subjects* into protected *citizens* is roughly contemporaneous with the circulation of antagonistic heritage culture criticism.[36] Furthermore, the state promotion of 'heritage' under successive Thatcher governments could be seen, by frustrated modernisers, as finding an echo in the state's own 'heritage' qualities.[37] From such a perspective the national Parliament was more accurately thought of as the Palace of Westminster, which was, in turn, understood not so much as a popular-democratic forum, but rather as an Old English institution in which power was designed to be concentrated in the hands of a privileged few and exercised over the many.[38] Autocratic, anti-consensual Thatcherism precipitated a crisis on the liberal-left – a crisis which the heritage film projection of a spectacular 'Heritage England' of social deference and patrician authority might easily find itself associated with. Indeed, as we will see in Chapter 7, it has been argued that it was partly the political frustration induced by Thatcher's abolition of the democratic forum, the Greater London Council, that laid the foundation for emergence of a literary, Gothic/'occult heritage' vision of London that flourished in the 1990s. Within the context of anti-consensual New Right politics, 'market' fundamentalism and the resulting liberal-left political crisis, 'heritage' became an overloaded sign. For the New Right, heritage might screen off the savagery of neo-liberal capitalism, the social consequences of which it preferred not to see, or better still, to pass off as the accumulated result of post-war, liberal-left social democratic decadence. This is one way of reading Stone's piece on British cinema of the time. For Stone, the 'heritage' films were to be welcomed as they offered an image of the nation which was felt to be familiar and reassuring whilst it could be imagined that middle-class malcontents and outsiders like Jarman and Kureishi had only their own 'revolting' imaginations to blame for the landscapes of social destruction they brought to the screen. For liberal-left, anti-heritage critics, such uses of 'heritage' were doomed as the latter was itself a key vector in the relentlessly destabilising commodification of all aspects of national life – in this instance the 'past' – that a society of neo-liberal 'enterprise' had spawned.[39] At the same time, 'heritage' was perceived as identifying the form of a dangerous, illiberal political power which was a relic of the pre-modern past and which had facilitated these economic depredations.

AMBIVALENCE AND THE HERITAGE FILM

Heritage films in the1980s certainly dramatised liberal discontents with Old England. In her response to one of the first anti-heritage film articles Alison Light made the point that to see Merchant and Ivory's films as an expression of neo-conservative Thatcherism was to miss this.[40] Subsequently, both Higson and Hill have argued convincingly that it is the contradiction between narratives aspiring to progressive, liberal sentiments and an indulgence in the spectacle of a socially conservative Englishness that gives these films a characteristic ambivalence.[41] In order to explore this ambivalence further let us consider Hill's account of a film which has been received as the progenitor of the 1980s heritage film cycle – *Chariots of Fire*. As he points out, the latter is steeped in the pleasures of patriotism. Additionally, the coincidence of its international success and the Tory-led military adventure in the Falklands, lent it a Thatcherite aura which belied its actual ideological complexity.[42] Whilst the film does provide images of bigoted and elitist Englishness, it sets such images against an ethnically and nationally diverse middle class seeking not the favours of privilege but to assert the pre-eminence of a meritocratic, open society.[43] Of the Olympic athletes the film features, Harold Abrahams (Ben Cross) and Eric Liddell (Ian Charleson) are both outsiders to the establishment – here represented by Oxbridge. Abrahams is a Jew of Lithuanian ancestry and Liddell is a Scot born in China whose strict sabbatarianism puts him beyond the Anglican pale. Despite representing a challenge to Old England these two figures carry unsympathetic associations – associations which bear a resemblance to the values and beliefs core to the New Right assault on old pieties.[44] The thrusting, 'aggressive individualism' of Abrahams and the inflexible zeal of Liddell, in the context of Thatcher's own 'conviction' politics, carry obvious ideological overtones.[45] Indeed, neither Liddell nor Abrahams is as attractive as the graceful and genially accommodating aristocrat, Lord Lindsay (Nigel Havers), whose selflessness gives Liddell the opportunity to win a medal.[46] Lindsay is reminiscent of that nostalgic profile of a stylish aristocracy to be found in the televisual adaptation of Waugh's *Brides-head Revisited* that was first screened in the same year of 1981. Emblematically, if it is the egalitarian geometry of the running track on which the film's narrative drama is concentrated, then visually the affective focus remains on cricket in the ballroom of an exclusive hotel; a ritually observed race around a Cambridge college quadrangle, or the vision of an elegant lord, in picturesque country house parkland, effortlessly clearing glasses of champagne balanced on hurdles.

Hill gives readings of other heritage films from the 1980s in which a similar effect is noticeable. Thus, *Another Country*, the story of the gay, communist 'traitor' Guy Bennett, appears to pivot on the latter's failure to accede to the most elevated position within his elite public school – an institution which is transformed into a 'source of visual pleasure and fascination'.[47] In *A Room with a View* the distinction between the Emersons and the Honeychurchs – a fraught leap in the class system arcana which the film details – is not the kind of class distinction which can support a contemporary sense of social exclusion.[48] Furthermore, despite its liberal, Forsterian themes of nature, spontaneity and the importance of the affections of the human heart, the film celebrates the cultural trappings and social ambiance of an Edwardian era of 'lost elegance and stability' that Forster himself was critical of.[49] Why then do such films take this detour – through a languid, stable and glamorous world – in their assault on establishment Englishness and its class system?

One way in which such divergent effects can be approached is as an expression of ambivalence about the social energies released by Thatcherism. The 'driven' characters, Liddell and Abrahams, not only provide a welcome assault on a complacent and unpleasant elite, they also conjure up an uncomfortable spirit of restlessness whose turbulence might just be indiscriminate. In this way, *Chariots of Fire* evokes both a sense of the need for change along with a fear of a particular kind of change – one which exposes everything, without exception, to the scouring blasts of political and economic neo-liberalism. On the other hand, a privileged English world of the past projects a sense of being immune to such destabilisation – the insouciant hurdling toff is a good example of such elevation. We might say then that a pattern is set early on and it is visible in *Chariots of Fire*. The heritage film seeks to imagine changes in the fabric of an Englishness whose illiberal oppressiveness it sees clearly, and at the same time it desires to retain the image of the Old Country's apparently timeless material comforts and social stability. But the significance of such nostalgia does not have to be confined to the endorsement of a political dream of empire and social hierarchy – Cannadine's 'ornamentalism'. It might also be seen as an attachment to a particular *special effect* of the English class system, one that is most effective at its apex, the screening-off of the unpleasantnesses associated with capitalism. On this level, the heritage film can offer the sensation of a 'breathing space' to those with political dreams very different to the neo-conservative ones dear to Stone. That is to say, if these films provide a 'vision of a more inclusive, democratic, even multicultural England'[50] then this attractive nourishing of difference in costume might well lean on the suspension of the coercive power of neo-liberal capitalism whose ability to reach 'into every corner of our lives, public and private' was becoming oppressively insistent in this era.[51] The power to effect this suspension appears to be borrowed from the tranquilising effect induced by spectacle of the English upper classes of the past.

GROTESQUE OLD ENGLAND

If for those on the left political change seemed a frustratingly remote possibility in the 1980s, then with the downfall of the New Right heroine Margaret Thatcher in 1990, it became a more tangible expectation. In the case of the heritage film, if Hill seems right in arguing that in the 1980s it often seemed drawn into the enchantment of a narrow, privileged and stable world of class, then from the early 1990s there emerges a strand of the genre which seems more resistant to the charms of Old England. These films might be linked to changes in the general perception of 'heritage' culture; specifically, they might be read in terms of an intensification of that view of heritage which sees it as a symptom of national political and cultural backwardness. Retrospectively, Nairn cites as crucial the role of the House of Lords in the passage of the Poll Tax Bill in 1990 – the very debacle that brought down Thatcher. As he puts it, this was a moment when the 'undead' from 'every decayed estate in the kingdom' were called on to save Thatcher – the authority of their 'grotesque traditions' carried forth in 'uniforms, furniture and wigs' or in what might be called the *heritage properties* of state.[52]

However, as the decade progressed, political disquiet with the legacy of the *ancien régime* exploited so ruthlessly by Thatcherism was in part co-opted by New Labour's presentation of itself as 'modernising'. At the same time, the economics of neo-liberalism had become the unquestionable horizon of social life – on this Blairism promised and delivered, after 1997, a consolidation of the 'Thatcherite paradigm'.[53] This general acquiescence to the market principles of neo-liberal capitalism has perhaps been the most enduring achievement of Thatcherism. In this context 'heritage' Englishness was to be recast as an updated, stylish accompaniment to, rather than evasion of, neo-liberal capitalism. In the next chapter we will be tracing this development in the romantic comedy cycle produced by Working Title in the late 1990s. However, at this point, it is useful to consider the company's earlier film, *Four Weddings and a Funeral* (1994), which, whilst anticipating these future developments, also belongs to that moment in the 1990s when heritage culture helped to focus concerns with Old England. The film features a helplessly ineffectual but eligible Englishman, Charles (Hugh Grant) who falls in love with a bold, 'modern' American woman, Carrie (Andie MacDowell). What is interesting is the way in which Charles's difficulties in winning Carrie carry the imprint of an obstructive culture of upper-class Englishness. This is manifested on a number of levels. First, there are the iconographic references to an oneiric *heritage geography* that extends from churches in the picturesque Home Counties and the City of London to castles in the 'Royal Highlands' of Scotland. It is this space which Charles and Carrie need to free themselves from – the last location listed is the site of Carrie's own wedding to a member of the Westminster Parliament. Second, the problem of Charles's relationship to the world of upper-class Englishness is inscribed in the film's episodic narrative structure which follows the temporal logic of a *society* season. The latter, as represented in the film, is best described as a series of spectacular, enclosed events, not bound together in a developing sequence but following one another with a repetitive, self-sufficient and fatal momentum. Note the use of stylised intertitles as punctuation devices between each society wedding and the motif of Charles's oversleeping – the implication being that he is enchanted.

The ellipsis between the funeral and the fourth wedding draws attention to this helplessness. This last wedding is to effect his own marriage to a woman he has shown no previous interest in. The narrative enigma it represents – why is Charles marrying an ex-girlfriend who he previously sought to avoid? – can be explained by reference to the bewildered passivity of the character within this overwhelming English social world. The film concludes with a 'non-wedding' which joins Carrie and Charles together and at the same time keeps them out of the upper-class *social* world in which they initially meet.[54] Note that in the final shot, Charles and Carrie are carefully quarantined from the rich *mise en scène* of Englishness – they are dressed down rather than in upper-class 'fancy dress', and they leave us with an image of purged bourgeois isolation in an anonymous park.

Released the year before *Four Weddings and a Funeral*, Stephen Poliakoff's *Century* (1993) explores the frustrations endured by a progressive middle class that is attempting to defend the ideals of the Enlightenment project against the 'science' of eugenics and the indifference of wealthy patrons. This film makes an alliance between its middle-class doctor hero, Paul (Clive Owen), and his working-class lab-assistant lover, Clara (Miranda Richardson) – an alliance whose vigour and credible intensity contrast strongly with the faltering fantasies of middle-class patronage of working-class 'naturals' to be found in films like *Maurice* and *Howards End*.[55] In its passionate enthusiasm for humanitarian principles, the film draws attention to an English indifference to social and scientific progress and at the same time, as Mike Wayne argues, makes a case for the continuing relevance of the Enlightenment project.[56] *Century* is less marked by alluring heritage spectacle than another release of the same year, *The Remains of the Day*, which is, nevertheless, preoccupied with the subject of the political regressiveness of Old England. The film covers the interwar, aristocratic appeasement of the Nazis and is set in the country seat of Lord Darlington (James Fox). Unlike the impression made by the unproblematically elegant and picturesque parkland and house of Lord Lindsay in *Chariots of Fire*, here stately heritage spectacle contains, within its labyrinthine structure, the lord's appeasement and the butler's complicit self-effacement. Whilst the *mise en scène* is certainly loaded up with a sumptuous and beguiling vision of Old England, we are nevertheless encouraged to read the same images in terms of a sinister patrican–plebeian conspiracy. The use of slow dissolves, providing superimposed images of the interiors of the house, intensifies the tainted atmosphere of intrigue. Spectacular views of Darlington enframe the narrative and consequently the house appears to enclose within itself the stories that have struggled to emerge, including the voice of dissent and modernity, the American, Lewis (Christopher Reeve). Ominously perhaps, Lewis steps into the disgraced English lord's place and becomes the new proprietor. Furthermore, the film distinguishes the political delinquencies of the lord and his butler from a genuinely democratic culture in which there is no place for deference or the deferral of political opinion up the social ladder. In one scene Cardinal (Hugh Grant), attempts to turn the butler, Stevens (Anthony Hopkins), against the compromised lord, urging him to remember that he is a free-born Englishman and not just an aristocrat's flunky.

Angels and Insects (1995) sets a gallery of aristocratic grotesques against the virtue and scientific talents of a governess and a 'gentleman' whose origins are working class. William Adamson (Mark Rylance), a brilliant naturalist and son of butcher, finds himself duped into providing cover for the incestuous relationship between Eugenia Alabaster (Patsy Kensit) and Edgar Alabaster (Douglas Henshall), the daughter and son of his aristocratic patron. Edgar is depicted as a brutally arrogant believer in the genetic superiority of his class who openly despises William for his low 'breeding'. The family's governess, Matty Crompton (Kristin Scott Thomas), assists William in his work – a project on worker ants which acts, symbolically, to contrast the useless splendour of the aristocrats against the values of co-operative labour – and helps to enlighten him as to his conjugal deception. In the scene which leads to William's discovery of Eugenia and Edgar's relationship, 'heritage space' itself seems to participate in generating a sense of class antagonism – having just set off hunting, William is called back, supposedly by his wife. He re-enters the house which is now empty of those whose class he has allied himself with through marriage. Directed by a servant, he makes his way to the bedroom in which he discovers his wife and her brother. In this scene the grand house is animated by the 'invisible' powers of the servant class and works to disabuse the hero.

William and Matty leave the estate not as social subordinates but as independent naturalists and lovers. Their intention is to resume the grand scientific task of mapping the insect world beyond England's shores. It should be noted that whilst the narrative has prepared a grand exit for them after William asserts his moral authority over Eugenia and her brother, the couple are pictured leaving in the dark and not by the front entrance. It is as if in these shots darkness is experienced not as the obscurity and humiliation of the lower classes skulking in the shadows of magnificence, but as the intimate and protective cloak of those whose seriousness and resolve place them beyond the reach of their nominal masters. Throughout the film heritage spectacle remains suggestively sensitive to the narrative enigma – what is wrong with Eugenia? – and rather than acting at cross-purposes with the critique of the upper classes, it directs attention towards the unpleasantly unrestrained appetites of the family. Thus, the ugly, sexual predatoriness of the racist bully Edgar is complemented by his mother's unbecoming teatime gluttony. Heritage feeding is usually an exquisitely decorous activity which enables the co-ordination of various aspects of the genre's *mise en scène* – precisely aerated enunciation between measured mouthfuls, elaborate dressing, fine crockery, hovering servants, imposing dining rooms etc. However, in this film repeated teatime scenes show the mother devouring elaborate pastries – an activity which culminates in speechless convulsion and death.

This strand within the heritage film of the mid 1990s which appears, as Pamela Church Gibson puts it, to represent a 'new departure' in the genre, one in which a 'social critique' is wrapped up in the problem of the English class system, can also

be seen in Michael Winterbottom's 1996 adaptation of Thomas Hardy's novel
Jude the Obscure.[57] *Jude* pits working-class interests and desires against the
inequities of Oxbridge. It also adopts a style which consciously avoids any suggestion of conventional, picturesque, heritage pastoralism – the English countryside is depicted as a place of pain, suffering and frustration.[58] Here was a film
in which it seemed difficult to argue that the frustrations of the outsider were
mitigated by a splendid *mise en scène* – the same might be said about a later Hardy
adaptation, *The Woodlanders* (1997). In the same year as *Angels and Insects*, *The
Madness of King George* was released. It was followed in 1997 and 1998 by *Mrs.
Brown* and *Elizabeth* respectively. As Kara McKechnie points out, the return of
the monarchy film 'after a hiatus of nearly twenty years', appeared to respond to
'a need arising from the public mood of the time'.[59] Both *The Madness of King
George* and *Mrs. Brown* deal with what were effective interregnums within two
of the most important reigns in the reinvention of the modern monarchy.[60] It
is difficult to avoid the conclusion that these films address, through the theme
of the disrupted functioning of royal public ritual, the domestic, dynastic and
institutional difficulties faced by the institution's contemporary occupants. Only
a few years earlier, during the pomp and circumstance of the royal marriages of
the 1980s, such developments would have seemed inconceivable.

Although not a heritage film, Keiller's *London* contains references to the relationship between heritage culture and the apparatus of the state, including the
role of its capstone, the monarchy. This relationship is articulated by Robinson
in terms of the Nairn–Anderson theses. As the narrator puts it: 'The failure of the
English Revolution is all around us.' This 'failure' and the later, fearful response
to the French Revolution which drove the bourgeoisie back into the arms of the
ancien régime, have had consequences which, according to Robinson, we are
still living with. For instance, he sees London heritage spectacle – Trooping the
Colour and the Lord Mayor's show – as the index of a general cultural-historical
regression that has reached a point of crisis in the present. Again, as the narrator
puts it, London's public spaces are 'either void or the stage set for the spectacles
of nineteenth-century reaction endlessly re-enacted for television'. Robinson's
response is to adopt the postures of republican incendiarism, turning up at royal
events in the capital and shouting out his political objections to the House of
Windsor: 'Pay your taxes you scum!'

The Tichborne Claimant (1998) stages a confrontation between the servant
class and its aristocratic employer and enables us to consider in greater detail
some of the issues concerning the politics of Englishness that have emerged
out of the recent history of the heritage genre. The film is based on a true story
in which a butcher from Australia sought to claim he was the amnesiac Lord
Tichborne who had been presumed lost at sea twenty years earlier. This plot
to dupe the English aristocracy is attributed to a Tichborne family servant – an
African called Andrew Bogle (John Kani) – who, as an infirm, destitute old man
in the Pentonville workhouse of 1895, provides a retrospective narration of the

deception. He tells of his journey to Australia on behalf of his employers in search of the lost Sir Roger Tichborne and his decision, upon the failure of this mission and his abandonment by the family after fifty years of service, to perpetrate a fraud on them. He selects Tom Castro (Robert Pugh), a drunken butcher from Wagga Wagga, and teaches him to play the part of Sir Roger. Initially successful, the Claimant is quickly abandoned by the family when his only ally, Sir Roger's mother, dies. Penniless, Castro and Bogle seek to persuade figures from the real Sir Roger's past into legitimising their imposture. Obstructed and outmanoeuvred by the family and on the verge of quitting, they find their cause adopted by a music hall impresario who suggests transferring the con into a political register. The Claimant is to tour the halls as an aristocrat who, denied his 'birthright', is in the same position as the working class who are also denied their rights of 'life, liberty and the pursuit of happiness by factory owners and coal owners'. As the Claimant puts it: neither the government nor the 'Queen herself' believes that the working class is good for anything more than 'making them a profit'. Audiences are encouraged to support the Claimant by acquiring Tichborne bonds which are to finance a legal challenge to recover the estates. If this action is successful the bonds can be redeemed as a percentage of the Tichborne fortune – thus allowing the working class to 'buy into the oldest and most profitable firm in the British Isles, the aristocracy'. The money duly collected, the Claimant goes to court; at this point, however, the family mobilise the 'full malevolent weight of the British establishment' – corrupt judges and expensive, amoral barristers – and produce what is presented as a counter-performance in which Tom Castro is turned from the Claimant into Fred Orton, a bigamous butcher from Wapping, London.[61] Orton/Castro/the Claimant is promptly arrested and imprisoned. However, in a coda which brings the narration up to date, Bogle is rescued from the workhouse by his protégé and is set up in a luxurious hotel as part of the entourage of the Claimant, who goes back on the stump, proclaiming the justice of his cause. Ultimately, the film suggests that ruling-class authority and legitimacy are grounded solely on the successful expression of a ruthless power and, in this way, the theme of impersonation, performance and the con implicates not only the working-class chancers of the film but the Establishment as well. Of particular importance is the film's choice to narrate the story from the point of view of Bogle. This places us within a transoceanic perspective – Africa, America, Australia and Ireland are all referenced through the alliance made between Bogle, Castro and his Irish wife – and leads to an image of a racially and nationally heterogeneous working class which is unusual for the heritage film.

Old England in this film is malicious and hypocritical. As the narrator, Bogle, puts it: 'the older and sicker the beast [the "old lion England"] the more savage it becomes'. However, what makes the film particularly interesting from the point of view of the arguments about Englishness, the classes and capitalism pursued in this book, is that it gives an impression of the complexity of that 'savagery' which extends beyond that fascinating, dark theatre of the English class system.

There is, in other words, a reflection in the film on the political problems posed by the spectacle of Old England and this is perhaps clearest in the music hall scenes. Here, the aristocracy, the government, the Queen and factory owners are combined to produce a composite image of the exploiting class which is historically acute. Of course, the political resistance suggested in these same scenes is undermined by the fact that the Claimant is a conman. Also, the interest of the Tichborne case to the working class is presented in terms of a parasitic mid-nineteenth-century Liberalism. At one stage, the Claimant appears as a *Citizen Kane*-style demagogue/plutocrat abusively manipulating working-class political frustrations. However, there are also suggestions that the problem of Liberal-style, anti-aristocratic populism is more complex than it at first appears.[62] During the sea voyage from Australia to England, Castro and his wife decide that they have had enough of the Tichborne plot and make to disembark in America. Bogle dissuades them and gives his own reasons for preferring England to America as his destination. As he puts it: all that they can hope for in America is 'equality' and *competition* with the anonymous mass, whereas in England a society of marked inequality presents people like themselves with a *visible enemy*. There is much packed into these brief comments. Let us first consider them in relation to the character of Bogle himself. As an ex-slave, his preference for enemies who are visible is on one level a reflection of his experience – a slave who does not own his own labour power is beholden to a 'master' who does. The slave owner is a clear target. However, Bogle is an ex-slave who has also worked for fifty years for a wage as a servant in an aristocratic family. As he puts it: 'I made my family with the Tichbornes but unfortunately they did not see their obligations.' What the character's life story exposes here is the impact of what Richard Johnson refers to as the ideological 'defence in depth' of the dominant classes of English society.[63] That is to say, historically, the strategic convergence of different sections of the ruling class – aristocratic and bourgeois – in the pursuit of capitalist priorities was complemented by a tactical divergence at the level of its ideological and political resources in dealing with the threat of the working class. The latter has historically faced a double whammy in which bourgeois and aristocratic ideological forms were combined.[64] In Bogle's case, it is the tactical switching between the distinct ideologies of deference on the one hand, and self-help on the other, that leads to his predicament.[65] If in patrician ideologies of the master/servant relationship there is a paternalist bond of obligation and reciprocity – whose advantage for the master lies in the sustaining of the relative unfreedom of 'deference' – then in ideologies of self-help the relationship between the employer and employee is contractual and the latter is 'free' whilst the former has no obligations beyond contractual ones.[66] Bogle the 'faithful retainer' who, when his usefulness is exhausted, is discarded in the colonies as a 'free' agent, is subject to this ruthless, ruling-class opportunism. In the circumstances Bogle's expressed preference for *visible* over *invisible* enemies indicates a desire to contain and pre-empt the forces against which he is struggling. However, the

Figure 4 *The Tichborne Claimant* – 'Lord Tichborne' and Bogle. Courtesy of Redbus Distribution Ltd

reality of those forces exceeds the image of them provided by a hypervisible, grotesque English aristocracy – this is precisely the lesson his own abandonment by the Tichbornes implies. An employer attached to the 'oldest firm' in England is able to depersonalise his actions by pointing to the impersonal mechanisms of the market. The Old England of the Tichbornes then forms a political target which is not entirely helpful and England is closer to capitalist America than Bogle admits.

In this way the film demonstrates how an exaggerated English culture of class – what Wood calls the 'pristine culture of capitalism' – works to exacerbate a problem that shadows working-class resistance to capitalism. If in pre-capitalist societies exploitation has an official visual presence – the 'embellishments' of aristocratic, feudal power for instance, which stand behind the process whereby a ruling class extracts the surplus from its social subordinates – then capitalist societies separate such extra-economic powers from the process of exploitation.[67] Capitalist exploitation does not require such 'embellishments' – the English aristocrat can maintain his wealth without insisting on any essentialised social pre-eminence.[68] Furthermore, because within capitalist society 'economic' transactions appear as un-coerced, contractual undertakings between 'free', individual economic agents, locating the systematic nature of the process of exploitation becomes difficult.[69] The 'capitalist' – understood as a member of a class whose interests are systematically opposed to those of the working class

– disappears. In the light of this, we need to recall that Bogle narrates his story from a workhouse – that grim embodiment for the working class of the time of the realities of the capitalist system. It is the workhouse that forms the fixed, largely unseen background for his exhilarations in vicariously mounting the same stage as that occupied by an imposing, amoral aristocracy. However, this is a stage which only partially circumscribes his class enemy.

The Tichborne Claimant makes a distinctive contribution to that aspect of the 1990s heritage film which responds to discontents brought into focus by the longevity of what Bogle calls the *sick old beast* – England. In an article on Nairn's diagnosis of 'late-British political culture' post 1997, Francis Mulhern comments that an obdurate focus on an unmodernised, 'Gothic' state and ruling bloc keeps assessments of the English past, present and future carefully away from the constraining problems induced by the logic of capitalism and class struggle.[70] It is the virtue of *The Tichborne Claimant* to raise these constraints at the same time that it explores the spectacle of Old England. Finally, the film demonstrates how the familiar landscape of the English class system represented in the heritage film can produce much more than nostalgic, timeless images of a stable past. What emerges in this film is something altogether more unfamiliar – the buried stories of the struggles of a transoceanic working class.

POST-HERITAGE

The Tichborne Claimant draws attention to the performative qualities of the English class system as it is represented in the heritage film.[71] It uses established English 'thespians' such as John Gielgud, Robert Hardy and Stephen Fry to pull off pleasurably malevolent enactments of upper-class types in all their notorious eccentricity and arrogant certainty. To an extent, this emphasis aligns it with that greater 'self-consciousness' about the representation of the past that critics have identified as a distinctive development within the heritage films of the 1990s.[72] Thus, for Monk the knowing, 'transgressive sexual politics' of films such as *Orlando* (1992) and *Carrington* (1995) – mistakenly assumed by those who made them to be more sophisticated in their representation of sexuality than critically derided heritage films of the 1980s such as *A Room with a View* – represent an attempt to reposition the heritage film as a critically respectable form of European art cinema.[73] Self-conscious, post-heritage representations of sex and gender now appear to be an established variant of the genre – a good recent example is *Stage Beauty* (2004).

Church Gibson's account of these changes in the genre also stresses the adoption of an eclectic, self-conscious postmodernist style in films such as *The Wings of a Dove* (1998), *Elizabeth* and *Shakespeare in Love* (1998).[74] As she says, such films seem to move away from the largely restrained naturalism of Merchant and Ivory Edwardiana, towards more dynamic, stylised and often generically hybridised heritage visions – she describes the James adaptation *The Wings of a Dove* as 'heritage noir'.[75] Such generic hybridisation was given particular emphasis in *Elizabeth* with its mixture of early modern Gothic and motifs from the thriller and gangster genres. As Moya Luckett observes, *Elizabeth* offers an updated, 'alternative vision of "heritage" for a contemporary nation'.[76] *Shakespeare in Love* is not dissimilar, with its ironic, playful intertextuality that mixes, in its casting, heritage 'repertory company' actors with Hollywood stars and consequently creates a sense of a 'happening' Britain/London within the framework of an early modern English iconography. However, beneath such aesthetic departures there are ideological continuities. As Wayne points out, the 'modernisation' of the heritage genre to be found in a film like *Elizabeth* actually works to revive the 'aura' of the institution of the monarchy with 'its attendant myths of national unity between the ruling and subaltern classes'.[77] Such convergences of new and old suggest the presence of what might be called an ideological *style-caste couplet*, one which operated not just in the heritage film of the late 1990s, but also in the political discourses of the time. That is to say, just as post-heritage film styling sought to maintain distinctions between Old Englishness and new Britishness, distinctions which barely concealed fundamental continuities of ideological substance, so too, New Labour's inflation of the difference between its 'newness' and the Tory past, a difference couched in terms of a farewell to a 'heritage' nationalism of castles and pageantry, barely concealed fundamental continuities with the Tories, especially economic ones.[78] The ideological effect of the style-caste couplet seems, therefore, to lie in its ability to assert the illusion of progressive historical discontinuities.

Monk observes that positive critical responses to 'post' or 'alternative' heritage films simply invert the errors committed by the earlier anti-heritage critics who were unable to see what for her are the progressive aspects of, for instance, many of the Merchant–Ivory films of the mid to late 1980s.[79] She is making a similar point to Wayne when she argues that *Elizabeth* is preoccupied with 'English sovereignty' in a way that speaks to a 'populist conservative anti-Europeanism and post-devolution English angst'.[80] Of the critical reception of *The Wings of the Dove* she complains that a 'Blairite image makeover' has been 'widely accepted as a "progressive" transformation in ideological substance'.[81] And of *Bridget Jones's Diary* – a film which in one scene explicitly cites the 'heritage aesthetic' – that it projects, 'a vision of the nation so uniformly young, white, wealthy, narcissistic and implicitly conservative, within a *mise en scène* cleansed of the urban poor, the homeless and ethnic minorities, that by contrast the 1980s heritage film looks like a paragon of socially inclusive, low-budget liberal filmmaking'.[82]

Monk's inclusion of *Bridget Jones's Diary* in her account of the heritage film 'debate' and her argument that the traces of a reactionary Englishness might be pursued not so much in the spectacle of period drama but in other generic cycles, including the 'gangster' films of the late 1990s as well as in romantic comedies, are interesting developments. The ideological elements found in heritage films are indeed 'not specific to films set in the past' and may be transferable across genres.[83] Fairytale London films such as *Notting Hill* provide *idyllically* complete, monocultural social worlds of Englishness. As we will see, such neo-heritage images of privilege are in an important sense orientated towards the 'pleasures of property'.[84] The updated heritage '*mise en scène* and milieu' used in such films as adornments of an Englishness coveted by a serene, contemporary possessing class, seems to take us far from the unstable, ambivalent vision of England found in the 1980s heritage film.[85]

Pandaemonium (2000) is an appropriate film with which to end this chapter as it helps to draw together some of the arguments made so far. It tells the story of the poetic and political adventures of the circle around Samuel Taylor Coleridge (Linus Roache) and William and Dorothy Wordsworth (John Hannah and Emily Woof). Set in the time of the Napoleonic wars, the film follows the fortunes of English Jacobinism and its influence on the middle-class radicalism and poetry of Coleridge and Wordsworth. The latter ends up betraying his friend and sister – along with the lower-class radical John Thelwall (Andy Serkis) – to the selfish pursuit of his career. In the film's opening scene we see Wordsworth as a respectable, middle-aged poet with his radical past safely behind him, waiting expectantly at a grand party for the King's messenger to appear and bestow the laureateship on him. The film is narrated from Coleridge's perspective. The latter's arrival at the party triggers a series of flashbacks cued by his continuing dependence on opium and we are transported back to the political and imaginative excitement of the 1790s which finds expression both in the poetry and private lives of the Wordsworths, Coleridge and their Jacobin comrades. Quickly, however, under the discouragement of the threat of government surveillance, the arrest and imprisonment of John Thelwall, and the internal domestic tensions amongst the friends, the hopeful sense of a new era of progressive social change in which poetry will play a part is replaced by a mood of retreat and isolation. Coleridge's poem ('Kubla Khan') stands as testament to this lost moment of utopian hope and struggle.

When the narrative flashbacks reach the present and we return to Wordsworth's party we discover that the latter's apostasy is not the victory of the sober reflection of age over the rashness of youth, but rather that it belongs to an earlier political betrayal. The laureateship is his expected reward for a long co-operation with government spies. Ironically, however, in a development which is supposed to indicate the ultimate indifference of the state towards matters of poetic value and its concern only with political conformity, the position goes to Robert Southey. The party is shot in a recognisably heritage style – our attention is drawn to the spectacular 'heritage properties', including the costumes and the lavish, authentic décor all of which is carefully choreographed around a high ceremonial occasion. It would seem difficult, however, to persuasively argue that the seductions of this spectacle work to take the edge off the radical libertarian sympathies of the narrative. The richness of the *mise en scène* is placed by the narrative as undesirable. Such sumptuousness is evocative of eighteenth-century ruling-class formality, and it is thus opposed in the film by a plain style that operates as an index of the poetic and political ideals of democratic romanticism.

Pandaemonium, as its Miltonic, allegorically post-revolutionary title suggests, seeks to excavate what Tom Paulin has called the republican 'puritan-radical' and 'popular' traditions from within the dominant 'aristocratic, hierarchical, conservative tradition' of heritage Englishness. It is what Paulin calls the 'syrupy drug' of monarchism, represented by the laureateship with its implied social conformity and deference to established authority, that the film's moral and political senses are set against.[86] As such, *Pandaemonium* belongs with those 1990s heritage films we looked at earlier which draw attention to the baleful qualities of the dominant, elite cultures of Englishness. Such films have continued to appear even after New Labour's attempt to co-opt such political energies through a kind of 'post-heritage', pseudo-modernisation of the national identity – the risible rebranding exercise of *Cool Britannia* – and a promised updating of state/constitution. Consider, for instance, the anti-Big House ethos of *Gosford Park* which puts on display an aristocratic England which is boorish, inelegant, philistinic, bullying and ruthless.

Like other heritage films before it, *Pandaemonium* contains ambivalences. However, these are not ones generated out of the contradiction between a progressive, liberal disapproval of an illiberal, privileged world and a covert

Figure 5 *Pandaemonium* – Coleridge's opium vision. Courtesy of Optimum Releasing

attraction to this same world's carefree solidities. The film is clear about wanting an end to the glamour of Old Englishness. However, its vision of the future is nevertheless problematic. We can see this in the narratively indeterminate supplement which accompanies the closing titles. In an innovatory anachronism, we find Coleridge wandering among the sites of contemporary London to the pop soundtrack of Lisa's 'Xanadu'. On one level this scene has been prepared for by the motif of time travel which accompanies Coleridge's drug experiences. At various points throughout the film we see the early twenty first century and the early nineteenth century brought together – often to indict the present in terms of Coleridge's nightmare visions. For instance, the contemporary 'anti-capitalist', eco-political imagery used to frame the nuclear facility at Hinckley Point is accompanied by Colerdige's composition of the 'Rime of the Ancient Mariner'. In the closing sequence, however, it becomes much harder to read the meanings generated by such constellations of past and present. We witness a thunderstruck Coleridge in various tourist/heritage locations – on the London Eye, rotating over the waterfront around the Embankment and the Palace of Westminster; walking through Piccadilly Circus near the statue of Eros; and sitting in City Airport from the windows of which can be seen the Millennium Dome. The first two sites in particular generate spectacular imagery through the use of time-lapse cinematography and fast-motion special effects. These scenes were shot at night and overexposed – the city's neon creates an intensely colourful, kaleidoscopic image. The panoramic views from the London Eye, in particular, appear to celebrate a contemporary London in which its venerable, 'historic' landmarks are transfigured into an intoxicating image of modernity. The saturated colour qualities of these images eclipse the more monochrome daylight shots of City Airport and of the Millennium Dome on the Greenwich Peninsula. The last shot shows the Dome reduced to a burning negative and clearly implies some sense of disenchantment. At this point, Coleridge's exploration of London seems to have exhausted itself and he is shown sitting apart, framed against the view of the Dome. The latter, as we will see in Chapter 7, was widely derided as a symptom of the hollowness of the New Labour vision for the future, and on some level clearly represented, for many, a disillusioning continuity between the new government and its New Right predecessors.[87] Notwithstanding this moment of dystopian doubt, on balance this 'epilogue', with its dazzling aesthetic effects, suggest not so much the stern verdict of the past on a future which has betrayed its hopes for progress, but rather the fulfillment of those hopes. This moment in *Pandaemonium* implies then that it is not just the ambivalently fascinating spectacle of an archaic Englishness which has the power to warp narratives of progressive liberalism, but also alluring images of a culture of millennial neo-liberal capitalism transmitted in spectacles of a transfigured London. It will be the aim of the next chapter to look more closely at this culture and its relationship with contemporary fairy tales of London.

CHAPTER 2

The Middle Classes: Fairy Tales and Idylls

The intention in this chapter is to consider the relationship of some of the most commercially successful British films of the 1990s to the culture of 'millennial', neo-liberal capitalism. *Sliding Doors*, *Notting Hill*, *Bridget Jones's Diary* and *Bridget Jones: The Edge of Reason*, all belong to a significant group of romantic comedies which have, in recent years, taken London as their backdrop.[1] Other relevant examples would include: *Jack and Sarah* (1995), *Martha – Meet Frank, Daniel and Laurence* (1998), *If Only* (1998), *This Year's Love* (1999), *Maybe Baby* (2000), *About a Boy* (2002), *Love Actually* (2003) and *Wimbledon* (2004). As Robert Murphy points out, 'London' in many of these films has been transformed into a 'fairy-tale' 'city of delights' and an 'enchanted village'.[2] This vision of an idyllic metropolis contrasts strikingly with the landscapes of 'underclass' decay and deindustrialisation which we will look at in the next two chapters. Nevertheless, a relationship between these outwardly very different types of representation is suggested by the structural features of neo-liberal capitalism. That is to say, a Manichean splitting between different worlds of class seems appropriate in a situation in which the widening material inequalities between the beneficiaries and victims of neo-liberal economics have been ideologically underscored, particularly in New Right political discourses, as a division between 'winners' and 'losers'. In this way, the culture of neo-liberalism differs markedly from its social democratic predecessor which sought to mitigate the fundamentally divisive effects of capitalism on the class structure. This does not mean to say that these fairy tale films make any neat fit with raw, New Right ideologies. They emerge during the years of the Tory party's post-Thatcherite twilight and the rise of New Labour. The accompanying shift in acceptable attitudes towards social deprivation is captured well in a scene from *Bridget Jones: The Edge of Reason* in which hard-faced Tory views on what the political right has traditionally called the 'undeserving poor' – in this instance beggars – are ridiculed by Bridget (Renee Zellweger). But Bridget's expression of sympathy and social concern belongs to a context in which the substantive existence of the social itself has become attenuated. Comaroff and Comaroff's general observations on neo-liberal culture help to clarify these points.[3] They pose what they rightly see as one of the most 'fundamental' questions about this culture, and that is, simply put: 'In what consists the social? Society? Moral community'?[4] That is to say, given that neo-liberalism, 'in its ideology and in its practice', seeks to 'replace society with the market', it is not surprising that the 'contours of "society" blur' and its 'organic solidarity disperses'.[5] What subsequently emerge are collectives built on a 'form of mechanical solidarity in which *me* is generalised into *we*'.[6] Bridget's confident dismissal of Tory contempt for 'losers' suggests that in this instance the *me* is capable of theoretically recognising the unpleasant consequences of neo-liberal political dogma. However, I will argue that both Bridget Jones films and *Notting Hill* remain particularly deficient in their conceptualisation of what lies beyond the special *me*. As we will see, it is the 'idyllic' form which appears to mediate this *blurred* social.

However, as well as *inter-class* differences between 'fairy tale' and derelict 'underclass' existences, we need to attend to *intra-class* differences and contrasts here, particularly within that most problematic of categories – the middle class. The chapter will open up this class categoristaion to the destabilising processes that tie it into the systemic imperatives of capitalism. Again, a good general description of the mobile, insecure world of class under neo-liberal capitalism is given by Comaroff and Comaroff: 'While the contours of the global proletariat are ghostly at best – and while the middle classes seem everywhere to be facing a loss of socio-economic security, their centre ground ever shakier – a transnationalist capitalist class is taking more and more tangible shape.'[7] I have already begun, in my introduction, to sketch the appearance of a ghostly 'global proletariat' of the past whose presence can be seen to impinge on its contemporary heirs; however, in this chapter my attention will be on the emergent *idylls* of a 'transnationalist capitalist class', particularly in *Notting Hill*, and on the insecurities of the middle class as it is presented within *Sliding Doors*. This is to divide up the terrain of these fairy tales and to study the films according to processes that link class to capitalism.

NOTTING HILL AND THE METROPOLITAN IDYLL

An atmosphere of untroubled contentment is unmistakable in *Notting Hill*. The film is imbued with an aura in which challenges to the social world it represents become unimaginable. In its highly crafted construction of public space it suggests an urban village whose foundations and limits are no longer tangible. That is to say, this idyllic space is exclusive and embedded but at the same time it is not a visibly enclosed, defended or class-contested space of privilege within the city. Such effects can be linked to the pacification of class landscapes which are a feature of the pastoral form. Here I have found Mikhail Bakhtin's discussion of the literary chronotope of the idyll useful.[8] What is a chronotope? Robert Stam succinctly defines it as a 'concrete spatiotemporal structure', one which mediates between 'the historical and the artistic, providing fictional environments where historically specific constellations of power are made visible'.[9] For Bakhtin the idyllic and pastoral chronotopes originate in what he calls the 'ancient matrix' of 'folkloric' culture.[10] In such pre-class cultures, the individual and the collective are not yet experienced as clearly distinct and there is a strong emphasis on the unity of humanity rooted in the 'gross realities of communal life'.[11] The idyllic chronotope evokes this unity in the special relationship of time to space it contains. Thus, in such forms, the life of an individual is grafted onto a 'familiar territory' in which the existence of the generations is encompassed.[12] As Bakhtin says, 'This little spatial world is limited and sufficient unto itself, not linked in any intrinsic way with other places, with the rest of the world. But in this little spatially limited world a sequence of generations is localised that is potentially without limit.'[13] This description suggests that the idyllic experience is characterised by a combination of disconnection, represented through spatial enclosure, and gratifying completeness, represented through temporal extension. We will return to these characteristics later.

As found in *Notting Hill*, the idyll resembles what Bakhtin calls the European novel's 'family' variant.[14] The latter adapts the motif of folkloric unity in bourgeois circumstances – unity of place is relocated to 'the ancestral family *town* house' which constitutes that 'immovable part (the real estate) of capitalist property'.[15] At the same time characters acquire a temporary mobility, moving out into a confusing world and eventually back into the limited, secure and known one which is figured in familial images. Bakhtin:

> The novel's movement takes the main hero (or heroes) out of the great but alien world of random occurrence into the small but secure and stable little world of the family ... where authentically human relationships are re-established, where the ancient matrices are re-established on a family base: love, marriage, childbearing, a peaceful old age for the in-laws, shared meals around the family table.[16]

When discussing the 'family novel' Bakhtin identifies its classic form in the English novel of the eighteenth and nineteenth centuries (Fielding, Smollet, Dickens).[17] Franco Moretti supplements Bakhtin when he isolates formal elements belonging to the ancient Greek 'romance' or 'adventure novel of ordeal' within the same tradition of the English novel.[18] Both forms present an essentialist, unchanging model of selfhood set against the confusions and complications of the plot. Moretti extrapolates from this, along the lines of the Nairn–Anderson theses, to argue the following: the English novel seeks to render the activity of capitalism – represented by the confused and confusing adventures endured by the heroes and heroines in an alien world – compatible with a classified, stable world in which property is not made but discovered, its origins and sustenance forever uncoupled from the activities of those who enjoy it.[19] The hero or heroine is charged with remaining true to their unchanging, essential self in order to trigger prosperity – they are therefore typically innocents and naifs.[20] In this way,

Moretti seeks to show how the English novel gives aristocratic legitimation to a bourgeois class that cannot – as a result of the thesis of aristocratic hegemony laid out by Nairn–Anderson – embrace the adventure of capitalist modernity without ambivalence. Moretti quotes Ross H. Dabney on this aspect of the English novel: 'Money is what counts, but making money is vulgar; a genteel young man must have wealth to begin with or acquire it passively. This is one reason for the recurrent fables in eighteenth- and nineteenth-century fiction of discovered identities and suppressed wills – one gets the inheritance, but actually one had it all along.'[21] Taken together, Moretti and Bakhtin's arguments offer a picture of an English cultural form, structured around a particular, *idyllic* conception of the social, which seeks to provide some insulation from capitalist realities.

By contrast, in nineteenth century Europe this idyllic 'little world' was seen as 'narrow' and isolated ('little' in the 'provincial' sense).[22] It might be argued that in cultures which were not yet dominated by the 'new' logic of capitalism, the idyll, as a symbolic form, was 'inadequate' for the purposes of the bourgeoisie.[23] (Thus, as both Moretti and Bakhtin point out, the European *bildungsroman* specifically set its face against the English novel's 'family idyll').[24] However, in an era in which capitalism has universalised itself, the 'little world' of the idyll becomes much more attractive. It offers an image of stability that draws on a dense heritage of Englishness that has been historically shaped, according to Wood, to respond to the problems of capitalism.[25] Thus, in the idyll's ability to transform the activities of capital accumulation into an interlude, an 'empty time' that 'leaves no traces'; in its related capacity to disconnect itself from what lies outside its always already established and solid world; in the impression it gives of the unchallengeable possession of property; and in its sense that the familiar repetitions of life are themselves a guarantee of their indefinite extension – in all these ways it offers security in a capitalist world.[26]

How can we apply the insights into literary history provided by Bakhtin and Moretti to *Notting Hill*? Certainly the film has the apparent self-sufficiency of the idyllic habitat. The opening voice-over of the principal character, William Thacker (Hugh Grant), is important in establishing the intactness of this world – as are the crane shots of the locale that begin and end the film. These *englobing* representations of the locale help to convey an atmosphere of proprietorial familiarity. As Thacker explains in this opening, 'Notting Hill' is a 'small village in the middle of London'. He adds, 'what's great is that lots have friends have ended up in this area'. The charmingly bemused passivity of the character, evident in the vagueness of this statement, fits with the convention which demands that such characters are kept innocent of the processes whereby wealth is created – here it is the characters' position within the booming London property market of the 1990s that hides, disingenuously, behind the configuration of their idyllic 'social' world'.[27] Furthermore, the proximity of friends, work and home creates the impression of the 'crowded little world' that Bakhtin identifies as typical of the idyllic form.[28] In the opening sequence, as Thacker walks down Portobello market, he refers to his bookshop as 'my *little* Travel Bookshop'. The bookshop and his house are in walking distance from one another – the house appears narrow, the blue door accentuating its position between what seem to be larger adjoining structures. The area offers a comfortable accessibility to Thacker and those like him – his friends. At various points he demonstrates – through the walks that punctuate narrative segments, or through his offers of help to Anna (Julia Roberts) after their second, accidental encounter – that the distances between home/shop/Portobello market are easy and advantageous.

This dimension of Thacker's world – its *littleness* – is chronotopic. It gives aesthetic shape to a social dimension or to a 'constellation' of power.[29] But what is the nature of that social dimension? In the opening sequence Thacker gives us a clue as to how it functions when he invokes the convention according to which scale figures social magnitude. As he puts it in his voice-over, Anna Scott – the film star who is to become his surprise lover – is a 'million, million miles away from the world I live in'. This social disparity between the elevated/stellar Anna and the humble/terrestrial William turns out to be illusory. What the narrative will demonstrate is how such a disparity of social scale can be accommodated by William's *little* world, thus proving wrong his own fear that 'Notting Hill' and 'Beverly Hills' cannot be brought together. Thacker's world can comfortably accommodate the star – who, as Church Gibson puts it, is 'enchanted' by the 'elegant village' he inhabits.[30] However, the enchantment is obviously not just a matter of topographical convenience. In a key scene Thacker and Anna enter one of Notting Hill's gated, residential gardens. As Thacker explains to her, 'all these streets around here have these mysterious, communal gardens in the middle of them, they are like little villages' and 'they are private villages, only the people who live around the edges are allowed in'. It will be just such a private garden that we discover the couple enjoying at the end of the film. We might say then that *littleness* signifies the *idyllic* experience of privileged possession. This is a privilege which includes a *mysterious* but pleasant social dimension, one which is capable of spanning apparently unbridgeable distances between people whilst remaining emphatically restricted and private. The film prefers to suggest that this privilege is the reward of an unassuming English charm; however, it is more materially grounded.

Clearly then, cosy-corner *Notting Hill* references what for Bakhtin are the significant topoi of the idyllic chronotope – precious enclosed space, children, marriage and collective meals are all given emphasis. One of the characters is a failed restaurateur and there are two scenes in his restaurant – one organised around a dinner for the friends. There are also regular dinner parties held at the house of William's ex-girlfriend, Bella (Gina McKee). The latter has been trying to have a child but in the course of the narrative discovers that she and her partner Max are unable to do so. The film ends with an image of procreative expectation at the heart of the urban village in a walled garden in which are found the pregnant Anna and partner. A scene that combines these idyllic motifs is the one in which Anna and William kiss for the first time in a gated garden at night. As the couple move into this enchanted space they discover a bench which is inscribed to the memory of 'June who loved this garden from Joseph who sat beside her'. The two couples become interchangeable as the idyllic location brings together, in one place, in a mystic communion, the lives of the 'various generations'.[31] Anna and William sit where June and Joseph sat – and later, at the end of the film, Anna and William will be seated on a similar bench, but now married and expecting a child, confirming the 'cyclic rhythmicalness of time so characteristic of the idyll'.[32] Here is that chronotopic combination of spatial enclosure and temporal extension that we have seen to be typical of the idyll. The time of 'nature' – parturition and the cyclic passage of the seasons – places us outside history. Possession is, in this way, accompanied by an unquestionable confidence.

Anna and William's kiss is accompanied by a distinctive, cinematographic flourish – an ascending, high-altitude crane shot which slowly rotates as it climbs over the lovers on the bench below. This camera movement seems to carry a complex combination of associations. The sensation of weightlessness might metaphorically reference love's ecstatic state; however, it also suggests that degree of confident expansiveness that is the peculiar quality of this particular idyllic form. The camera's motion combines elevation with circularity, and provides an image of a delimited place – when seen from above – that can be likened to the pastoral's traditional representation of 'temple space'.[33] For Angus Fletcher, temple iconography in the English Romantic tradition – such as the *hortus conclusus* of Spencerian Romance – designates 'hallowed ground' which, in the process of excluding the chaotic profane world, constructs a microcosm out of the 'quality of sacred centredness'.[34] This 'sacred space' can be both defensive and expansive – representing as it does, allegorically, the purified form of the larger world.[35] It is the stilled centre or 'omphalos' of the world where the experience of ritual recurrence 'collapses ordinary time'.[36] Note how the dialogue in the scene is mixed with music after the couple kiss. The only words are Anna's absorbed recitation of the inscription on the bench and her invitation to William to sit with her – this is language as heirurgic performance. Note also how her voice is detached from her image as the camera climbs, and mixed with the song, it resonates at the volume it would if our position remained close to where she is sitting on the bench. Her voice and presence – and his as addressee – fill the space opened up by the shot with the sensation of idyllic closure.

Whilst undoubtedly evoking a self-sufficient, privileged exclusivity, the idyll of *Notting Hill* does not represent a simple denial of the world beyond its borders. We can explore the nature of the outward directedness of the idyll if we attend to the range of unobtrusive, comic references to the 'world' throughout the film – references that have been overlooked by those focusing on the more marked representation of social exclusivity and homogeneity in the film.[37] For instance, there is the running joke according to which the everyday misfortunes of individuals are measured against more fundamental human tragedies. This joke illustrates what William refers to as the ability to retain a 'normal amount of perspective'. Thus, immediately after his voice-over introduction, the first character he encounters is his Welsh, proletarian flatmate, Spike (Rhys Ifans), who has an 'incredibly important' decision to make – which t-shirt to wear on a date. William's immediate and sardonic response is to ask if this decision compares with the importance of 'Third World debt'. Later, and in sarcastic retaliation, when William is himself urgently looking for his glasses before a date with Anna, Spike asks him if the inconvenience of frequently mislaying his spectacles might be compared to 'earthquakes in the Far East, or testicular cancer'. Finally, in the scene in which William is trying to persuade Anna that she needs to acquire a due sense of proportion about her concerns with the press besieging his house – as she puts it the images of her affair with him will be appear from 'here to Timbuktu' – Spike interrupts to inform her that in arguing against her overreaction, Thacker will probably ask her to consider 'the starving in Sudan'.

'Notting Hill' on the one hand – the 'Third World', the Far East, Timbuktu and the Sudan on the other. What are we to make of this juxtaposition of the metro-politan idyll and a chaotic, non-western world beyond its borders – a chaos in which unavoidable natural catastrophe (earthquake) is mixed with the kind of avoidable mass death (starvation) whose origins ultimately lie in systemic social forms such as capitalism? In Bakhtin's account it can be seen how the idyll – despite the emphasis on its lack of any 'intrinsic' relationship to 'the rest of the world' – is in a position to construct the illusion that it speaks for universal human life.[38] This illusion is a manifestation of the relationship between the idyll and what we have seen Bakhtin call the ancient folkloric matrices.[39] The 'gross realities'[40] of this ancient, pre-class complex – collective labour, food, copulation, birth, death – are absorbed within an 'all-embracing whole'.[41] As this breaks up, these elements diverge and are only apparently held together in forms such as the idyll which offer an echo, in the context of the divisions of class society, of the 'unified time of collective human life'.[42] The topos of the family idyll under capitalism, for instance, presents only a 'limited idyllic collective'.[43] Nevertheless, the family idyll makes claims to stand for 'authentically human relationships'.[44] At the same time, such claims are grounded on an opposition between 'the great, cold, alien world' on the one hand, and idyllic 'warm little corners of human feel-ing and kindness' on the other.[45] There is, then, a concealed logic of abandon-ment here – a self-justifying narrowing of the human community which, at the same time, presents itself as in touch with the basic collective realities and values of a universal humanity. The idyll, with its residual motifs of a pre-class collective, is a form serviceable in the context of class societies which are required to deny class in the name of humanity.

The examples cited above of William's ethical concern with what lies beyond the idyll are revealed, through Spike's mocking, proletarian skepticism, to be self-serving. One possible implication of Spike's sarcasm is that the 'coldness'/chaos of the world – duly acknowledged and regretted – can become an excuse to ignore the immediate social conflicts one is implicated in, as well as a means of intensifying, by contrast, the sense of one's own good fortune. The comic theme of the 'world' beyond the 'little village' then, despite its apparently incidental significance in the film, coherently presents that combination of explicit concern for others (charitable subjectivity) and covertly contented middle-class fatalism that can persist even in the face of the suffering of those others. The character amongst William's friends who literally embodies the importance of remembering human suffering is Bella, his paralysed ex-girlfriend. He cites her case to Anna as an example which illustrates why the fortunate need to retain a sense of due proportion in the face of their own difficulties. It is interesting that this same character makes the announcement during a dinner party, that the course of human life has no has 'no rhyme or reason'. Of course on one level Bella is refer-ring to her own unforeseeable and meaningless accident. However, her remarks also help to legitimate a diminishment of the sense of social implicatedness and responsibility, and in this way they echo the idyllic logic of abandonment referred to above. A world without 'reason' absolves us of the need to seek out the *causes* of social phenomena and a world that does not 'rhyme' absolves us of the need to make *connections*.

In *Bridget Jones's Dairy* and *Bridget Jones: The Edge of Reason* an ethical relationship between the idyll and the world is represented through the professional life of Mark Darcy (Colin Firth). In the earlier film he is a barrister defending the right of a Kurdish 'freedom fighter' to resist deportation. In the later film, however, there is a significantly different articulation of this aspect of his character. When Bridget is wrongly arrested in Thailand for drug trafficking, his professional concern for the injustice done to others is made to overlap with his personal concern for his lover, and the ethical dimension to his character expands, taking the form of a manifold power to *make things happen*. Using pro-fessional networks which pass through the Foreign Office, British embassies in the Middle and Far East, Interpol and MI5, he has Bridget discreetly exonerated and released. What seems particularly notable about the Bangkok jail scenes is the contradiction between the concern for others, represented by Mark's association with 'human rights', and the image provided of those others. Like William from *Notting Hill*, Bridget encourages herself to maintain a level of 'perspective' on her situation relative to the other women who surround her in the jail, some of whom, it is made clear, have suffered at the hands of abusive men. However, this difference is transformed into a conventional colonial figure – the fascination of the non-white for the white woman. On leaving, as if cloning herself, Bridget hands out gifts which reproduce the reference points of her own privileged identity. The *idyllic me* takes pity on those whose lives are abandoned to the 'great, cold alien world', and solipsistically offers itself, a 'warm little corner', as a foundation for an *idyllic we*. Critics' embarrassment and complaints about the bad taste of these scenes are a clear indication of their ideological dysfunction-ality.[46]

Bridget Jones: The Edge of Reason concludes with English kitsch. The camera rises above the terrain of Mark and Bridget's idyll to give us an encompassing, high-angle shot of a snow-covered churchyard, complete with ancestral tomb-stones and enclosed valley beyond. The fairy tale circle is joined. This sequel already constitutes the 'happy ever after' of the first film's ending. Indeed, *Bridget Jones: The Edge of Reason* begins by addressing the problem of how to start a narrative within a fairy tale. We see Mark and Bridget romping on Parliament Hill, the London skyline laid out before them. The beginning appears pre-empted by the already known end. Mark and Bridget are clearly 'destined' for one another – as Bridget's mother recalls, they even played together as children. Bridget does not have to do anything to end up with Mark who likes her 'just as she is'. In this way, the inconsistent use, in both films, of a feminist point about the oppressiveness of female 'self-improvement' culture easily shifts into another register – that symbolic legitimation of the innocent self that Moretti describes in the English *bildungsroman*. Recall that in Moretti's analysis the rewards of class privilege must not be struggled for; instead they are given as one's due. Bridget and Darcy's idyll is grounded in this tradition and of course Darcy is named after the aristocratic hero in Jane Austen's *Pride and Prejudice*. As Moretti points out, it is the old English, bourgeois–aristocratic capitalist ruling bloc which is celebrated in the marital union of this novel – a ruling bloc constructed on the denial of the capitalism from which its material comforts derive.[47]

It is this same bloc – updated – which, as Roger Bromley notes, is visible in *Notting Hill*'s Working Title predecessor, *Four Weddings and a Funeral*.[48] Bromley:

> The alliance of class fractions which represents the dominant power bloc is almost entirely invisible [in contemporary British film]: we catch glimpses of this bloc in a film like *Four Weddings and a Funeral* – although only in its 'decorative' role – but part of the achievement of this bloc has been its ability to slip through the prevailing currencies – visual and narrative – of identity and representation. Dispersed, international, corporate and impersonal, it eludes figuration... The power bloc's only consistent mediation is through the parasitic lens of 'celebrity', which focuses on lifestyle rather than on the specifics of its exploitative activities.[49]

It is interesting that Bromley draws attention to the mediation of this class through 'celebrity', as this is an explicit theme in *Notting Hill*. But more than this, these Working Title films appear to play with celebrity not only within the diegesis but also on its borders. *Bridget Jones: The Edge of Reason* seems to make reference to the arrest of Hugh Grant in Hollywood – after *Four Weddings and a Funeral* made him famous in America – on a charge of indecent behaviour with a prostitute. Thus, Daniel Cleaver, played by Grant, briefly becomes a Bangkok sex-tourist. Subtler links are to be found in *Notting Hill* which at times seems to work as a meditation, within the fiction, on its two stars' concern with their private lives. The film appears to allude, teasingly, to off-screen lives through the relationship between star persona and fictional role – for instance, Roberts, Grant's love interest here, played a Hollywood hooker in *Pretty Woman* (1990). With its self-conscious, ironic familiarity and solidarity between American and English celebrities, the film engages our sense of peering through Bromley's 'parasitic lens' of celebrity at a class which, as he says, tends to elude figuration.

Finally, we need to consider the production context of these films as it can provide another dimension to the image of capitalism and Englishness so far explored. *Notting Hill*, *Bridget Jones's Diary* and *Bridget Jones: The Edge of Reason* were produced by Working Title whose post-1980s history displays the contemporary alignment of the British film industry with, in the words of co-chairman Eric Fellner, 'filmmaking as a global business'.[50] Set up originally to produce 'socio-economic and political movies with a strong narrative' Working Title was behind *My Beautiful Laundrette* and *Sammy and Rosie Get Laid* – two films which are very different from the later productions under discussion here.[51] Taken over by Polygram Film Entertainment in 1992, and then by Universal-Seagram in 1998, it shifted its approach and sought to 'exploit British cultural materials in the American market'.[52] The commercial success of *Four Weddings and a Funeral* in 1994 provided a formula which thereafter became a 'brand identity: neo-heritage locations, white middle-class characters and films with a geographical awareness that points firmly across the Atlantic'.[53] The use of American actresses is perhaps the most explicit aspect of the last mentioned aspect of the new formula – thus the presence of MacDowell (*Four Weddings and a Funeral*), Roberts (*Notting Hill*), Dunst (*Wimbledon*) and Zellweger (*Bridget Jones's Diary* and *Bridget Jones: The Edge of Reason*).

As Mike Wayne points out, Working Title's post-*Four Weddings and a Funeral* output has neglected to address the 'antagonisms, complexities and diversity of life in the UK'.[54] He describes Working Title's dependence on the American market as involving a form of neo-colonialism. The company, a subsidiary passed from one 'Cultural Transnational Corporation' to another, provides a profitable one-dimensional Englishness that assists in 'the ideological role of giving advanced capitalism the appearance-form of plurality and diversity'.[55] The clichés of the upper reaches of the English class system become a means of 'screening off monopolistic tendencies' of a global media corporation. This same process is particularly well-illustrated by Working Title 2, which was set up to exploit a 'slightly more differentiated' Britishness rather than the Englishness of Working Title's earlier efforts. *Billy Elliot* was the first Working Title 2 production and, as Wayne points out, it provides a 'disembedded', middle-class view on a 'cultureless' working class which is of interest only in as much as it provides a tame degree of regional and class colour.[56] Of course the Englishness of Working Title's core business is already marked by that cultural simulation which is a characteristic of the 'pristine culture of capitalism' – a culture in which, as Wood has it, the infrastructural shells of older social forms, particularly archaic class images, have covered over the dynamic forces of capitalism. When viewed in this way the timeless, kitschy England of *Bridget Jones: The Edge of Reason*'s closing provides, paradoxically, an appropriate image for the contemporary transnational capitalist class whose presence such fairy tales allude to.

SLIDING DOORS: THE FEVERS OF THE NEW MIDDLE CLASSES

Sliding Doors is more troubled than the assured *Notting Hill*. It displays the contradiction between the idyll and the 'larger world' because it puts the category of the middle class under pressure. What becomes apparent in this film, when it is compared with the representations of class found in *Notting Hill*, is that the middle class is itself a site of struggle. In fact, the post-war 'new middle class' is, from some perspectives, not really a class at all – as Alex Callinicos puts it:

> the NMC ['new middle classes'] are not a class in the sense that the bourgeoisie or the proletariat are a class. Workers and capitalists have each a distinct and coherent set of interests deriving from their position in the relations of production. This is not true of the NMC because they occupy contradictory class locations that pull them in two directions… In other words, it [the NMC] is a collection of heterogeneous social layers who have in common an ambiguous and intermediate position with respect to the fundamental contradiction between capital and wage-labour.[57]

Sliding Doors opens up the cracks in this 'new middle class' – its identity is seen to unravel under the impact of a capitalist dynamic. But how do such larger questions of class experience manifest themselves in the film? The reading of *Sliding Doors* offered here rests on the peculiarity of the film's bifurcating narrative structure which presents two alternative and concurrently running plot lines for the same characters. Often in such narratives, the protagonist's initial situation motivates the temporal anomaly of 'splitting'. Thus, the need for a character to remodel the past or halt the present in order to grasp or investigate other, possible futures is conventionally behind such innovative, 'alternative reality' narrative forms.[58] No such premise is provided in this film. Instead the metaphor of 'spooling back' the tape of someone's life – represented literally in the image as a ghostly video-rewind – sets up the initial bifurcation between Helen (Gwyneth Paltrow) and her double.[59] The gratuitousness of the initiation of the narrative encourages us to consider whether the relationship between the two plot strands might in some way be understood as seeking to resolve an inexplicit problem whose existence is betrayed in this beginning. On the manifest level of the narrative the problem is the difficulty of resolving the romantic dilemmas of the heroine. The first Helen's partner, Gerry (John Lynch), is having an affair with Lydia (Jeanne Tripplehorn) who is his previous girlfriend. This Helen (Helen 1) is unaware of Gerry's infidelity at the beginning of the story but eventually discovers the deception. The second Helen's story is a variant of Helen 1's. Helen 2 discovers Gerry's unfaithfulness as a result of catching the tube train. However, whether or not the stranger – James (John Hannah) – she has met on the same train is a genuine suitor or a charming adulterer is left unclear until the final scenes.

Considered thus, the issues that seek resolution in the narrative are those which are conventionally found in the plots of mainstream, heterosexual romantic comedies. However, we can reformulate these manifest narrative concerns in terms of what they suggest of the difficulties that lie within the middle-class urban idyll. Marshall Berman's work on the history of the experience of urban modernity is useful in providing a more detailed sense of these difficulties.[60] According to Berman's reading of the writings of Charles Baudelaire, urban modernity challenges us to dialectically overcome the opposition between an uncritically positive 'modern pastoral' and a one-dimensionally negative 'counter pastoral'.[61] That is to say, the experience of urban modernity demands a recognition not only of the exhilaration of modern technologies, new forms of public space and the crowds of strangers within them – an exhilaration which Baudelaire describes in his poetry in terms of the intoxicating possibilities of city romance – but also of the disfiguring evidence of class struggle and poverty whose causes cannot be painlessly resolved through the progress of capitalist modernity.[62] The neo-liberal urban idyll of London in the 1990s, as it is represented in a film like *Notting Hill*, not only excludes such disfigurements but is not engaged, in the way that *Sliding Doors* is, with the exhilarations of urban modernity. The problem that disturbs *Sliding Doors* is that an invocation of such exhilarations, in the generic form of the romantic comedy, brings with it the dilemmas of the experiences of class.

In order to examine more fully these dilemmas, it is necessary to continue interrogating the narrative and generic features of the film – that is to say, the parallel plot structure and the conventions of romantic comedy. Starting with the latter, if the utopian aspects of romantic comedy have often been associated with the experiences of urban modernity, then increasingly, in the context of the socially segregated forms of urban postmodernity, the thrills of the anonymous crowd, public transportation, modern city architecture and chance encounters with the 'stranger' – all key elements in the genre – have diminished. If we now reconsider the beginning of the film it is apparent that the tube encounter between Helen 2 and James foregrounds the difficulty of their exchanges – a difficulty which his confident and comically self-deflating performance only partially obscures. That is to say, this conversation at least raises the suggestion of harassment, stalking and aberrant public behaviour. The dialogue in this scene makes this problem explicit. After mentioning the general absence of conversation on the tube, James, who continues to talk to Helen despite her silence, assures her that he is not 'a potential psychopath or drunk'. Helen assures him that she does not think that he is a 'psychopath'. Before getting off the train, James warns her that if they get off at the same station that he is 'not following' her. Having got off the train, she apologises in case she has given the impression that she thinks him a 'nutcase or psycho'. It is the counter-pastoral 'contamination' of public space by the ejectees of the old welfare state – in this instance, those suffering mental health problems – that appears to lurk behind these exchanges.

The end of the film re-imagines this meeting as a chance encounter in a lift. Helen 2 is dead, however, because Helen 1 retains memories of her experiences as Helen 2 she is able to respond to James spontaneously, without consciously knowing how or why she can complete his conversational cue. In other words, the final scene attempts to present an authentic beginning – the redemption of the romance of urban modernity in London's fairy tale world – that the film appears to recognise is difficult to accommodate in the contemporary middle-class urban idyll. The fact that these *strangers* are, from the spectator's perspective, really *friends* who do not recognise each other, indicates the extent to which the narrative fails to generate a solution to this problem. True strangers, in other words, remain excluded from the idyll and the difficulty of the first meeting between the two remains unresolved.

But this film is not just about the exhaustion of the culture of urban modernity, and again it is important to attend to the bifurcated narrative structure which provides two different class trajectories for the heroine. The film actually begins with a sacking – Helen is dismissed from her job in a male-dominated company on the pretext of office theft. Helen 2 recovers from this setback – in fact this plot strand suggests, in classic neo-liberal fashion, that her sacking is actually a blessing in disguise as it provides her with the opportunity to recognise her own strengths and set up in business for herself. Helen 1, however, does not recover from her sacking and slips down into a casualised, rigorously exploited labour force rather than rising 'upwards', drawn, like Helen 2, towards the capitalist class. The social milieu of the film suggests then the 'contradictory class locations' of the new middle class. This is a class whose apparent unity of status actually conceals a diversity of different class positions – proletarianised in peripheral, insecure jobs at one extreme and an intimately related professional-managerial adjunct to the capitalist system at the other.[63] After she loses her job, we see Helen 1 repeatedly subjected to humiliation in menial occupations. It is the exploitation of the working class inherent in the neo-liberal culture of customer sovereignty that emerges in these scenes. Take the scene in which Helen 1, as sandwich delivery girl to the gleaming office blocks of the city, is unknowingly ambushed by her partner's lover, Lydia. Here the complexities of the generic plot pattern (the spite of a love rival) are inflected with class antagonisms (Lydia uses the discourse of consumer pre-eminence to browbeat her opponent). Note how cowed and submissive Helen 1 appears in this scene – when internalised by workers this peremptory culture of customer sovereignty helps to further secure the conditions of exploitation. Another, perhaps the key, example of this effect is to be found towards the end of the film when Helen 1 goes for what she thinks is a job interview. In fact she is being set up once again by Lydia. The latter, pretending to be a potential employer, arranges for Helen to arrive at her flat at a time that coincides with one of Gerry's clandestine visits. The interview is intended as a form of romantic intimidation and dismissal. At this point Helen 1 is pregnant and the shock of discovering her partner's infidelity plays a part in the accident that leads to her losing her baby. The film here is mixing together the melodramatic plot turns of romantic comedy with representations of class antagonism that belong to another story world. If we recall the first scene of the film in which the convention of the purposeful, energy charged middle-class working day in the shiny city is abruptly and embarrassingly terminated as soon as Helen enters the office, then this penultimate scene, with blackly absurdist logic, completes the process by which her life is crushed. Her story turns out to be dominated by the despotic power of the neo-liberal job market – from unjust sackings for which there is little protection to this final absurdist scenario in which the power of the employer over employee is imagined as a kind of omnipotence that is no respecter of the 'private' person. Helen 1 stands no chance of making the transition made by her successful double. Thus Helen's 1's story is an ironic comment on that of Helen 2.

But the question that then poses itself is this – why does the successful Helen die and the comprehensively defeated Helen 1 survive? Robert Murphy is able to explain the death of Helen 2 by claiming that the film follows the conventions of the fairy tale. Thus the two lives are judged according to the moral polarisations common to the form:

> *Sliding Doors* begins as an archetypal 'Cool Britannia' film with its trendy, prosperous, classless, young people. But in the story where Helen follows the New Labour path to happiness by starting her own business she is run over by a white van – the embodiment of untamed proletariat aggression – and dies. The Helen who survives is the one who works like a dog in low-paid jobs and learns the lessons of life the hard way. [64]

In what ways then does Murphy's reading of the *Sliding Doors* fit with the one proposed here? There seems little to support the idea that the successful Helen dies because she is crassly 'New Labour' in outlook. In fact it might be argued that Murphy's allegorical reading works, in this instance, to prematurely resolve and therefore conceal this symptomatic awkwardness in the narrative. There is little sense of the character's failings being a cause of her death (likewise the allegorising of the white van as a force of 'untamed proletariat aggression' is perhaps overly schematic and an unfortunate endorsement of middle-class views of the working class as a natural force of violence). As I have been suggesting here, it might be useful to pursue the sense of this difficulty in the narrative further and to seek to understand whether or not this formal feature might be symptomatic of underlying social contradictions. It may be the case that these two plot patterns need to be understood as working together to address concealed problems, rather than separated according to the textual logic of the fairy tale with a virtuous Helen on the one hand and a fallen Helen on the other.[65]

I began by arguing that the film struggles to revive the form of the romance of urban modernity. The values of mobility, self-transformation and freedom associated with modernity are thus placed in a social space which is increasingly unable to sustain them. In this respect it is interesting that the success narrative, premised as it is on the early and liberating discovery of infidelity which the deceived Helen 1 is deprived of, does not break open new social perspectives for Helen 2. What is striking about this story is the way in which Helen 2 is drawn deeper into a familiar social world. That is to say James, her new partner, is known to her old partner, and clients introduced to her through James know of her professional reputation – a reputation established in her earlier advertising/publicity job. A key scene in this respect is the restaurant opening which Helen 2 is employed to host by friends of James. It is at this moment that Gerry reappears and Helen 2's new social world is made to overlap with her old one. That this coincidence occurs in a restaurant is significant – the latter appears as a contemporary version of Bakhtin's 'warm little corners' of the idyllic 'little world'. We might say then that this film foregrounds the difference between the contemporary metropolitan *idyll* and the older urban utopianism of modernity as described by Berman.

At this point the question of who dies and why becomes more interesting. Superficially, it does indeed appear, as Murphy argues, that the virtuous and embattled proletarianism of Helen 1 succeeds over the fashion and privilege of Helen 2. However, the suggested development of the story at the conclusion of the film is for Helen 1's life to converge with Helen 2's. Helen 1's meeting with James in the lift and the déjà vu of the exchange between them points the way. Moya Luckett is making the same point when she argues that 'The death of blonde Helen [Helen 2] at the end suggests a return to authenticity, but the film inverts this, strongly hinting that brunette Helen's [Helen 1] life will follow the same trajectory trail-blazed by her blonde counterpart.' [66] Helen 2 dies then not just because she is successfully entrepreneurial and too visibly resident within a 'warm little corner' but because in sacrificing her, the film can remodel the equally unattractive fate to be glimpsed in the crushing humiliation of proletarianised drudge Helen 1. With Helen 2 dead, Helen 1 can restart the adventure of modernity whilst avoiding what Berman calls the 'darker potential of its economic and political drives'.[67] At the same time, however, if Helen 1 is destined to step into the idyllic little world vacated by Helen 2, then that older, 'heroic' experience of modernity can only be present as an anticipation, never an actuality.

The last conversation between Gerry and Helen 1 is one in which the sliding 'doors' of the film's title finally become an unproblematic division of space/life marking an outside and an inside against which Helen can locate herself. That is to say, Helen – now returned to herself as her double is dead – asks Gerry simply to walk through the door of her hospital room and to close it behind him. This gesture of clarification is required – the new Helen needs to distance herself from a world so clearly sustained on naked class hostility (Lydia) and solipsism (Gerry).[68] Equally, she needs to be distanced from the other extreme of 'victimhood' – the Helen that closes the door on Gerry is a woman whose exploitation in the neo-liberal labour market is matched by her exploitation by her own partner. (Gerry is not only unfaithful to Helen 1, he is also living off her wages whilst he writes a novel.) With the rebirth of a Helen equipped with an unconscious aptitude for striking up promising relationships based on patterns of cultural and social recognition – the 'Monty Python' test – what disappears is the sense of the bottom range of the *sliding* social scale on which the middle classes must exist. Thus, as much as the film strenuously works to avoid the embarrassment of a middle class drawn into the cosy orbit of the capitalist class, equally, it seeks to close the door on the fear of a *working middle class*. Which is to say, it wants to find what it cannot: a class that is in the middle.

CHAPTER 3

The Working Class: Elegies

Whilst the 1980s saw intense political conflict and economic restructuring, it was only towards the end of the period of continuous Tory rule begun in 1979 that films addressing the epic struggle and defeat of the industrial working class began to appear. These films, including *Brassed Off*, *The Full Monty*, *Among Giants*, *Dockers* and *Billy Elliot*, are all affiliated to the tradition of British social realism; however, there are, as we will see, significant differences in their ideological orientation. Critical responses have stressed their presentation of class through the prism of gender.[1] Nostalgically patriarchal, impotent and domestically confined – this is a male working class that is pictured as struggling to cope with economic superfluousness along with the perceived irrelevance and anachronism of its masculinist cultural and political traditions.[2] Some have drawn attention to the links between the films and Blairism.[3] From such a perspective, *The Full Monty* and *Billy Elliot* can be read as calling on the assistance of superficial, multicultural images of collectivity in order, like New Labour, to banish an older world of class and class conflict, and move into a stylish, modernised future.[4] For Cora Kaplan, films like *The Full Monty* suggest a more complex, nuanced relationship with Blairism. She sees fantasies of 'radical communitarianism'[5] in *The Full Monty*'s inclusion of alternative identities – fantasies which perform a critique of the Blairite 'conservative modernity' that in other ways the film endorses, particularly in its investment in the 'enduring values of family'.[6] For Hill, on the other hand, *The Full Monty* and *Brassed Off* reference an older, social democratic ethos in which images of the working-class community are mobilised in order to construct national allegories of unity.[7]

My own approach will be to explore the relationship between the films and the world of neo-liberalism. As Huw Beynon puts it, this is a world in which a 'growing complex of jobs and labour contracts' have combined with 'gender and ethnic difference' to produce a 'mosaic' of 'fragmented labour' that is not easy to represent in 'simple images'.[8] In view of this, the chapter covers a range of films which permit us to explore both the diversity *and* the common ground shared by this evolving working class. I will not, in other words, restrict myself to studying images of Yorkshire miners, Sheffield steel workers and Liverpool dockers, but will include a consideration of the representation of those whose existence is often deemed to lie somehow 'outside' the working class – either as

a result of belonging to an unemployed 'underclass' or because such individuals
are thought of more in terms of some sociological attribute such as 'youth'. It is
for this reason that I have selected two 'youth' films to add to the post-industrial
'elegies' of *Brassed Off*, *The Full Monty*, *Dockers* and *Among Giants*, namely
Human Traffic and *Late Night Shopping* (2001).[9] There are common experiences of exploitation figured in *Human Traffic* and *Late Night Shopping* which
I have chosen to approach through the paradoxes supplied by a Department of
Employment advertisement from the late 1980s whose slogan ran: 'Let's train
the workers without jobs, to do the jobs without workers'.[10] On a literal level
this statement suggests the neo-liberal state's continuity with the objectives of
social democratic inclusion and full employment – thus *workers without jobs*
are to be found employment in an exercise whose disarming simplicity suggests
that the problem of unemployment is merely one of training and the subsequent
matching of supply and demand within the labour market. Intriguingly, however, this palindrome also implies a new conceptualisation of employment
which can no longer be understood within the political discourses of social
democracy. Thus, *a job without a worker* might be understood as a new kind
of job altogether – one in which the expectations and defences relied on by
a person who would once have claimed the status of 'worker' are no longer
available. Whilst social democracy recognised the legitimacy of unionised labour
and the category of 'worker', within the culture of neo-liberalism the protected
relationship between 'worker' and 'job' is severed. As the bosses in Ken Loach's
The Navigators (2001) put it – echoing an admonition which has become part
of a new common sense – 'jobs are not for life'. Indeed, as I will seek to show,
these 'jobs' have a particular, parasitic relationship to the 'life' of the 'worker'.
One name for such jobs within the neo-liberal labour market is the 'McJob'
– or 'low prestige, low paid' employment associated with the intense levels
of exploitation common to casualised and 'flexible' working practices.[11] It is
just such employment which is featured in *Late Night Shopping*, and whilst I
would not seek to disregard the different perspectives and probable prospects
of 'twentysomething slackers' and those of redundant dockers, miners, steel-
workers or railway labourers, nevertheless the representation of both groups in
these films, when taken together, can help us to develop an image of the neo-
liberal labour market 'mosaic' along with the values and beliefs that support it.

GHOSTS OF '84

As if by a process of delayed action, *Brassed Off* gave expression to a popular
mood disturbed by the legacy of the struggles between the neo-liberal state and
organised labour that had taken place a decade earlier in the mid 1980s. The
film presents the superior value of an older culture of mutuality and collective
belonging over a newer, dishonourable one dedicated to the pursuit of individual

gain. Its representation of money helps to convey this distaste. Take the character of Gloria (Tara Fitzgerald), a local who has moved away to train as a surveyor and who returns, at the behest of Grimley colliery's management, to conduct a survey on the future viability of the pit. After realising how her work has been used to cloak the management's determination to close the pit with the appearance of dialogue and concern, she hands over what she calls the 'dirty money' of her salary to the colliery brass band. 'Dirty money' can be cleansed, turned into honest 'brass' by being donated to the impoverished band. In the moral structure of the film 'dirty money' represents a bribe which in turn is the monetary transaction which typifies a ruling class seeking to buy off or divert political opposition to its attack on King Coal. The redundancy payment offered by the management to the miners is the key example of dirty money – its primary function is to divide the miners and to encourage them not to vote to seek a review of the 'economic' status of their pit. Money distorts the vote by making it an unreliable representation. The agony of Phil (Stephen Tomkinson), a miner who wants the pit to remain open but feels constrained to vote for a redundancy pay-off, is a good example of this process. His predicament is a result of the strike of 1984 during which time he was imprisoned for his union activities, and then later dismissed by the pit. Eventually reinstated, his level of indebtedness threatens to split his family up. Loan sharks hover around his house; his wife cannot afford the family groceries. His situation is only made worse when he incurs further debt in order to continue playing in the colliery band. According to the arguments of his bandleader father, Danny (Pete Postlethwaite), this brass band represents a collective tradition which requires asserting even in the face of what all the miners recognise, from the beginning, as the inevitable closure of Grimley. With his trombone falling apart Phil purchases a new one. However, neither the IOU accepted by the seller nor the loan/gift of a five-pound note folded into his wife's receipt at the supermarket by a checkout assistant sympathetic to the family's impoverishment, can rescue him from voting for his own redundancy.

What is *given* in this film cannot contain the destructive effects of what is *taken*. The *taking* is represented by the pitiless logic of the neo-liberal 'market' and its representative, the pit manager Mr McKenzie (Stephen Moore) – I will return to this character shortly. The *giving* includes: the 'subs' from the members of the band to their collective 'kitty'; the 'collection' to buy something for the hospitalised, dying Danny; Gloria's donation; the 'credit' given to Phil by the music shop; and the gift given to his wife in the supermarket. We might even include in this cycle of giving, the hopeless bets that Gloria's childhood sweetheart, Andy (Ewan McGregor), makes with his mates in the pub. Such exchanges are an example of the kind of 'non-productive expenditure' whose object is to sustain precious rituals of working-class socialisation.[12] *Brass* – kitties, gifts, collections and donations, bets, IOUs – stands for what passes between the working class outside the circuits of capitalist exchange. It represents a rejection of the competitive individualism of the market and symbolises a working-class moral economy whose values are co-operative and communal. Perhaps one of the most vivid images of this culture is provided at the very beginning of the film. As the miners exit the pit lift at the end of their shift they place dull-coloured tokens in the palm of an outstretched hand – presumably a tally system designed to ensure they are all accounted for after their shift. The relationship between the token and each life is peculiarly powerful. The coin is an arbitrary symbol of the individual carrying it, but it has the power to link that individual to the solicitousness of the collective. On surrender this worthless *brass farthing* secures a life.

Although set in 1992, *Brassed Off* is a coda to the convulsive national strike of 1984. However, rather than simple nostalgia for the past powers of the industrial working class this backwards view involves a process of clarification. As Seumas Milne points out, at the time of the pit closures of 1992 there was a 'sea-change in popular attitudes' towards the strike of 1984.[13] In the intervening years it had become difficult to avoid the conclusion that the Tories' 'economic' arguments against the miners were hostage to their anti-union political project.[14] Ironically, given the principles of neo-liberal capitalism, to finally bury the miners and establish the futility of resisting market imperatives, it had been necessary to 'fix' the energy market. Thus, in the period after 1984 subsidies had been provided to gas and nuclear power companies so that they could compete with coal.[15] What had been presented by the Tories at the time of the original strike as the pre-eminence of markets, competition, profitability and modernisation over the regressive 'class-war time-warp' of the National Union of Mineworkers was, therefore, in 1992, easier to see as part of an ideological offensive.[16] In the circumstances it was the government that harboured the most vigorous class ideologues prosecuting a ruthless class war. If for the New Right coal was 'history' this was first and foremost because of its determination to see through to the bitter end a political struggle with the organised working class. Milne accounts for the power of *Brassed Off* in terms of its retrospective clarification of this unequal political struggle between the neo-liberal state and the mining communities.[17] By the early 1990s, the President of the NUM, Arthur Scargill, had become a political leader whose judgement was retrospectively vindicated, whilst Thatcher's own unpopularity had seen her political career unceremoniously ended.[18] Kaplan sees Scargill's 'ghost' animating Danny during his Albert Hall speech as the latter turns down as irrelevant the national prize won by the band and berates the liberal politics of the metropolitan audience.[19]

Brassed Off's awareness of these post-1984 developments can be seen in the characterisation of the pit manager, McKenzie, and in the process of narration. McKenzie is presented as a suave, reasonable and well-prepared antagonist. He is as confident of duping Gloria as he is in going through the motions of union consultation, and events unfold as he foresees. What is important to recognise here is the way that the film works to exploit the foreknowledge of the audience. If McKenzie is in a position of apparent omniscience *vis-à-vis* a character like Gloria who is seduced by illusions generated out of her acquired professional and class position, he is not in the same position in relation to either Grimley's sceptical miners or the audience, for whom the unravelling of the fuller picture behind the 1984 strike and its relationship to later developments makes his role in the film's plot transparent. What comes as nasty surprise to Gloria – McKenzie's smirking confession that the decision to close the pit was made two years prior to the public announcement – is only what the miners are presented as already knowing.

This narrative of inevitable failure is not, however, unproblematic. That is to say, it places female characters such as Gloria and the Women Against Pit Closures – who are encamped outside the colliery – as somehow 'naive' in struggling for something the wiser male characters know to be doomed. Indeed, in as much as it suggests that the colliery band without the colliery is pointless – a position argued against by Danny until he finally adopts it himself in the Albert Hall – the film implies the necessity of a kind of correspondence between the political culture of class solidarity for which the band is a symbol, and a delimited socio-economic group who are deemed to own that culture. Analogously, to the extent that miners' wives are not themselves miners their endurance is somehow suggested to be pointless – possibly even, although the film does not go this far, their protest is an example of the 'meddling' that Gloria is accused of when she seeks to argue that the miners' cause is her cause.

The eclipse of the economic base which once supported a white, masculine, industrial working class does not invalidate a political culture rooted in working-class solidarity – even if it makes such a culture harder to construct and sustain. *Dockers* attempts to argue just this case. The film is a drama-documentary on the Liverpool dockers strike of 1995. It seeks to show how the predicament of industrial labour – the undermining of its ability to go on strike – does not make older forms of class-based resistance any less relevant to post-industrial workers struggling against neo-liberal forms of exploitation. In this instance, the employer, the Mersey Dock and Harbour Company, dismiss an already heavily exploited group of workers belonging to a contract labour firm.[20] The immediate issue is the obligation to do unpaid overtime. When 329 of the remaining 500 core workforce refuse, out of the principle of solidarity, to cross the picket line set up by their fellow employees, they are also sacked. The dispute raises the issues of the impact of casualisation on workers' lives and the relationship between workers and a union movement cowed by neo-liberal, anti-union legislation.

Like the other films under investigation here, *Dockers* explores intra-class conflict by mapping it onto an opposition between fathers and sons. The narrative revolves around the experiences of the Walton family. Andy Walton (Lee Ross) is one of the sacked contract workers; his father, Tommy Walton (Ken Stott), is one of those who refuses to cross the picket line that Andy and others like him have set up. The crisis in their relationship occurs when Andy decides to give up the dispute whilst Tommy, who has been sacked as a result of his act of solidarity, continues to fight. Witnessing an accident at a building site on which casualised labour is subject to dangerous working conditions, Andy returns to the picket line and is reconciled with his father. The case that the film is trying to make is that the dockers struggle is not motivated by a regressive attachment to the class conflicts of the past – what this film and *The Full Monty* refer to as the time of the 'dinosaurs' – but by the necessities of the contemporary working conditions of many different types of worker. Jean (Crissy Rock), mother of Andy and wife of Tommy, makes this same argument in her speech to a union meeting of sympathetic teachers. Rather than 'class' suffering the double contraction whereby its relevance is limited, first, to the social experience of the industrial working class and, second, to the lost world of 'embarrassing' fathers – Danny in *Brassed Off*, Gaz (Robert Carlyle) in *The Full Monty* and 'Dad' (Gary Lewis) in *Billy Elliot* – *Dockers* tries to lift the horizon within which class struggle remains a relevant experience in the here and now.

Nevertheless, Judith Williamson, who is generally sympathetic with the ambitions of the film, argues that it exhibits a kind worthy, didactic naturalism which fails to engage with the ways in which the larger, ultimately 'historic' narrative of the struggle between labour and capital – represented in the film by banners, marches and a language of working-class solidarity – intersects with the actual complexities of existing working-class lives.[21] Despite such arguments, there is evidence that *Dockers* addresses the increasing impingement of neo-liberal forms of exploitation on everyday, working-class life. In one scene, Jean receives a phone call from a foreman demanding to know why Tommy has missed a night shift which he has in fact completed. This phone call – an intrusion by the employer within the 'private', domestic sphere – provokes in Jean the erroneous suspicion that Tommy is having an affair with another woman. Later on, when addressing a meeting of trade unionists, Jean recounts how telephone calls from the company demanding extra shifts would be fielded by children who were told to reply that their parents were out. In ways such as these, the film attempts to provide a representation of the culture of work and the texture of everyday life installed under neo-liberal conditions.

However, what distinguishes the situation in this film from that found in *Brassed Off* and *The Full Monty* is that there is no seemingly unarguable 'economic' premise grounding the narrative – what occurs to the workers is not presented as the result of inevitable economic processes whose end point is redundancy. Here the issue is dismissal. The dock's profits are not in question. For the company, the dispute appears to be one of principle. As Patrick Keiller puts it in his gloss on the script of *Robinson in Space*, the company's actions seem to be 'a concerted attempt to rid the port of any memory of its culture and traditions'.[22] As with the miners' strike in 1984, the significant point for the employers is the excision of the defenses of the labour force. However, the film is ultimately less interested in the employer than it is in those who might have been expected to be allies of the dockers. A 'narrative of betrayal' implicates the dockers' union, the Transport and General Workers Union, and New Labour.[23] (It is interesting to note that the film makes it clear, through the role of a sympathetic American longshoreman played by Shane Rimmer, that the dockers' ultimate allies are other workers, in this instance, from other nations.) In the case of the TGWU, the film indicates that the problem is not just the threat of legal action if the union becomes involved in the dispute, but also the organisation's compliance with New Labour's insistence that effective political action can only take place within the limits prescribed by neo-liberal capital.

Those who might have been expected to support the dockers are bound by what they tacitly support as the new political 'reality' – the freedom of capital. This draws attention to what Žižek refers to as a 'post-political' era's ideological 'big Other' – Capital.[24] The 'big Other' is a psychoanalytical concept drawn from the work of Jacques Lacan. It stands for the particular forms in which we experience what Lacan calls the order of the 'Symbolic' or our sense of a received 'reality'.[25] For Žižek the only authentic political response or 'act' that can be made is always one which challenges the position of society's ideological 'big Other'.[26] Thus, in an era in which the domain of the political cannot be imagined to extend beyond the framework of 'existing socio-political relations' as defined by neo-liberal capital, authentic 'left' political acts simply disappear.[27] By definition a 'political act' is a risky, courageous, even 'impossible' gesture as it seeks to suspend this 'framework'.[28] Žižek uses *Brassed Off* and *The Full Monty* as examples of films which figure such political acts – in the former, the act lies in the impossible fidelity to the lost cause expressed through the apparent pointlessness of keeping a doomed pit's band in existence, and in the latter it is to be found in a heroic sacrifice of 'false male dignity' by physically unprepossessing 'strippers'.[29] Žižek goes on to argue that these are the acts of 'losers' which for him symbolise the deadlock on the left after the collapse of communism and social democracy.[30] Either one sticks to the 'brass' orthodoxy of the Old Left or one strips away the remainder of those traditions and accepts that global capitalism is now the 'only game in town'.[31]

Dockers makes the case that the traditions of the Old Left remain relevant – that there are for the left fundamental political principles which cannot be given up. Of course, the film is also a story of defeat; however, it too stages a political 'act' in Žižek's terms – one which cannot easily be written off as the deluded, 'ritualistic incantation of old formulas'. If refusing to cross a picket line has become a 'political act' in the sense that it can no longer be deemed to belong to the 'art of the possible' but has crossed over into the 'art of the impossible', then such a situation provides a means of measuring the strength of the grip of the priorities set by our present ideological 'big Other'.[32] In the vocabulary of the government employment training scheme referred to earlier – *Dockers* depicts the struggle between capital and labour in terms of an opposition between jobs and workers. When the dockers act as *workers* they lose their entitlement to *jobs*. The 'job', in other words, has been annexed by the 'big Other' – thus giving us the preferred mode of neo-liberal employment, *jobs without workers*.

This same idea of a world without workers forms the subject matter of *Among Giants*. Like the others under discussion here, this film unfolds in an industrial north which has seen its traditional industries gutted in the 1980s. It is self-consciously elegiac and uses an allegorical landscape to evoke a 'lost world' as the context for its depiction of post-industrial forms of labour. Set on the Yorkshire moors surrounding Sheffield, it relates the efforts of a gang of men brought together to paint miles of electricity pylons over the summer months. The men are not directly hired by the electricity company who own the pylons but by one of its management employees who is illegally subcontracting the work. There is a compact here – typical of neo-liberal labour markets – in which the convenience of undocumented arrangements between capital and labour circumvents an older world in which capital and labour are subject to 'regulation'. As the film makes clear, this new arrangement is to the advantage of capital not labour. This is emphasised in the deployment of two different types of 'freedom'. According to the first, the workers are 'free' of the enclosure and supervision of factory and plant – 'kings' on top of the pylons, the gang have that giddy sense of being in absolute control of their own lives. The film constructs an opposition between nomadic and sedentary characters which partly supports this illusion of omnipotence. Those who range beyond the boundaries of an older, fixed working-class world of family and place retain some hope for change. They are the 'goers'. Those who cannot work their way out of these older patterns of life, the 'stayers', are likely to slip into the oblivion that has overtaken those other disappearees, the industrial working class whose ruined monuments scatter the landscape. This opposition is explored through issues of age and gender. The two younger characters, Gerry (Rachel Griffiths) and Steve (James Thornton), are presented as nomads whereas the gang boss, Ray (Pete Postlethwaite), is a middle-aged man who is separated from his wife and children and who wants to settle down again with Gerry. However, the opposition is a complex one which does more than simply set off age against youth, the mobile against the sedentary. Gerry is an Australian who has been on the road for a considerable time and her experience is used to reflect critically on the emptily masculinist aspirations of easy sex and travel that motivate Steve. Her summary of her life as a 'goer' is that it is repetitive and unfulfilling – it is this which tempts her into trying to settle down with Ray, an option which she finds equally problematic in terms of his suffocating assumptions about conventional heterosexual coupling. The film documents therefore a desultory search for new forms of livelihood, community, sexual partnership and culture which undercuts the simple endorsement of the 'freedom' of the road as a response to the reshaping of working-class lives in the post-industrial moment. The 'second' type of 'freedom' in the film is that of capital itself. The arrangement between the company boss and the painters ensures the avoidance of union interference – it is characterised by the principle of deniability which extends to the relationships amongst the workers themselves. As Ray puts it to Gerry when he takes her on: 'If anyone asks, I don't know you and you don't know me.' The film figures this freedom of capitalism from burdensome regulation as a kind of paradoxical, demiurgic *absence*. That is to say, in one of the few moments of narrative surprise, the sudden and nearly fatal reconnection of the current on the pylons aligns the force of electricity with the 'anonymous', unlocatable agency of capital which is displaced down the chain of subcontraction. Capital is thus represented as possessing an inscrutable and complete control over the fate of the labour it exploits.

Alongside this invisible force, the film's complex aerial and high angle cinematography depicts a landscape which bears witness to a disappearance – the industrial 'giants' of the title. A motif of heroic, industrial giganticism is used in order to suggest a 'lost civilisation' whose ruins are dotted across the moors and the city. To a degree the narrative is subordinate to this visual spectacle – thus the romance between Ray and Gerry is organised within the decayed grandeur of derelict cooling towers on decommissioned power stations; on top of an urban gasometer; and dangling off pylons whose rudimentary, anthropomorphic qualities suggest both stationary sentinels and mobile, striding colossi. In this poetic exaggeration of the iconographic traditions of 1960s 'northern realism', the film begins to suggest the emerging outlines of an unfamiliar, post-industrial image of the working class.[33] To capture this image it is necessary to reconsider the opposition between the space of the road and the settled place of established territory. Take the scene in which Ray and Gerry stand on the gas tower in the city and view the entire horizon of Ray's life and that of his forebears. The image provided is clearly *idyllic-nostalgic* in the sense that it merges the individual life with the life of the generations who have lived, worked and died in this delimited area. However, Ray is also acutely aware of how this space is breaking apart. What the scene figures is the passing of 'community' – that essential feature of that chronotope of northern realism which found its most vivid articulation in the immediate post-war period when it was felt to be under threat from various quarters, including 'youth', 'working-class affluence' and Americanised mass culture.[34] Note the characteristic circling, aerial cinematography in this scene which helps to draw the enchanted circle around the idyllic place. Whilst Gerry finds this image of working-class community attractive, she also complains that it is suffocating her – within its boundaries conceptions of sexuality and gender remain 'traditional'. Her discomfort with Ray's expensive engagement ring seems to epitomise this difference between them.

In contrast, consider the alternative images of the working-class present that emerge in space of the moor encampment. It is the nomad Gerry who is associated in the beginning with life on the moors – she pitches her tent beneath the pylons. One evening after work a tanker arrives driven by a friend of the gang who is stopping off on his return route between Scotland and Japan. The giant cylindrical tank is full of whisky and is a suitable image of a Rabelaisian appetite – an idea reinforced by the gang drinking the whisky from a bucket as they sit around a campfire on the moor singing country and western songs.

This scene appears to represent an attempt to imagine a space and life beyond the rooted, regional, national, ethnic and gendered boundaries of the past. It is a temporary, 'gathered' space, one that is open to international migrants and labour routes – the black intercontinental trucker and the Australian backpacker/ undocumented woman worker helping to support a sense of destinations lying on routes other than the one that runs back to Sheffield along the line of the pylons under which they sit. The presentiment of temporal discontinuity and dispossession which hems in Ray's view of Sheffield from the gasometer is left behind in this scene – the space constructed around the campfire on the moors is not threatened by the break-up of the older community but emerges out of that same process. The scene does record the scars of the working-class experiences of post-industrialisation – one of the gang members breaks down after an abusive, drunken outburst whose origins the narrative has encouraged us to ascribe to his indebtedness. However, the gathering on the moors also avoids any nostalgia for an industrial north of the past – Ray's *idyll* which is incapable of including Gerry or Steve – and provides intimations of future, post-industrial forms of working-class connection and collectivity.

The script for *Among Giants* originated from the writer behind *The Full Monty* – Simon Beaufoy.[35] Both films are set in post-industrial Sheffield and involve the search for new forms of livelihood by those made redundant through the restructuring of the steel industry. *Among Giants* was written earlier although filmed later – this difference might be used to explain the more insistent optimism of *The Full Monty* which was produced closer to that time when the hopefulness which accompanied New Labour's challenge to an exhausted Tory party was intensifying. In its preoccupation with the 'recovery of community'[36] *The Full Monty* film relies on what some have seen as a facile populism and multiculturalism which act to conceal class struggle and continuing ethnic division and conflict.[37] Thus, for Luckett, the film's gestures towards inclusiveness – for instance, the presence of the black character, Horse (Paul Barber), which she sees as an example of the way in which cultural difference is subsumed into an exotic, updated regional ethnicity – are 'superficial' and only exist 'at the level of the unifying image'.[38] Likewise the film's display of sexual difference – the troop of unemployed men turned strippers includes two gays – and its questioning of a traditional masculine, working-class subjectivity are equally problematic. There is a strong, defensive homosociality at work in the narrative which works to qualify the process of dismantling the older, oppressive culture of masculinity. Note also that the gay characters are quickly turned into a hand-holding couple.[39] Whilst recognising such shortcomings, Kaplan is less severe on the film than other critics. For her its 'sentimental' representations of a community in which gender roles are in flux do at least point in the right direction – towards a 'possible reinvention of agency and community'.[40] This aspect of the film remains particularly important in view of the Blairite fear of any persistent, disruptive collective dimension to social life – a fear which she suggests is expressed in New Labour's occlusion of class.[41]

Monk, however, is more critical of the film's politics and argues that the final scene – in which unemployed steel-workers, endorsed by their community, appear to transform themselves into paid performers in the 'creative and entertainment industries' – represents a Blairite celebration of neo-liberal entrepreneurialism which neglects the realities of working-class life.[42] In this respect, her position on the film's finale is not dissimilar to the one eventually arrived at by Danny in *Brassed Off* when he argues that the performing band is an irrelevant distraction from the community's pressing economic/human needs. However, rather than just being an evasion of economic realities, 'entertainment' can also be thought about in these films as providing a figuration of key aspects of the evolving relationship between labour and capital. Within the 'millennial' ideologies of neo-liberal capitalism, *opportunities* demand strenuous efforts of improvisation and self-reinvention. Success seems to depend on a relationship in which there is nothing the worker will not do or be asked to do, and in which there is nothing that the magical world of neo-liberal capitalism will deny such compliant workers. In *The Full Monty* such imperatives are figured as 'putting on a show', and the activity of stripping is represented as a pitiless test of the willingness to do whatever it takes, in the name of self-help, to successfully trigger the apparently magical logic of accumulating good fortune which Luckett likens to that of the 'Lottery'.[43] Note the way that Gaz discusses the monetary rewards of stripping in terms of a miraculous multiplication sum.

A similar relationship between capital and labour is being referenced in Loach's *The Navigators* by the managing director of a newly privatised track company in his take-over video address to his new workforce. After intoning the neo-liberal maxim that 'jobs for life are gone' he adds: 'There are no limits to what this team can achieve together'. Again, what is being advised is the acceptance of a situation of material insecurity and jeopardy, which, if endured, promises limitless rewards. (Note also that these rewards pretend to abolish the division between 'worker' and 'boss' with a new collective – the 'team'.) A similar example of the maximalist rhetoric and euphoric euphemism of neo-liberal employment practice is identified by the vigilant, sharp-eyed Robinson in *Robinson in Space*. In Sheerness, the narrator dryly informs us that Co-Steel – a scrap reprocessing plant – imposes 'total team culture' on its workforce. He goes on to explain that this means that 'overtime is unpaid and union members fear identification'. Here again the 'worker' – identified by union membership – is unwelcome and placed outside the 'team'.

The audition for *The Full Monty*'s stripping troupe – Hot Metal – is interesting, as it provides an example of a character backing out of this compact with a new world of opportunity. The first to be auditioned is Reg (Bruce Jones) who is either unwilling or unable to transform taking his clothes off into a *performance* of stripping. A limit is reached with this character which cannot be passed beyond. His literalisation of the task is a means of refusing it whilst seemingly complying with it – he stands largely motionless and simply undoes and removes his clothing until he gets to his trousers at which point his unenthusiastic hesitation prompts Gaz to end the audition. Reg's self-confessed desperation is embarrassing. He and his like are not entertaining and have to be forgotten in order to give the success of those who do go 'the full monty' any wider resonance. Reg is similar to Phil in *Brassed Off.* The latter reaches the limits of what he can tolerate as Mr Chuckles the party clown. The difference between the two films is clarified by a comparison between these two figures. Reg is the 'worker' as party-pooper, whereas Phil's refusal to reinvent himself as Mr Chuckles is something which seems eminently reasonable.

The neo-liberal relationship between labour and capital, figured in the theme of the business of entertainment in *The Full Monty*, has implications for the concept of unemployment. In deindustrialising elegies like *Brassed Off*, unemployment still appears to indicate a break in the lives of traditional industries and communities – it marks the shifting of the macro-economic gears which threatens to leave entire workforces on the 'scrap heap'. Here 'unemployment' is a sign of political crisis – as it was under the consensus conditions of post-war social democracy. However, in *The Full Monty* unemployment is emerging not so much as an end-sign but more as an accepted challenge to labour and as a structural part of new, post-industrial labour markets. The moment of unemployment becomes a crisis not for a community or for a political regime held accountable for its stewardship of such communities, but for individuals who, even when out of a job, must meet the challenge posed by a force which is far from done with them – capitalism. In *The Full Monty* note the presence of the mandatory 'job club' for the unemployed. Such clubs are associations of the unemployed demanded by a welfare apparatus that has been redesigned, according to neo-liberal principles, to place greater emphasis on self-help and responsibility as opposed to *entitlement*. Amongst other things the name – 'job club' – indicates a de-differentiation of the realms of leisure and voluntary association on the one hand and that of employment on the other. (A distinction maintained in a previous era even if leisure activities such as football and brass bands were organised around a place of employment.) Indeed, the opening titles of *The Full Monty* feature a short civic promotional film – 'Sheffield: A City on the Move' – which makes a clear, if increasingly obsolete, distinction between work and leisure. New labour markets depend on an ever more invasive process whereby what was once considered to lie beyond the 'job' – leisure time and the skills and talents it supports – is henceforth to be considered part of those exploitable resources which the individual must place at the disposal of the market. (*Among Giants* begins with Ray and Steve rock climbing – the 'job' they take on parasitises this skill.) Qualities once viewed as outside circuits of commodification are called-up, and distinctions between 'life' and 'work' become much harder to sustain.

As we have seen, *Dockers* suggests one way in which one might reclaim 'life' from the 'job' – the seemingly archaic, political route of becoming conscious of oneself as a 'worker'. And as we will see in the next section, films like *Late Night*

Shopping offer a very different solution to the same dilemma. However, I will close this section with an analysis of *Billy Elliot* which is markedly different in several respects to those films which appear to be its immediate predecessors. Set in a northern mining town during the strike of 1984, it is centred on a small boy, Billy (Jamie Bell), and follows his struggles to convince his father and brother, both miners involved in the strike, to accept the importance of his talent as a dancer. Rather than dealing with the strike's depressing aftermath, as shown in *Brassed Off*, the film provides a representation of its actuality. Also, the strike in this film, unlike that in *Brassed Off*, does not function as a symbol of a general, precious and endangered sense of social connectedness. When Billy is taken to London for his interview at the Royal Ballet School, the panel of exaggeratedly middle-class aesthetes offer their 'solidarity' to his father. Such a gesture, in the context of a scene in which the same individuals are represented as patronising and intimidating their working-class interviewees cannot help but seem inauthentic. The scene declares that the miners really are on their own – Kaplan seems right when she describes this moment as 'an exemplary scene of class confrontation'.[44]

It is also interesting to see the ease with which the film dispenses with the 'economic' argument against the miners. It does this by putting it in the mouth of the unprepossessing husband of Billy's ballet teacher – an adulterous, alcoholic, petit bourgeois patriarch whose class *ressentiment* matches the tones popularised by Tories of the same era. In a deftly compressed speech he damns the strike as the responsibility of a few 'commies' undemocratically imposing themselves on the unwilling majority, and argues that the politics of the strike are simply irrelevant anyway because: 'it costs more money to pay everybody to dig the coal than you can get for the coal when you sell it'. Of course such arguments miss the loaded political context in which the 'economic' case was made.[45] The film shows that it is aware of this context in its representation of the paramilitarised policing of the strike. From the first scenes the police presence in Billy's pit town is presented as sinister – this is achieved by the understated use of the backgrounds of shots in which the ranks of a police army are seen to be either encamped or drilling whilst in the foreground Billy goes about his life, not unaware but precisely what is worse, habituated to this 'enemy within'. In one scene a tracking shot shows Billy and a little girl walk down a street together. The brick wall against which they are framed becomes, as they cross a road, a wall of waiting, strategically placed police riot shields along which the little girl continues to run her stick. The scene achieves its effect not just by its surprise substitutions within a recognisable iconography of childhood – the trailing stick, the roaming and unaccompanied children suddenly surrounded by a police army – but also by the refusal to re-frame the image. That is to say, the camera does not immediately pull back in order to offer an establishing shot which might act to mark the anomaly in the children's environment more clearly. In this way, a continuous lateral movement, held at a steady height encourages us to view the extraordinary as the ordinary. These and similar representations of the police throughout the film suggest an appeal to audience foreknowledge – the meticulous, strategic positioning of the police army in the landscape metonymically representing the forethought and planning of a political power whose deepest resources were recognised, by the time of the film's release, to have been covert forms of state-sponsored class struggle.[46]

Perhaps the most striking example of this effect is provided in one of the most important 'dancing' sequences in the film which features the striking miner, Billy's brother Tony (Jamie Draven). The editing of the strike sequences predominantly supports a perspective which is indifferent to the class logic of the confrontation. Usually, the police and miners form two interlocking parts of an atavistic male world which is cross-cut with the fantasy/aspirational world of Billy in ballet shoes surrounded by little girls in tutus. However, in the scene in which Tony is trying to run away from the police who have sealed off the town, we are encouraged to identify with the miners and their community. Tony's flight is choreographed around the architecture and everyday activities of the community who assist his attempted escape. Vaulting walls, darting down back alleys, passing in and out of numerous houses as their occupants unblinkingly open and close doors to assist – he appears untouchable. The community itself dances and Billy, the escapee virtuoso, struggles to keep up for once. However, the agility with which Tony negotiates and uses this protective labyrinth is rendered pointless by a complete encirclement of the town by the police. Rapid, reflex motion inspired by an intimate knowledge of the resources of the space – *the ballet of community* – confronts an immobility which represents a superior strategic anticipation.

Whilst the film shows sympathy towards the miners then, puncturing some of the myths which accompanied the strike and demonstrating a grasp of the implacable forces which sought to destroy the industry, it does none of these things with the intention of retrospectively endorsing the logic of working-class struggle. What is conveyed instead is an impression of the futility of working-class struggle. Sympathy with the striking miners in no way contradicts a dismissal of what they stood for politically. But given that this political judgement is in some respects clear-eyed – it is distanced from the ideological animus of the Thatcherism which accompanied the strike – it is perhaps more disturbing. The film is only interested in drawing lessons from the outcome of the strike not from the nature of the struggle involved. It is on the premise of the political failure and historical obsolescence of the miners that Billy's narrative of success and escape is constructed. His departure from the town is narratively synchronised with the collapse of the strike – acceptance by the Royal Ballet School coming at the same time as the miners' exhausted capitulation. It is as if the end of one narrative finally releases the other. Note the miners return to work. As they enter the lift cage they hand over safety tokens. In *Brassed Off* the same exchange was made at the other end of the shift and represented a restitutive ritual in which those who have gone underground are counted back into the light. This scene fitted with *Brassed Off*'s desire to place moral value in the miners' struggle and it stands out in the film as a whole for its cheerfulness. In *Billy Elliot*, however, the miners' sombre act of faith suggests something more emphatically terminal.

It is the film's flash-forward coda which makes explicit its politics. Billy is now a lead dancer in the Royal Ballet and his 'family' turns up to watch him in a performance of Swan Lake. This 'family' includes not just his father and brother – how they earn a living is left unaddressed – but Billy's transvestite school-friend (who is sitting next to a black man who might be his lover). Subordinate sexual, racial, regional and class identities are combined in a metropolitan culture which is presented as enlightened and inclusive – one which finally liberates Billy's awestruck father and brother from their various, sexist and homophobic prejudices concerning boys who dance. Billy himself appears, as Kaplan puts it, 'hypermasculine and androgynous' and the freeze-frame on his leap, like the euph-orically suspended action at the end of *The Full Monty*, suggests a transcendent gesture which resolves all previous conflicts and struggles.[47] *Billy Elliot* is at its closest to the ideology of Blairism here in its representation of the glittering trajectory of individual talent and success as an adequate answer to structural social problems, problems which, in as much as they raise the spectre of class and class struggle, are censored in mainstream political discourse just as they are peremptorily forgotten about in this film.[48]

JOBS WITHOUT WORKERS – 'YOUTH'

'Unemployment' in *Late Night Shopping* and *Human Traffic* is not the issue it is in an industrial elegy like *Brassed Off* – the problem for the characters in *Late Night Shopping* is, as Saul Metzstein, the director, puts it, not the struggle to hang on to a job but the unattractiveness of the many 'McJobs' which are available.[49] In both *Human Traffic* and *Late Night Shopping* the characters do not identify with their jobs. Labour here is no longer 'heroic' industrial toil which sustains a lifetime, a family and a community, but rather a necessary, unpleasantly menial, boring and poorly re-numerated distraction from the 'life' one wants to live. However, this does not mean to imply that these films are 'escapist' or that they have nothing to say about the material necessities of contemporary life. As Karen Lury has pointed out, 'youth' in contemporary British cinema appears to participate in an 'emerging cultural and economic dynamic played out between local and global cultures'.[50] Both *Human Traffic* and *Late Night Shopping* are set outside the metropolitan 'centre' – the former in Cardiff and the latter in Glasgow; however, they largely minimise their use of local cultural difference and address issues of class and employment which are common to the diverse communities and identities of contemporary, multinational Britain and beyond. It is this dynamic played out around 'youth' themes of 'slacking' and drug-culture hedonism that I will focus on.

Human Traffic is a celebration of the 'chemical generation'. It features a group of friends who come together to take drugs – cannabis, ecstasy, cocaine – and party. Based in Cardiff, the group includes a wide range of ethnic, racial and regional identities. Such differences are not, however, in themselves the central focus of the film. What is emphasised is common experience – 'clubbing' and working. The film's title offers a useful image of its predominant social affect – it suggests the exhilaration of a humanism whose emblematic images are not just the crowded, intimate spaces of clubs where strangers become friends, but also city nightscapes across which coloured lights track the constant motion of other, related human beings. In one club scene the 1960s metaphor of the drug taker as astronaut in orbit is recalled – the image track shows us close-ups of the ecstatic faces of Jip (John Simm), Koop (Shaun Parkes), Moff (Danny Dyer), Nina (Nicola Reynolds) and Lulu (Lorraine Pilkington) as they appear to float in a dazzling white space. On the soundtrack Jipp's voice-over describes an 'overwhelming feeling of love' and the desire for a 'universal level of togetherness where we are comfortable'. Such sentiments of utopian collectivity co-exist with the dystopian drudgery of paid work. In an early scene an exasperated Jipp defines his job as fattening 'the arses of the corporate wankers at the top'. Required to 'brown-nose' the customers and submit to the tyranny of the store manager, his corporate uniform carries the slogan of a recognisably evangelical form of neo-liberal business – *Go For It!* The original theatrical release of the film contained footage from London's late-1990s anti-capitalist demonstrations in the opening titles, and Jipp uses the idiom of this movement when he observes: 'The anti-Christ has been with us for long time, and he means business, big business.' This statement is immediately followed by a surreal scene in which a reprimand by the store manager is represented as a sexual assault. The manager, a barcode imprinted on his forehead, pushes Jipp over the counter, seals his mouth with a £20 note and delivers a tirade of increasingly incoherent instructions and threats whilst simulating sexual intercourse. The theme of exploitation figured in sexual terms also manifests itself in Jipp's family life as his mother is a prostitute. It is implied that Jipp's own sexual crisis – a 'monumental case of Mr Floppy' – may be related to his mother's occupation and his subordination at work. However, *Human Traffic* avoids the misogyny that some critics have seen in contemporaneous films dealing with crises of masculinity.[51] Jipp is tender towards his mother and overcomes his fear of impotence by allowing himself to be guided by his female friend Lulu.

In the scene following the 'assault' on Jipp, Nina is shown working in a fast-food restaurant. Her co-workers are body popping; however, their performance is presented as a distressingly involuntary display. (The scene manages to effectively convey the loathing felt by the employee for the translation of working practices into the register of 'entertainment'.) As in the scene with Jipp, it is as if the bodies of the workers are not their own – they resemble a collection of hijacked 'metabolic vehicles'.[52] At this point Nina walks out of the job and later we see her celebrating being unemployed with Lulu. However, despite such examples of the combative refusal of exploitation and alienation, it might be argued that the film's emphatic division between an ecstatic 'weekend' and 'mundane Monday' mitigates our sense of how it is not just utopian moments of escape but also grinding levels of everyday exploitation which unify the group. The complex links between the problems of the 'job' and the pleasures of 'life' are, however, at the centre of *Late Night Shopping* and as a consequence, despite the impression of Generation X or 'slacker' apoliticism, it is a more politically challenging film. Like *Human Traffic* it features a group of friends; however, unlike the earlier film, the status of the friendship is uncertain. This uncertainty hinges on the relationship between the 'mickey mouse' jobs of Sean (Luke de Woolfson), Vincent (James Lance), Jody (Kate Ashfield) and Lenny (Enzo Cilenti) and their social/'personal' lives. These characters work nights and regularly meet up in a café before and after their shifts. As Jody puts it, their association is more properly thought of as an *acquaintanceship* or a 'convenience' determined by their jobs. By definition then, actual friendship would be a social arrangement which exceeds or challenges the coincidences provided by their jobs. Jody's bruising comments have a telling accuracy as what the group is doing is precisely exploring the peculiar capacity that their undervalued jobs have to organise, shape and even suspend their lives. In Sean's case his job allows him and his girlfriend to avoid the pain of unequivocal separation after a row. As they work opposing shifts – she day to his night – they are never in their shared flat at the same time. Sean calls this the comfort of 'limbo'.

It is the liminal status of these 'twentysomethings' – as the characters are referred to in the film's promotion – that permits the maintenance of a protective distance from the reality of what Vincent calls 'mickey mouse' jobs.[53] The material basis for this prolonged period of being in-between 'youth' and 'adulthood' has in part been provided by the expansion of British higher education in the 1990s and the development of 'flexible', casualised labour markets which many students have been forced to enter as a result of statutory shifts in the economic burden they bear for their studies. In this way a certain kind of working life is sustained in parallel with periods of study. As Lury puts it, whilst for some the twilight world of 'low paid, low status' jobs is only a temporary fix, for others it represents something more substantially predictive of the future.[54] Lury argues that 'slacking' is in part a defensive attempt to fend off this unwelcome possibility by the development of 'elaborate, and often antipathetic lifestyles'.[55] In an interview, Saul Metzstein locates the characters in a post-university/pre-adulthood phase. He adds that this situation is not characterised by the 'despair' of the unemployment of an older era but rather by the key 'slacker' qualities of 'aimlessness' and 'distraction' which a plentiful supply of McJobs enable. Such jobs allow a deferred reckoning with 'adult issues'.[56] Vincent is perhaps the best example of this. He views his 'mind-numbing' work as a supermarket shelf-stacker as a means to pursue his 'hobby' – the serial dating of vulnerable women with emotional problems. The 'job' is irrelevant, interchangeable and of no interest to him. Around his 'hobby' he has developed an elaborate postmodernist persona modelled on Errol Flynn.

The film shows how it is possible to construct, on the basis of a 'Mickey Mouse' job, an eccentric, detached, defamiliarised, almost enchanted view of the world – summed up in the film's title as *late night shopping*. It is Joe (Laurie Ventry), Vincent's middle-aged co-worker, who is critical in undermining such pleasures. Over the opening titles, in what is a flash-forward, we hear him intoning to himself and Vincent that they are 'little cogs in a big machine' and that such a life – arithmetised as a 40-50 hour week sustained for 40/50 years – has no identifiable purpose. For Joe, working as a supermarket shelf-stacker represents a different kind of *late night shopping*, one that is always overshadowed by what he grimly refers to here as the 'bigger picture', or the threat of an unrewarding and wasted life. However, this possibility is not something which is necessarily restricted to jobs which are clearly and perhaps comfortably marked as 'McJobs' – such as Lenny's in a call centre, Jody's in a micro-electronics factory and Sean's in a hospital. When Vincent attempts to answer Joe's question about what he is going to do with his life – reduce his debts; leave his job for a better one; move to a nicer flat – he finds himself struggling to counter what the film suggests is Joe's unanswerable supplementary question: 'And then what?' Later on, and in recognition of the impact Joe has had on him, Vincent uses the same question to disrupt Sean's attempt to imagine a future with Madeline in terms of new jobs. Likewise, shortly afterwards, Jody ponders the same problem in her notebook. Having lost her job she is considering what she will do when she returns to the city after the excursion to help Sean find Madeline. The list she constructs has three steps:

1. Get a job.
2. Get a life.
3. And then what?

The comic touch of puncturing the apparent completeness of the combination of 'job' and 'life' enables the question of a fulfilled, purposeful existence to hang in the air. Like Joe, Jody's 'And then what?' registers an unappeasable dissatisfaction inherent in the system or 'bigger picture'. If there is a *politics of slacking* it might be summarised thus: given the unsatisfactory nature of the entire system, 'bad' jobs have the advantage of leaving you psychically disengaged and still able, at least, to pose Jody and Joe's critical question. A 'Mickey Mouse' job is the best worst option. However, slacking remains haunted by the possibility that that disengagement – the grace of liminality – might also be the origin of various dangerous illusions. Once again, the character of Joe is critical here – he dies of a heart attack in the supermarket after he has witnessed the clock go into reverse. Previously he has discussed with Vincent various methods of 'clock-watching' designed to make time on the job pass more easily – speeding up the work or slowing it down, segmenting the hours into discrete blocks of time etc. His conclusion is that there is no way to beat the clock. (Vincent's own slacker strategy is to rely on a watch that no longer counts the time – Errol Flynn's.) Joe's 'clock-watching' simulates the 'out of time' experience of slacking; however, what it also indicates is that such activities do not leave the precious substance of life intact in some enchanted, parallel, 'limbo'. What the 'bad' job does is to stealthily consume life without pain – it is, as Vincent puts it, 'numbing'. Joe's reversing clock of death signals the reality behind Vincent's temporisations.

In another scene designed to convey the oppressive repetitiousness of time at work, Sean watches his co-workers clocking in and out. As he gapes at them there is no particular sense that, in a process of displaced abjection, it is the spectacle of the individuals themselves – who are middle-aged *and* young – that appals him. What does this is the deadly nature of the rhythm of the work. A series of looped dissolves bring the same men back to the clock whilst Sean stands transfixed. The scene ends with Sean stepping up to the clock and looking back at himself. (We looked at the strategy of doubling in *Sliding Doors* where it seemed very much part of an anxiety about processes of proletarianisation.) Here is that extreme state of alienation described by Joe. Sean observes the process in which the clocking-in machine reduces his life and the lives of his co-workers to an extension of its own soulless mechanism.

Such perceptions of a common experience and fate – denied vigorously by the superstitious Vincent who refuses to believe that Joe's life might anticipate his own – are, nevertheless, resisted through the operation of the film's plot which takes a providential form. Whilst thematically the characters are drifting aimlessly, the complex narrative contradicts this impression, giving their lives a shape and direction through a series of coincidences and synchronicities. The infidelities of Sean and Madeline are represented as occurring in parallel; Madeline's infidelity is by chance with Sean's friend Vincent; Gail, the woman Lenny is secretly in love with, is a friend of Madeline's; Madeline walks into the same café in which Jody is sitting and therefore allows the latter to set up a reconciliation with Sean; the punishment Vincent has to endure for sleeping with Sean's girlfriend is to have his Errol Flynn watch destroyed – consequently he begins to fail with women and there is a suggestion that the attraction between himself and Jody might develop. The general direction of these incremental nudges is away from the blind alleys of their 'night-shift' existence towards the 'light at the end of the tunnel' which they approach in Lenny's car in the film's final image. By contrast, when Joe collapses beneath the reversing clock of death, Vincent is unable to find the key to the supermarket doors to let the medics in. Lenny's earlier comment – that the doors are shut at night not so much to keep the public out as to keep people like Vincent in – actually represents a forewarning of Joe's fate. Clearly then, the providential power in the film works to inscribe, from the point of view of 'twentysomething' slackers like Vincent, 'safe' class distinctions. Joe is marked by his Scottish accent and his age as working class. The film is shot on location

Figure 6 *Late Night Shopping*. Courtesy of Film Four

in and around Glasgow; however, the four principal characters are not given recognisably Scottish identities. In this way the constrictions of class are confined to the realm of 'identity', with male *Scottishness* signalling *working-classness*.

Certainly the film celebrates the ingenuity with which the characters tackle the task they have set themselves – an ironic transfiguration of alienation. Certainly also, the stylishness of the film itself – its eclectic soundtrack; its slick cinematography; its ironic *mise en scène* – energises this effort. The cinematographer, Brian Tufano, had previously worked on *Trainspotting* – a film whose combination of stylisation and grim subject matter has been received, as we shall see in the next chapter, as seminal in dislodging the social realism associated with the representation of working-class themes and culture in general.[57] However, it needs to be remembered that *Late Night Shopping* remains uncertain about the relationship between its characters and the world of class and capitalism. Whilst slacker 'youths' and their working-class elders are divided by the exercise of a providential power, the character of Joe points to common problems and dangers. Furthermore, Jody is distanced from the superstitious, ironically magical belief in immunity which sustains Vincent. In the final scenes we learn that she has been sacked but has continued to turn up at the café at night as if she was still working. Her sacking is a result of her dissatisfaction with her life – her sensitivity one could say to the 'And then what?' When she explains that she was dismissed for her negative attitude and for bringing her workmates 'down' she is aligned with Joe who does the same to Vincent. Jody is prepared to stare into what she calls the 'black abyss' of her life. In sum, if *Late Night Shopping* gives us a view of a world of *jobs without workers*, this is not simply because the apparently obsolete social category – *worker* – is separated by a gulf from a contemporary identity like the *slacker*. It is also because the slacker world depicted in the film is recognisably a world shared with working-class others who struggle under not dissimilar conditions of life in neo-liberal job markets.

CHAPTER 4

The Underclass: Fantasy and Realism

In this chapter I will be primarily concerned with one film in particular – *Trainspotting* – in which the treatment of extreme working-class or 'underclass' subject matter is brought into collision with an aesthetic of hyper-stylised, 'glossy anti-realism'.[1] Indeed, *Trainspotting* appears to be a bold reformulation of a debilitating aesthetic and political opposition between social realism and fantasy which, it is claimed, has marked, on a number of levels, the history of British cinema.[2] Its drug-taking, criminal, 'non-working' working-class youths – serenely out of it on heroin and at the same time fizzing with the unpredictable social energies released by the decolonising, post-industrialising Celtic periphery[3] – are represented in terms of a novel aesthetic ably described by Murray Smith as 'black magic realism'.[4] Smith's book on the film allows us to examine in detail how a sense of aesthetic innovation raises questions about changing conceptions of politics and class. Key to this examination will be a discussion of what is too often taken as a solid sociological datum – the 'underclass'.

Originating in New Right political discourse in the early 1990s, the notion of the 'underclass' was used, by Charles Murray for instance, to refer to the emergence since the late 1960s of a section of the working class whose existence is characterised by a combination of 'illegitimacy, violent crime' and 'the tendency to drop-out from the labour force' – what social conservatives have traditionally called *idleness*.[5] The causes of the *de-civilising* process which has, it is claimed, produced this parasitic 'New Rabble', are supposed to lie in the welfare state's bias towards entitlement and neglect of individual responsibility; in the influence of the radical politics of the 1960s – including feminism – on institutions such as the family; and in a perceived weakness of repressive state apparatuses such as the police whose inefficiency has allowed crime to flourish.[6]

Generally, the concept of the 'underclass' conceals the systematically destructive effects of capitalism on particular sections of the working class, including the young, single mothers, ethnic minorities and the unemployed. It does this by moralising these same effects in terms of individual and cultural failings. Furthermore, it locates the source of value in society outside the working class. As I argued in the previous chapter, the scope of the working-class contribution to society is thus restricted to the presence or absence of the ability to grasp the opportunities that capitalism is understood to offer. In this way, the 'underclass' represents more than an identification of a fragment of the working class that has gone astray. Indeed, by realigning the position of the entire working class to capitalism the concept announces itself to be very much part of the same world which has produced a millennial, renovated capitalist fundamentalism.

By contrast, in contemporary, male-centred films such as the Welsh *Twin Town* (1997), the English *Lock, Stock and Two Smoking Barrels* and the Scottish *Trainspotting* – films which Claire Monk associates with a 'commercial underclass cycle' – the milieu of the criminal, 'unrespectable' working class is a source of pleasurable spectacle rather than an object of moralising disapprobation.[7] It is this pleasure attaching to the vision of a wasted 'underclass' that suggests Stallabrass's account of Britart's contemporary urban pastoral might be of relevance for the analysis of such films. For Stallabrass, the urban pastoral effects a dual displacement of the working class in time and space.[8] *Spatially* it uses images of dilapidated urban environments to provide figurative traces of their abject inhabitants. Commenting on Lynne Ramsay's *Ratcatcher* (1999), for instance, Paul Quinn observes that, despite the film's best intentions, it reduplicates a traditional representation of the proletariat 'from above' – one in which 'garbage, rats and the poor engage in a dance of substitutions'.[9] *Temporally*, the urban pastoral often displays an obsession with working-class cultural formations that are located in the past. For Stallabrass, Britart's exploration of this working-class past and the associated pleasures of caricature, mimicry and voyeurism are related to the destabilising forces of contemporary capitalism. Increasing exposure to the discipline of the market necessarily intensifies the inherent economic instabilities fissuring the middle classes.[10] In these circumstances the post-war economic boom becomes the object of an intense nostalgia which fixes on certain images – in particular the 1960s swagger of a working class 'that was increasing its wealth and exercising its power effectively due to a labour shortage' and whose 'lifestyle was seen as cool'.[11] Indeed, beyond the boundaries of Britart, working-class culture of the 1960s is frequently the focus for contemporary 'retro' obsessions. The 'New Lad' of the style magazines and the gangster film cycle of the late 1990s both carry the physiognomy of the young working-class male of the 1960s. In both cases, contemporary anxieties of class and gender appear to express themselves as an admiring emulation of a stylish, masculinist, often 'unrespectable' individualism of the past.

Of course there are films which approach 'underclass' themes of industrial decline, poverty, social dislocation, unemployment, crime and shifting lines of gender power with altogether different emphases than those found in the urban pastoral. Thus, *Essex Boys* (2000) and *Shooters* (2001) both feature a criminal working class, but this is one stripped of charismatic, stylishness masculinity. Likewise, in the gangland thriller *Going Off Big Time* (2000), the least attractive character is the one most insistent on the codes of competitive masculinity. Films like *The Last Resort* (2001) and *Dirty Pretty Things* (2002) look at what has been called an 'immigrant underclass' and do so from the perspective of the economic exploitation of a social group whose constitution is fluid in terms of nationality, ethnicity, 'race', gender and age.[12] *Purely Belter* (2000) looks at the child's experience of the 'underclass' milieu and does so in such a way that the temptation to offer the image of the ideal father as a means of resolving the problem of the bad/absconded father and the 'single mother' is resisted. In this film it is the son's relationship with the mother which is presented as mutually sustaining.

In Shane Meadows's *TwentyFourSeven* (1997) the issue of 'underclass' masculinity is subtly detached from what appears to be a story of hapless youth and is relocated in the fragile subjectivity of the boys' older mentor, Darcy (Bob Hoskins). The 'lads' Darcy tries to help with his boxing club are shown to have problems – including gang tribalism, drug taking, a violent, abusive father and the law. At the same time there is a sense in which they already possess the resources and values that Darcy is seeking to instil in them. Indeed, Darcy's 'failure' with the boxing club is perhaps more a reflection on his own struggle to come to terms with an era in which, as he puts it in his diary, working-class men such as himself feel that they are 'casualties' who are 'not really living'. When Tim (Danny Nussbaum) – the boy who rejects Darcy's violent response to his own violent father – takes in the destitute, mortally sick Darcy and subsequently arranges the funeral, his undemonstrative maturity and compassion are not presented as a revelation but appear more as a confirmation of pre-existing characteristics. By the end of the film the success or failure of Darcy's lads' response to the challenge of that emblem of male, working-class self-help – the boxing ring – becomes largely irrelevant. Alongside the theme of 'underclass' abjection then, *TwentyFourSeven* is concerned with the protective, reciprocal and collective aspects of working-class culture – the scene in which Darcy washes, feeds and puts to bed one of his elective sons is echoed by Tim's actions as he gently assists the destitute and dying Darcy. Such images of an ethic of abiding working-class tenderness and mutuality contest what Chris Haylett argues is an important aspect of the ideology of the 'underclass' – the representation of 'working class differences as divides'.[13]

Gary Oldman's *Nil by Mouth* (1997) has been received by some as an 'underclass' drama.[14] It examines male violence within working-class domestic space. The patriarchal rage of the central male character, Raymond (Ray Winstone), is unbounded – he beats up his wife Val (Kathy Burke), who miscarries as a consequence, viciously attacks his heroin-taking, identifiably 'underclass' brother-in-law Billy (Charlie Creed-Miles), sexually taunts Val's grandmother and refers to his own daughter as 'it'. These reflexes in Ray represent the psychopathology of a certain kind of working-class 'respectability' – as Glen Creeber argues, the film rips open the 'charade of old-fashioned working-class respectability' and undermines any residual nostalgia for its masculinist charisma.[15] This is done through the distinctions made between a positively accented social world of women and the violence of the homosocial world of Ray and his friend Mark (Jamie Foreman). This opposition is elaborated in terms of different models of dialogue – from the compassionate, interrogative forms used by the female characters which place an emphasis on listening, to the anecdotal eloquence and rhetorical sophistication of Ray and Mark which dominates the first half of the film and which only offers interchangeability of the position of speaker and listener within a delimited, exclusive male world.[16] Moretti's problematising of Bakhtin's association of heteroglossia with dialogism is useful here.[17] Moretti makes the point that cultures marked by heteroglossia are typically 'status' societies.[18] Such societies, he argues, do not offer opportunities for dialogue. Instead, they are marked by an atmosphere in which 'idiosyncratic monologues' dominate and 'speaking has lost contact with listening'.[19] In the case of *Nil by Mouth*, Ray and Mark clearly exist within the aftermath of a 'rigidly classified' male, working-class world and they are adepts of its 'expressive idiosyncracies'.[20] In contrast, Creeber seems correct in his contention that the film permits the emergence of a 'female voice' that has been obliged to be silent in this world.[21] However, I am not sure that this sufficiently captures the full significance of the role of language in the representation of class here. One of the most notable things about the film seems to be the uniformity of the diction, in particular the insistent and 'unspectacular' use of profanity – this is a quality that cuts across the gendered division of language in which men silence women. A common idiom of profanity is, in the context of the prominence of heavily stylised, 'heteroglossic' representations of the male working class – consider the 'remarkable level of vernacular sophistication' in Ritchie's films – an important novelty.[22] *Nil by Mouth* then is a film whose intensely felt divisions between young and old, male and female, respectable and unrespectable working class are recapitulated and simultaneously put in suspension by a community which endures in a common idiom.

Indeed, the final scene of the film provides an image of communal/familial working-class inclusivity. The pretext for this gathering is a collective visit to see Billy who is now in prison. All the characters are assembled (despite the fights) and they all leave together (despite hints at continuing difficulties in individual relationships). The image of domestic space offered is one of intimate complexity – some are sitting, some are standing, all are relatively close to one another in the cramped kitchen. The conversation – led by Val – clearly engages all those assembled. It is also clear that Billy is still considered part of this community even though he is absent. The observation of the details of character interaction is also interesting in this scene. Ray's daughter is sitting on his lap and he kisses her. This action recalls his earlier discussion of his own father's failure to demonstrate affection and reminds us of the latter's empty mouth, from which, as Ray ruefully admits, 'not one kiss' emerged.

Crucially, as Kerry William Purcell argues, the film's aesthetic is distinguished by a style that captures not just the disconnection and isolation of characters like 'underclass' Billy, but also the sense of a 'shared predicament' underlying the fragmentation of working-class life.[23] This is achieved, according Purcell, through the cinematography of Ron Fortunato, which adapts the style of photographers

such as Paul Graham and Nick Waplington.[24] Thus, stylistically, the film manages
to convey the 'brutality'[25] and confinement of its domestic and exterior spaces,
whilst at the same time suggesting, in the manner of Graham and Waplington,
that these working-class individuals are 'conscious of the dynamics of their lives,
not slaves to them'.[26] Purcell makes the point that Graham and Waplington's
style is to be distinguished from that of contemporary photographers such as
Martin Parr. For instance, the subtle use of colour in Graham's documentary-style
photographs of working-class subjects that have traditionally been shot in black
and white achieves a 'poetic vision' and 'respect' for 'everyday life' that Parr's
ironic use of 'excessively vivid colours' does not.[27] Indeed, in referring to the
implications of Parr's *odious* aesthetic, Purcell goes on to describe effects which
overlap with Stallabrass's account of the urban pastoral.[28] As he puts it, Parr's use
of colour is typical of the 'fetishising' vision of the working class that appeals to a
fascinated middle-class voyeur.[29]

TRAINSPOTTING AND THE POLITICS OF STYLE

Trainspotting participates in the break-up and re-imagining of older, apparently
homogeneous class and national identities – including those founded on the
'working class' and 'Scotland'. This is reflected in the film's distinctive relationship
to established cinematic traditions. As Duncan Petrie observes, it rejects both
'Celtic romanticism and naturalistic grit' in favour of a 'new sophisticated urban
aesthetic'.[30] An important part of the cultural energy and excitement behind this
aesthetic is borrowed from 'style culture'. Consequently, before considering the
film in detail, a brief account of key aspects of this cultural formation might be
helpful.

Most commentators recognise that in the 1980s the concept of 'style' acquired particular connotations as it was used to refer to developments across
wide areas of the mass media including fashion, design, popular music and
advertising. Thus, for Michael O'Pray, early 1980s style culture in the work of the
British film-makers collectively referred to as the New Romantics, represented a
postmodernist mixture of the influences of club culture, dance, music, journalism,
fine art and design.[31] 'Style' here signified an attachment to the 'surface of things'
along with alternative representations of sexuality and gender understood in
terms of 'lifestyle'.[32] For Matthew Collin, style culture from the mid 1980s to
the early 1990s forms 'a shadow history of the Last Days of High Thatcherism:
one part aspirational materialism (i.e. flash), one part entrepreneurial verve
(i.e. blag), plus a whole lot of self-referential hype'.[33] The emphasis here is
more on the suggestion of economic vitality and individual resourcefulness
('entrepreneurialism', 'materialism', 'blag', 'hype'). There is also a link made with
Thatcherism which casts the phenomenon in an ambivalently alluring, decadent
light ('shadow history', *High* Thatcherism'). If we take the descriptions of

O'Pray and Collin together, the impression given is of a culture characterised by a flamboyant aesthetic of excess and an interest in unconventional identities on the one hand, and by its close relationship to the transformations brought about by economic neo-liberalism on the other. This last aspect of style culture was, for some commentators, its defining feature. Thus, for Robin Murray, style culture was an index of a post-Fordist 'designer capitalism' that was more sensitively attuned to a range of consumer tastes and lifestyles than had been possible under mass, Fordist models of production and consumption.[34]

It is the suggestion of the simultaneous flourishing of cultural difference and the entrepreneurialism of neo-liberalism which helps to explain the complexity and ambivalence of response to style culture on the left. Take, for instance, the approach of Dick Hebdige who, in the mid 1980s, described 'style' as one of the decades 'keywords'.[35] Hebdige's approach was to place the phenomenon in the complex force field provided by progressive aspects of postmodernism and regressive aspects of neo-liberal capitalism. He was concerned with what he called a style-related 'monetarist imaginary' in which 'social and identity formation' was restricted to what could be grounded in 'consumption'. This was a world operating according to a 'New Realism' of Hobbesian individualism, one in which 'natural' appetites ruled through the agency of 'market forces'.[36] However, at the same time, Hebdige recommended avoiding what he referred to as left 'miserabilism' in response to these developments and consequently he applauded style culture's investment in 'emancipation narratives' which were helping to construct 'collectives other than the imaginary community of nation or the international brotherhood of socialist *man*'.[37] In place of class and nation, Hebdige placed his hopes in contingent, topical and impermanent alliances of individuals to be found in new, utopian 'communities of affect' such as those formed in popular music.[38] Within such frameworks of postmodernity – the 'transnational media systems'[39] – style culture might be viewed as providing the resources for new, improvised 'communities' and 'identities'.[40] To that extent it implicitly represented a release from the English class system in which identity is seen to be immutably fixed.[41]

However, there remained problems with Hebdige's hopes for a progressive 'politics of style'.[42] The same process in which desirable, unforeseen and dynamic communities and identities were being constructed was also producing a historical *residuum* defined in terms of its incorrigible social backwardness – often an 'underclass'.[43] This process became progressively more apparent as the 1980s passed into the 1990s. Thus, there are examples from the style press of this era of working-class collectives finding themselves represented as dangerously atavistic – their profiles drawn from a social bestiary of grotesques. Style culture often helped to exacerbate this social conspicuousness through its valorisation of consumption. In comparison, for instance, with the complex lifestyle choices offered in the style magazines, the working class was in danger of being cast as a collection of offensively inept consumers. For example, in a piece for *Arena* entitled 'The Tattooed Jungle', Tony Parsons produced a polemical version of antagonistic middle-class social, cultural and political attitudes towards the working class that were typical of the period.[44] He presented the working class as tainted by xenophobic nationalism, sexism and grotesquely incontinent forms of consumerism – qualities which for him could be appreciated most clearly in what he saw as the decline of football culture. Interestingly, there is a sliding in the article between the characteristic features of a working-class 'underclass' that struggled under Thatcherism and a working class that prospered in the same context. The point of convergence is expressed in terms of consumption – for instance, the 'mindless desire to consume to excess' of what he calls the prosperous 'prole nouveau' is aligned with the anti-social gluttony of those drinking 'bruise-blue cans of Tennents' in public, in the morning.[45] Hill's comments on Peter Greenaway's film *The Cook, The Thief, His Wife and Her Lover* (1989) are relevant here.[46] He argues that Greenaway's critique of Thatcherism becomes an attack on those who, in Parsons's article, are referred to as 'Thatcher's unruly children'.[47] Like Parsons, Greenaway organises his allegory of Thatcherism around images of grotesque corporeality and consumption. For both, it is this philistinic 'race of mindless gluttons' who are made to stand as representative of the devastation of the New Right moment.[48] Parsons's phrase for these working-class 'traitors' – 'prole nouveau' – is a designation which fits well with Greenaway's central character, Albert Spica (Michael Gambon).

If *Trainspotting* is reliant on style culture to deconstruct older notions of class and nation, it might well be the case then that it too reproduces complex class antagonisms. In what follows I attempt to elicit the evidence of such antagonisms by attending to the film's *stylish* aesthetic. This is an aesthetic which has been appropriately described as 'black magic realism'.[49] According to Smith, the latter concentrates on 'the most dismal aspects of realist *mise en scène*' – in the manner of traditional social realism from Grierson to Loach, Leigh and Douglas – and at the same time manages, through the use of 'effervescent style', pop music and the 'fantasy' of magic realism to suggest the redemption of a sordid, fallen world.[50] Smith cites the example of Renton's (Ewan McGregor) dive into a toilet in pursuit of two opium suppositories as typical of the way the film seeks to transform 'the most impoverished real existence into one of sensual richness' – once inside the 'worst toilet in Scotland' Renton discovers a paradise lagoon and retrieves the suppositories as if they were pearls.[51] Generally, *Trainspotting* takes what Smith calls the 'garbage culture' represented by 'domestic squalor, cramped tenements, ruined council estates, [and] industrial wastelands' – and through 'set design, lighting, visual composition, musical scoring and so forth', manages to offer 'possibilities of escape as well as stories of entrapment'.[52] Its aesthetic verve draws 'a kind of vitality from grinding poverty' and is not 'a betrayal of reality, but an insistence that destitution need not stifle all imagination and will'.[53] Smith concludes this section of his text with the following defence of the film:

Figure 7 *Trainspotting* – Ewan McGregor and 'The Worst Toilet in Scotland'.
Courtesy of Andrew MacDonald

The unalloyed awfulness of poverty is thus continuously off-set by the processes of imaginative and aesthetic transformation. Such transformation does not amount to an escapist sugaring-of-the-pill, because the unpalatable realities of the world are still evident; but neither does it pretend to effect, or substitute for, the actual elimination of these realities. Rather, the claim of aesthetic redemption is, precisely and modestly, an aesthetic one; that it is a more subtle, more inclusive – one might say more realistic, if this didn't immediately conjure paradox – mode of representation than either conventional social realism or pure escapism. [54]

How might we assess these claims for *Trainspotting*'s black magic realism? The most important issue here seems to lie in the conceptualisation of the 'reality' which the aesthetic is described as capturing. A complex 'real' in which the awful and the wonderful can co-exist may be 'more inclusive'; however, within that formulation there exists a simplification of class realities. This simplification exists in both the film and Smith's analysis. Thus, in the film there is a slippage between the 'unalloyed awfulness' of what Smith describes as a 'very particular social world' – that of heroin addiction – and the wider, working-class context in which the drama concerning a group of young addicts is played out.[55] The attributes of the 'garbage' world of heroin-use – it's grey, listless and befouled limbo-time between fixes – stand in for this wider world. In this way, a 'traditional working-class culture' receives the image of the truth of its own 'spiritual poverty' from a prostrate, zonked-out, drug-taking 'underclass'.[56] In terms of the Nietzschean system of transvaluations that Smith accurately describes in the film, the working class, by 'choosing life' (jobs and consumer culture), has chosen *death*. In particular, it is consumption which is the necessary background to this transvaluation. The only difference between the working class that works and the one which has stopped working is that the consumption of the latter achieves an intensity absent in the experience of the former. The down-time of the heroin addict's existence can therefore be understood as an exaggeration of what is already felt to lie at the heart of working-class existence. (Note that the grotesquely soiled toilet that Renton dives into is located not in the trashed domestic space of the addict but in the larger, working-class world of the betting shop.)

Trainspotting's covert class commentary can be seen most strikingly in the opening sequence, and Smith's analysis is helpful in clarifying its drift. He views this sequence in terms of a 'tradition of conscious dissent from the values and lifestyle represented by modern consumer capitalism'. This tradition is expressed forcefully in Renton's first monologue which Smith describes as displaying a form of countercultural 'contempt' for the 'ethos and rewards of mainstream society'.[57] As this speech is important to the argument that follows, I include verbatim a large part of it here:

Choose life. Choose a job. Choose a career. Choose a family. Choose a fuckin' big television. Choose washing machines, cars, compact disc players and electrical tin openers. Choose good health, low cholesterol and dental insurance. Choose fixed interest mortgage repayment. Choose a starter home. Choose your friends. Choose leisure wear and matching luggage. Choose a three-piece suite on higher purchase in a range of fucking fabrics. Choose DIY and wondering who the fuck you are on a Sunday morning. Choose sitting on that couch watching mind-numbing, spirit crushing game shows stuffing fucking junk food into your mouth. Choose rotting away at the end of it all, pissing your last in a miserable home, nothing more than an embarrassment

to the selfish fucked-up brats you spawned to replace yourselves. Choose your
future. Choose life.

Smith's discussion of this speech in terms of an opposition between the
'counterculture' and 'mainstream society' sustains the impression that the animus
voiced here is not class specific. It is true that the list of rejected 'choices' given
by Renton includes ones which are both recognisably middle class and working
class; however, the speech remains class sensitive in ways that ultimately make
its universalising pretensions – as an attack on 'modern consumer capitalism' –
problematic. Let us consider its details in terms of the tactics of class differentiation
and antagonism. Whilst the speech's rhetorical structure – the repetition of a
single syntactical formula – does help to establish a formal equivalence between
the signs of working and middle-class forms of consumption, at the same time it
builds towards the grotesque outcome of this series of lifestyle choices: 'rotting'.
The latter is class-accented – it evokes a middle-class fear of the bodily and 'spiritual' consequences of a working-class culture of *couches, game shows,* and *junk
food.* (It is hard to link the more suggestively middle-class forms of consumption
and lifestyle listed – 'good health, low cholesterol and dental insurance'; 'fixed
interest mortgage repayments' or 'careers' – so directly with such outcomes.)
But perhaps most significantly, this judgement reproduces the middle-class belief
that the damaging aspects of working-class life are a matter of poor *choices.* Such
beliefs represent the recognisable, confining edges of the middle-class conception
of working-class existence – a conception according to which the latter would
be fine if only it was a little more disciplined, sensible and tasteful. These latent
class difficulties in Renton's opening speech reoccur in Smith's analysis. In a
section of the text that points to Renton's disdain for the working-class culture
of his parents, Smith cites 'compact disc players and electrical tin openers' and
'mind-numbing, spirit-crushing game shows' as evidence of Renton's perception
of its 'spiritual poverty'.[58] However, in the next paragraph Renton's rejection
of this world is couched in less class specific terms – now its target is 'modern
consumer capitalism' and 'the rewards of mainstream society'.[59] Smith's analysis
acknowledges and conceals such class distinctions in Renton's speech.

   A not dissimilar problem of a loss of focus on different class experiences within
'consumer capitalism' arises when Smith seeks to comment on those aspects of
the speech which make reference to middle-class lifestyles. Thus, in one passage
he points out how the references to 'good health, low cholesterol and dental
insurance' along with 'fixed interest mortgage repayments' that are targeted
by Renton's countercultural hedonism, provide evidence of traditional middle-
class 'deferral of gratification'.[60] However, this sub-list does not entirely support
the distinction between, on the one hand, a 'countercultural' championing of
the 'immediate pleasures of bodily intoxication', and on the other, a traditional
middle-class investment in the 'potential rewards of self-denial, sobriety and hard
graft'.[61] Such middle-class services and products do not necessarily demand self-
denial. Moreover, if it is true that the immediate pleasures of heroin use may not be

compatible with 'good health', it is perfectly possible for the prosperous middle classes to remain healthy and indulge in many immediately realisable pleasures. Indeed, to the extent that Smith's class landscape seems rather static here, it is tempting to destabilise his opposition between the 'underclass'/counterculture and the middle class. That is to say, it might be possible to establish links between those sections of the hedonist 'new middle class' that have done well under neo-liberal regimes, and the countercultural 'underclass' represented by Renton. This would be to render unsafe the older opposition between 'counterculture' and 'bourgeoisie'/'mainstream society'.

At this point, it is useful to consider the form of this opening speech as it makes reference to the complexities of the film's title and helps to throw more light on the transformations of middle-class culture that I am suggesting the film explores. The speech is structured as a list and listing is the recognised activity of the 'trainspotter'. Within style culture, 'trainspotting' becomes a trope for the self-conscious adoption of the grand gestures of canonical advocacy in the interests of apparently lowly or overlooked cultural phenomena. Indeed, what ultimately identifies the gesture displayed by the 'trainspotter' seems to be its ability to establish unarguable cultural value.[62] In this respect, the 'trainspotter' is the *omnipotent* consumer. Bearing this in mind, if we attend to the way in which Renton's opening speech adopts the rhetorical vehemence of the trainspotter's list, then the punchline is significant. 'But why would I want to do a thing like that? I choose not to choose life, I chose something else – and the reasons? There are no reasons. Who needs reasons when you've got heroin.' The consumer of heroin has chosen the ultimate commodity – the one that trumps all the others. This sense of omnipotence can be seen in the novels of Nick Hornby where the 'trainspotterish list' functions not only as the symbol of eccentric and 'self-involved' cultural consumption, but is also presented as the definitive and *essential* selection of popular cultural items.[63] Likewise, Renton's identification of one essential commodity is announced with such absolute confidence that it does not require any explanation or defence ('There are no reasons'). It is, therefore, not so clear that Renton's anti-list (what Smith calls the countercultural underclass's 'addict's manifesto')[64] is ultimately distinct from the society of consumption it appears to reject. Rather than standing outside consumer culture, the trainspotter is at its epicentre.[65]

Taking this further, we might say that Renton's superior hedonism represents, from a certain perspective, less the self-consuming indulgences of the 'underclass' than it does certain shifts in middle-class culture – shifts such as those captured by Danny Boyle's earlier film, *Shallow Grave* (1994), in which a group of middle class, 'egoistic ... anti-heroes' also seek out extreme and dangerous pleasures.[66] Perry Anderson's comments on the metamorphoses of the European bourgeoisie in the era of postmodernity are useful here.[67] Anderson argues that although in the immediate post-war period the bourgeoisie retained 'its own sense of collective identity, characteristic moral codes and cultural *habitus*'[68] – what Smith refers to as middle-class 'orderliness and decorum'[69] – by the 1970s this class 'was all but extinct'.[70] Thus, a 'democratisation of manners' and a 'disinhibition of mores advanced together',[71] and rather than focusing on what has perhaps been the dominant class narrative of the post-war period – the *embourgeoisement* of the working class through the post-war 'affluence' – we need to recognise the 'more striking phenomenon', the '*encanaillement* of the possessing classes'.[72] In a recent text Eagleton concurs with Anderson's assessment of these changes, observing 'It seems, then, that we have moved from the high-minded hypocrisy of the old middle classes to the low-minded effrontery of the new ones.'[73] The idea of a middle-class *canaille* helps to illuminate the conjunction of counterculture and underclass described by Smith and it substantially transforms our sense of Renton's journey of 'character formation'.[74] Smith seems right in seeing the film's narrative as a variant of the one found in European *Bildungsroman* – such a comparison directs our attention to how, in both cases, the story is structured around a youthful, central character's journey to find their 'place' and to become integrated into society.[75] However, unlike the classic European *Bildungsroman*, the society which the film imagines Renton being integrated into is no longer one best described in terms of the 'orderliness and decorum of bourgeois existence'.[76] It is just such a world, with its middle-class 'deferral of gratification' and its 'self-denial, sobriety and hard graft', whose substantiality Anderson and Eagleton would claim is now chimerical. Smith recognises this when he points out that Renton's ironic capitulation to society at the end of the film – 'I'm going to be just like you: the job, the family, the fucking big television' – is qualified 'by the kinship between the junkies and self-interested consumerism that the film has established'.[77] In important respects the hedonist junkie already resembles those he appears to be joining for the first time. This convergence of what are typically perceived to be opposed worlds – the counterculture and the mainstream – fits with the characterisation of the structural problem of the middle class provided by Eagleton. The latter argues that historically this class is typified by a 'fatal doubleness' in which the desire for stability, respectability, responsibility and order – the foundational metaphysics of traditional bourgeois civilisation – co-exists with the voracious opportunism of self-invention and excess.[78] The ulti-mate figure for this doubleness in the film is the *trainspotter* or Renton, who is 'decent' and therefore uncool, and at the same time 'bad' and therefore cool.[79]

THE POLITICS OF BLACK MAGIC REALISM

In the passage quoted earlier in which Smith describes the film's strategies of aesthetic redemption, he remarks that Renton's toilet fantasy 'off-sets' rather than *sugars* or *eliminates* the awfulness of working-class poverty.[80] One might argue in response to this that the use of *off-set* underestimates how 'unalloyed awfulness' and 'aesthetic transformation' generate and support one another. Stallabrass's work on the urban pastoral, for instance, describes a process whereby images of working-class abjection are folded into middle-class pleasures and anxieties. Black magic realism and the urban pastoral might be mutually illuminating. From such a perspective, the claim that Smith makes for the greater inclusivity provided by the aesthetic redemption of black magic realism depends upon an illusory *pastoral universalism* of a kind similar to that found in Renton's opening speech. In this speech the junkie is presented as the ultimate truth teller – all are implicated through the judgement of those who have fallen so far that they can reflect back to society, without distortion and with brutal honesty, the corruption of its 'consumer capitalism'. In the most extreme conditions, the junkie holds onto the endangered 'spirit of resistance' that heroin use, despite everything else it involves, remains faithful to.[81] But we must remember that such authority is actually founded on rigorous class division. Renton's opening speech borrows this pastoral authority or *truth-telling* of the low Other/junkie for the purposes of vehemently rejecting the mediocrity – the 'rotting' – of working-class life. At the same time, middle-class consumption, as we have seen, is more elusive. It may appear to be included in Renton's grand gesture of refusal, but it actually persists uncontradicted and even covertly supported in new, unrecognised forms. In sum, if we read black magic realism as an aesthetic which is closely allied to shifting class relationships, then what is noticeable is not so much its brave embrace of human aspiration and beauty even in the most degraded of conditions, but more the way it works to distinguish a particular class-inflected experience of the social damage generated by neo-liberal capitalism.

However, in order to fully address the complex politics implied by black magic realism we need to consider the political associations of the long-standing opposition in British cinema between social realism and fantasy – an opposition which Smith claims *Trainspotting* deconstructs. As Joe Brooker points out, since the early 1940s, a national cinema of 'quality' based on an aesthetic of 'mimesis and moderation' has asserted itself against a popular cinema in which 'fantasy, spectacle, trance, masquerade are the watchwords'.[82] The critical neglect of this cinema of 'spectacle and show' – associated with the output of Gainsborough and Hammer studios as well as maverick *auteurs* such as Powell and Pressburger – has, however, been more than compensated for in recent years.[83] A 'new consensus' appears to be replacing the older one, and as Brooker puts it, there is a sense of a 'hierarchy being reversed, with Gainsborough replacing Grierson at the top of the aesthetic pile'.[84] What ultimately interests Brooker is the question of the 'historical roots' of these competing valuations – roots which lie 'beyond film studies or the cinema itself'.[85] He goes on:

It seems plausible to surmise – as an empirical observation rather than an inevitable logical consequence – that the surge of theoretical interest in spectacle, melodrama, costume and fantasy have corresponded to the greater importance and prominence of 'social movements' or 'liberation' politics – feminism, gay rights, anti-racism – in the 1980s and 1990s, as against the visibility and plausibility of class discourses and politics in the 1970s and earlier.[86]

If it is this division between class politics and 'liberation' politics that is behind competing critical evaluations of realism and fantasy, then what kind of politics is implied by black magic realism with its attempted deconstruction of the couple 'social realism' and 'pure escapism'? [87]

One film in which we can explore this issue further is *My Beautiful Laundrette*. Smith claims that the latter offers a rare precedent for *Trainspotting*'s aesthetic strategies.[88] Critics have long recognised that Frears and Kureishi's film uses irony to undercut Old Left 'sectarianism and puritanism'[89] and seeks to celebrate vital, living, 'multidimensional characters' rather than one-dimensional 'political certainties' – certainties groundlessly supported by the belief that certain social groups possess a 'monopoly of virtue or wisdom'.[90] Described in this way the film clearly fits with the sympathies of a post-1960s libertarianism for which a socialism built on the assumption of the centrality of the working class is not only in principal undesirable but also inherently improbable. Recall the judgement of Papa, the film's washed-up socialist, who pronounces with simple finality: 'The working class are such a great disappointment.' The aesthetic traces of these political shifts are manifested in the film's 'heightened' and stylised *mise en scène* – stylistic features which are clearest in scenes featuring the 'magical' and 'whimsical' space of the laundrette business set up by Omar.[91] However, the stylisation of the film does not displace the continued use of the conventions of social realism.[92] Like *Trainspotting*, the film sites itself in a degraded, 'crappy' environment.[93] The difference is that this world is defensively shrugged off by the earlier film's central metaphor – the washing machine – whereas in *Trainspotting* a toilet is the means by which 'paradise' is 'regained'.[94] In the later film it is *through* not *despite* an excremental vision of the working class milieu that its aesthetic redemption achieves, by contrast, the lustre of its effects.

For Smith, despite the magic, *My Beautiful Laundrette* remains weighed down by the 'generally realist world of the film'.[95] If Brooker is right, this sense of an aesthetic struggle might be connected to a political one, in which case the difficulty the film has in establishing its magical vision of the world, especially when compared with *Trainspotting*, may reside in more than just a stylistic deficiency – the absence, for instance, of a 'lively pop-inflected narration'.[96] We might speculate that what needs to change, as it indeed does between 1985 and 1996, is the political position of the working class. 1985 is a political watershed – it marks the defeat of the miners – but just as important is 1989 and the start of the collapse of the Soviet bloc. Between the release dates of these two films the working class was being busily consigned to the past. A political disappointment in *My Beautiful Laundrette*, by the time of *Trainspotting* the working class as an independent political force has vanished. The 'garbage' that constitutes the context of this shared aesthetic needs to be thought about in terms of that vanishing. Black magic realism appears to mediate a particular class-inflected exploration of the destructive social consequences of triumphant neo-liberal capitalism – its vividness requires as its background a posthumous or exhausted working-class world.

But if this is so, we need to make adjustments to Brooker's formulation. That is to say, there is a perceptible shift in the political associations of fantasy/'magic' as we pass from *My Beautiful Laundrette* to *Trainspotting*. Whereas the equation aligning non-realist techniques ('spectacle and fantasy') to the often utopian countercultural traditions of the 'new social movements' ('liberation politics') still seems relevant in the case of *My Beautiful Laundrette*, it is much harder to see *Trainspotting*'s strategies of 'aesthetic redemption' supporting such political aspirations. Indeed, the degree to which *Trainspotting* gives expression to any countercultural ambition might be questioned given the characters' lack of interest in the 'possibility of transformation'.[97] As Smith himself points out, 'With their parallel commitments to self-interest, greed and short-term gain, the junkies constitute a revealing mirror-image of the political and economic neo-conservatism of the 1980s.'[98] This is interesting as *My Beautiful Laundrette* is also characterised by a certain admiration for Thatcherism which co-exists with its complex, postmodern politics of difference. Leonard Quart describes the film's 'deepest commitment' as 'a rejection of bourgeois life and an affirmation of sexuality and disorder'.[99] In this way it can be anti-Thatcherite through an opposition to the conventionally conservative morality of the New Right and at the same time enthusiastic about neo-liberal enterprise culture – as Hill points out the laundrette is at least in part a 'symbol' of the power of 'self-help'.[100] One of the unresolved issues raised by Quart's sympathetic account of what he identifies as Frears and Kureishi's liberal scepticism concerning all political projects, is the degree of substantive engagement in the film with the Left.[101] In reality, *My Beautiful Laundrette* proposes a liberal-libertarian 'politics of irony' that has a relationship of flat rejection towards traditional forms of left politics grounded in class. Indeed, it might be argued that the main zone of its political engagement lies in the conflict between residual, welfarist traditions of liberalism and a libertarian politics which, licensed by Thatcherism, is seeking an exit from this increasingly defunct social democracy. (Quart points out that the film seeks to undermine 'notions of political correctness' which is code for welfare liberalism.)[102] The 'energy' and the 'drive' of the libertarian permissiveness in the film effects a condensation of the sexual and the economic which expresses this conflict well – those who embrace the enterprise culture have learnt, as Nasser (Saeed Jaffrey) puts it, how to 'squeeze the tits of the system'.[103] The *system with tits*, vulnerable to the depredations of 'enterprise', can be identified through its New Right cognate – the 'Nanny' or social democratic state. Furthermore, Frears and Kureishi's libertarian transgressiveness might be thought of in the same context as the metamorphoses of the middle class described by Anderson and Eagleton – images of 'consumerist excess' in *Sammy and Rosie Get Laid* would support this conclusion.[104]

The sensibility on display in *Trainspotting* is by no means an isolated one. Stallabrass's account of the class culture and political flavour of Britart in the 1990s is also very much along these lines. Smith also draws together *Trainspotting* and

Britart on aesthetic level. Both share a 'flashy, self-promotional style; [and] a dark
and sometimes grotesque humour, which is nevertheless alive to the unexpected
places and ways in which beauty can be found'.[105] Stallabrass draws our attention
to what he calls the 'twilight of ideals'[106] and the disappearance of the expectation
that 'things' will 'improve' amongst the yba's (young British artists) – an outlook
matching *Trainspotting*'s particular inflection of counterculture cynicism.[107] In
sum, the common aesthetic identified by Smith in *Trainspotting*, anticipated in
My Beautiful Laundrette and ascribed by Stallabrass to Britart, seems to suggest
a politics that responds to and helps to shape shifting middle-class experiences.
This is a politics which systematically seeks to antagonise left-liberalism from
a position which has recognisably been influenced by the New Right. Both
Trainspotting and Britart characteristically look to achieve a suspension between
'crude visual pleasures' and this atmosphere of scandalised left-liberalism.[108]
Images of the working class as 'underclass' provide an important part of the
material for this provocation. These images transform the working class into an
entertaining 'spectacle of degradation'[109] and ally it with 'the wild body, with
unregulated hedonism, with violence, drug abuse and filthy sex'.[110]

    In the case of Britart, the emotive and disturbing content to the work is
matched by a refusal to 'make consistent comment'.[111] Stallabrass refers to a
consequent nihilistic suppression of 'meaning and morality'[112] along with 'social
responsibility'[113] – and once more, this corresponds quite closely with the
sensibility Smith discovers in *Trainspotting*'s countercultural 'underclass'. There
is, nevertheless, an important exception to this cultivation of complex, ambiguous meanings that exceed any political message-making or moral certainty.
Stallabrass: 'These artists seek our admiration for their honesty, for giving us a
view of life in all its horror and beauty together, and not comforting us with hollow
parables.'[114] His examples include figures like Damien Hirst, Chris Ofili and Sarah
Lucas who create the impression in their work and in their own commentary
on it that they 'know about "real life" and tell it like it is'.[115] And once again, this
approach to 'reality' is not unlike that which Smith finds in *Trainspotting*. This
can be seen most clearly in those passages in which he proposes the superiority
of the aesthetic of black magic realism over social realism in capturing a complex
world in which horror and beauty are to be found side by side. In his analysis of
Renton he sees a similar complexity represented in the way that the character
recognises himself to be both 'hero and anti-hero'.[116] It is instructive in this
respect to compare the presentation of Hirst's persona as an artist with the
fictional character Renton. This is Stallabrass quoting Hirst:

> I want the viewer to do a lot of work and feel uncomfortable. They should be
> made to feel responsible for their own view of the world rather than look at
> the artist's view and be critical of it. I try to say something and deny it at the
> same time. I'm a hypocrite and a slut and I'll change my mind tomorrow.'[117]

Here Hirst's desire to challenge complacencies and his disarming confession of unreliability would work just as well in describing Renton. We have seen how at the end of the film we return to the terms of the latter's opening speech. Our uncertainty about Renton's intentions and position, within or outside 'mainstream' society in this final flourish, mirrors the privilege of changeability that Hirst reserves for himself in this piece of self-promotion. The degree to which such forms of self-consciousness represent a connection with the honesty of 'real life' is doubtful. Such gestures of self-incrimination – 'I'm a hypocrite and a slut' in Hirst's case and Renton's judgement on himself as a 'bad person' after double-crossing his friends – could just as easily be seen to forestall consideration of the ways in which the 'honesty' appealed to is no less ideologically interested than other, less self-conscious and more apparently defensive acts of self-justification.

Renton and Hirst. Despite the working-class/'underclass' appearances, here is the delineation of a certain kind of middle-class cultural and political sensibility. It needs to be remembered, however, that this sophisticated and even appealingly 'honest' sensibility is dependent on a particular image of the working class. There is an illustration in Smith's book on *Trainspotting* which helps to emblematise this particular conception of the working class that I have argued is implicated in the film's aesthetic. It appears in the section detailing the diverse cultural in-fluences at work in the film and is placed to support the connection Smith makes between the film and Britart. After remarking that Hirst made the video for Blur's song 'Country House' and that in turn Blur contributed to the soundtrack for *Trainspotting*, Smith includes a reproduction of Hirst's photograph *With Dead Head* (1991). This photograph shows, in the style of a comically posed snap of two friends, Hirst's grinning face, cheek to cheek with a severed and grimacing corpse's head. The head is bald, the face fleshy and the features 'coarse' – the rictus suggests a working-class *gimper* or *gurner*.[118] This image presents itself as both a kind Bakhtinian populism of the grotesque body, consonant with Britart's self-consciously iconoclastic, anti-liberal provocativeness, and as a memento or trophy of what Stallabrass refers to as a species of lurid 'middle-class porn'.[119] Here is the working-class body – grimacing, broken, unprotected – and alongside it the grinning, baby-faced artist. The image's relationship to Smith's text is revealing as although its inclusion is clearly justified in terms of his general argument about the 'black' humour shared by both the film and Britart, it nevertheless contains a recognition, safely screened by the uncertainty of the artist's intention – is it solidarity or derision? – that this humour is related to a particular view of the working class. The photograph is an extreme example of the way that the melancholy spectacle of decay and destruction – in this instance that of a human body, one which is comically identified as working class and reduced to mortuary garbage – from a certain point of view, no longer inspires any redemptive or restitutive desires. These energies are short-circuited in Hirst's photograph so that here the death's head becomes the source of the scandalous pleasure that lights up his own cherubic countenance.

CHAPTER 5

The Lumpenproletariat: Countercultural Performances

Recently Colin MacCabe asked the question of *Performance* (1970): 'Is this the best British film ever?'[1] The answer would appear to be 'yes', not only for MacCabe, but also for many of those putting their energies into late 1990s gangster cycle, albeit for very different reasons.[2] My discussion will take as its starting point MacCabe's impassioned contextualisation of the film in terms of the social, political and cultural ferment of the mid to late 1960s. I will argue that his account of a struggle between Old England and the revolutionary promise of the counterculture – a struggle played out in the life of the film's central, working-class protagonist, Chas (James Fox) – neglects the evidence of 'another' working class in the film, one which is marginal to its privileged countercultural site of 81 Powis Square, Notting Hill Gate. I conclude the chapter with an analysis of *Withnail and I* (1986), a film which looks back with ambivalence at the bohemian class mixing or 'classlessness' of the late 1960s. The narrative of *Withnail and I* suggests the terms of a middle-class exit from the political challenges of the era and can therefore provide an interesting gloss on the relationship between class, 'the possibilities for liberation in Britain', and the counterculture – the key themes of MacCabe's analysis of *Performance*.[3]

OLD ENGLAND

For MacCabe, *Performance* seeks a utopian fusion of two separate worlds – 'pop and crime' – represented by Turner (Mick Jagger) and Chas (James Fox) respectively.[4] After committing a murder Chas goes on the run from both the police ('the filth') and the other members of his gang ('the firm'). Hiding in the house of fading rock-star Turner, he is exposed to a countercultural lifestyle of drugs and alternative sexuality before being retrieved by the gang and driven off to what we presume is his death. Crucial for the release of the 'energy and mobility' of Chas and Turner are the countercultural sexual and gender performances of two 'foreign females' – Lucy (Michèle Breton), and Pherber (Anita Pallenberg).[5] These two succeed in transforming Chas to the extent that when he is driven away at the end of the film he has become a hybrid being, both Chas and Turner at the same time. As MacCabe puts it: 'The final fusion of Chas and Turner brings together the two elements in English society which have the power and the energy to transform "old England"'.[6]

Let us start then with the place of 'Old England' in the film. This phrase is spoken by Turner towards the end of a musical number referred to as 'Memo from Turner'. The line in full is 'Here's to Old England' and it is delivered by Turner directly to camera as an ironic toast. His immediate reference is to the criminal underworld of Harry Flowers (Johnny Shannon), an East End gangland boss modelled on the Krays. In the context of this scene Turner is drawing our attention to an aspect of the English class system that I have previously discussed in terms of the patrician/plebeian figure. That is to say, he is pointing to one of the most potent myths of English nationalism – the collusion of the social polarities of the class system. From this point of view, as MacCabe puts it, the criminal underworld is the double of the 'vicious and cynical ruling class'.[7] This point is made in the *mise en scène* through the painting that hangs behind Flowers's desk in his 'office'. As Andrew Hill observes, 'Flowers is shown attempting to run his operations with a certain respectability, or "a touch of class"'. His office is oak-panelled and has leather furniture; behind his desk hangs what could be a Stubbs – an archetypal image of the eighteenth-century squire on his mount.'[8] Further evidence of this attention to the class system of Old England can be seen in the narrative structure of the film. The opening and closing scenes feature images of chauffeur-driven Rolls-Royces. These emblems of class power are associated with both the ruling elite and the criminal underworld. The black Rolls we see at the start remains un-owned, the occupant(s) unidentified – the interior 'a mysterious space hiding one knows not what infamy and perversion'.[9] The impact of this opening sequence in which an enigmatic black car glides through a rural landscape suggests both the gilded, landed-conservative symbolic repertoire and a darker gothic pastoral. Equally sinister is the white Rolls in which purring gang boss Harry Flowers arrives to take Chas away at the end of the film. In comparison with the utopian alliance that MacCabe sees the film setting up between Chas and Turner, these images of the patrician and plebeian form the prototype of what MacCabe calls the film's 'sordid alliances'.[10]

Chas, however, is a working-class figure who redeems himself. A potential redemption is to be seen in his confrontation with the upper-class barrister Harley-Brown (Allan Cuthbertson) in which he challenges the 'Law in its full psychic authority and class power',[11] and demonstrates the 'enormous vitality' of a working-class London which 'mocks a ruling class' that it does not 'recognise'.[12] (Harley-Brown also owns a Rolls-Royce – one which Chas pours acid over.) Notwithstanding such acts of defiance, actual redemption for Chas is only to be found through his transformation in the countercultural, 'heterotopic'[13] space of 81 Powis Square, Notting Hill Gate, which MacCabe argues is the 'locus of the sex and drugs and music which has the potential to transform the society'.[14]

Despite this argument – one which is so sensitively attuned to the liberatory intensity of the film – the 'class system that so rigidly rules British society' retains a bewitching fascination for MacCabe.[15] His text is peppered with references to this system, including: 'old fetters',[16] 'barriers',[17] 'the rigid class divide'[18] and 'ancient' and 'secure' English class relations.[19] The emphatic use of such metaphors works to persuade us of the overwhelming reality of this English prison house of class. *Infamous, perverted, corrupt, ancient, imprisoning* – as with Nairn and Anderson, *Old Englishness* takes on the qualities of an enduring, fossilised *ancien régime*. It might be added that the utopian fusion of crime and pop, 1960s counterculture and the working class rests, as MacCabe is aware, on a view of the latter in which it is likely to remain 'irredeemably stuck' if left to its own devices.[20] Such a perspective reproduces that assessment of the working class central to the Nairn–Anderson theses.

Aside from this pessimistic assessment of the political potential of the working class, there is a tension in MacCabe's argument which affects the opposition it is required to sustain between a credible, realisable countercultural pressure for change and the object of his loathing (Old England). This can be seen most clearly in his handling of the idea of 1960s 'Swinging London'. The 1960s were discussed in the mass media of the time – and since – as a moment of 'emergent classlessness'.[21] MacCabe is rightly wary of this commonplace. At the same time, his discussion of the representation of class in *Performance* conveys an acute sense of some revolutionary pressure warping the solidities of the English class system. Thus, he talks of pop catapulting 'mainly working-class men through the barriers of class' and follows this with a reference to the Rolling Stones meeting the 'Chelsea set' in 1964.[22] The latter offered a 'protean' bohemian milieu in which 'debs', 'public schoolboys', 'criminals', 'jazz musicians' and 'black men' partied together.[23] From one viewpoint, the Chelsea set embodied the spirit of 1960s classlessness and MacCabe celebrates this.[24] However, he also endorses the skepticism of *Performance*'s co-director, Donald Cammell, and sardonically comments that the Chelsea set remained 'lodged within class relations as secure as they were ancient'.[25] A distinction might be drawn here between classlessness as class 'mixing' and classlessness understood as the experience of going beyond the exploitation at the heart of capitalism as a social system.[26] The former involves the transgressive derangement of a hierarchical system of status in which the fundamental structure of the system remains intact whereas the latter, needless to say, suggests something far more profound. Take another example from *Performance* – the casting of James Fox. MacCabe recounts an anecdote concerning Fox in which the old Harrovian earns the respect of the 'chaps' at the Thomas a Becket pub in South London whilst researching his part as an East End gangster. This arrangement had been brokered by Chelsea set intermediary with the Krays, David Litvinoff. Having won the acceptance of his handlers, Fox is described as successfully crossing the 'great divide of British society'.[27] At such moments, MacCabe authenticates and celebrates a movement between social extremes which carries a charge of transgression and which can be read as an example of 1960s class mixing. Thus, in casting an 'old Harrovian as an East End gangster' MacCabe claims that the directors, Cammell and Nicolas Roeg, were 'crossing class as transgressively as Pherber was to encourage Chas to cross gender'.[28] However, such vivid movement within the confines of the class system might be understood as the intensification of the signs of the English patrician–plebeian polarity across the performance of the actor. Whether such an intensification works as a proleptic deconstruction of the class system, as opposed to an exploitation of its taxonomic resources, is less clear.

A skeptical view of 1960s class mixing is only strengthened when it is noted that nostalgic accounts of the bohemianism of *Performance* as a lost or suspended moment of possibility for radical politics appear reliant on reconfirming a belief in the abiding realities of an English atavism of class. Consider this quote from an appreciative article on the film by Jon Savage:

> Indeed, much of the attraction of this period lies in its class mix: that extra-ordinary cross-pollination of criminals, upwardly mobile street urchins, disaffected middleclass artists, and bohemian aristocrats ever on the lookout for sensation. Britain is a country where this mix is actively discouraged: since the 70s the class walls have gone up again, explicitly re-erected by New Right ideologues and politicians.[29]

Savage's comments endorse the notion that Britain is a country in which, as Gareth Stedman Jones puts it, class is a 'life-sentence'.[30] Sixties class mixing acquires its impact principally against the background of this image of a society stuck in class proprieties and fetishisms. We might talk here of a *carceral* model of class which Savage and MacCabe share, one which is closely associated with their sense of Englishness, and which is needed to lend credibility to their belief in the wider political significance of 1960s class-traffic.

I will return shortly to the theoretical implications of this view of Englishness and class; however, at this point I would like to look in detail at another aspect of Savage's comments on the film – their evocation of a contentious, conjoined figure of class and politics, the *lumpenproletariat*. As Hill observes, Savage's article echoes Marx's description of the lumpenproletariat or 'la boheme'.[31] For Marx, the lumpenproletariat represented those bohemian social elements who had become detached from their class backgrounds – an 'amorphous, jumbled mass of flotsam and jetsam' including, amongst others, bourgeois 'wastrels', aristo-cratic bankrupts, as well as vagabonds, pimps and pickpockets.[32] Marx argued that these declassed forces of social confusion rendered more complex the essential struggle between capital and the proletariat. Also, as the 'refuse of all classes' this 'free floating mass' was vulnerable to being recruited for reactionary movements and was, therefore, politically dangerous.[33] Taken as a figure for the social and cultural tumult of the 1960s, however, the lumpenproletariat has been retrieved as a positive political sign. Thus, Peter Stallybrass uses it to represent the vital 'heterogeneity of political groups and processes' that bloomed in the 1960s.[34] In this way, it comes to stand for a progressive politics of new, unforeseen alliances between different, oppressed constituencies – a politics which is no longer reliant solely on the revolutionary vocation of the proletariat. This use of the concept of the lumpenproletariat fits with the tenor of MacCabe's arguments about *Performance*. As we have seen the latter stresses the fact that the film seeks to bring into existence in Chas/Turner something that has not existed before – 'a new hybrid being' representing the utopian fusion of the insubordinate energy of the working class and the sexual and social *otherness* of the counterculture.[35] Perhaps the most striking images of this political articulation are provided in the bedroom morphing of Chas/Turner/Lucy/Pherber in Powis Square. As MacCabe writes of the scene in which Chas both embraces Turner and makes 'love to the boyish Lucy' – 'This is a Chas not only comfortable in his own skin but able to open himself to the foreign and the other'.[36]

Like Stallybrass, MacCabe is uninterested in a politics based in any claims of 'certainty about social relations'.[37] Such comments are directed at the centrality of the working class in Marxist visions of socialist politics. The suggestion is that 'scientific' forms of Marxism are only sustained by the belief that political positions emerge directly out of the structure of interests objectively given in the socio-economic base.[38] Whilst it is easy to agree with MacCabe's dismissal of such beliefs, what needs to be remembered is that he has an additional reason to be skeptical of a politics which would put the working class at its centre – the fear of 'Old England' and the associated 'tragic impasses of British life' most accurately captured by the prison-house of its class system.[39]

Returning to Savage, we can now consider in greater detail the theoretical and political implications of this carceral model of the English class system. As well as providing a vivid background for bohemian transgression, it tends to imply that class is principally a political and ideological problem which prevents social mobility. The rhetoric of imprisonment ('walls' in the quote from Savage) aligns class struggle with the liberation struggles of the era in which *Performance* was made and thus blurs the critical, political differences between the concepts of class, race, gender and sexuality. Freedom from class – classlessness – cannot be achieved without challenging the most basic laws of exploitation that structure the capitalist mode of production. If the idea of transgressive class mixing conceals this, it helps to support an illusion of freedom. However exhilarating and utopian, class mixing has no intrinsic link to the political task of liberating society from the source of class exploitation.

But equally, if class mixing is not necessarily a good thing, then neither is class necessarily a 'bad thing' in the way that Savage's liberationist rhetoric suggests.[40] We can agree that racism, sexism and homophobia are bad, but such forms of oppression and domination can be distinguished from the exploitation that is at the heart of class. Marxism, of the variety espoused by Eagleton or Wood, sees historical change itself emerging from the class struggle that this exploitation necessarily entails – but certainly not in any simplistic or 'scientific' fashion whereby the working class acts directly on its objective interests, as given by its position within the relations of production.[41] Struggles against racism, sexism and other forms of oppression, whilst essential, do not have the same social scope as class struggle. Indeed 'Sexual and racial equality ... are not in principle incompatible with capitalism' and the massive material inequalities it involves.[42] Capitalism 'subjects all social relations to its requirements' and can 'co-opt and reinforce inequalities and oppressions that it did not create and adapt them to the interests of class exploitation'.[43] If it is accepted that class struggle is the Achilles heel of capitalism, then class politics hold out significantly more hope for any project of general human emancipation than other forms of liberation politics. When class is detached from the system of capitalism – as it has been in Savage's article – it loses this pivotal position within society and history and becomes little more than an offensive anachronism.

ANOTHER WORKING CLASS

MacCabe's interpretation of *Performance* seems motivated by his concern with marking the unfulfilled promises of his own countercultural generation; however, it is possible to interpret the film in terms of a significantly different image of the working class than the one he gives emphasis to – an image, moreover, which lies outside his opposition between the rigid confines of the Old English class structure and the 'transformative' social fluidities of the counterculture. In order to detail this image – which is a fugitive one – I have found it useful to attend to the representation of space in the film. It is important not to focus exclusively on the countercultural space of 81 Powis Square, as there are other spaces and other stories at work in the film – spaces and stories which suggest complex relations between representations of class, gender and 'race'.

Take the film's working-class spaces. The bedroom of Chas's cousin Tony (Ken Colley) is a space of a 'straight' working-class culture which lacks glamour – it is the site where the trap which will catch Chas and prevent his escape to America is set. The space here is 'straight' in the sense that the characters are presented as heterosexual – the implied sexual activity is procreative (note the distance between the single beds and the presence in one scene of a child). In the affective economy of the film this bedroom represents that somnolent and deadening working-class world which the countercultural bedrooms of 81 Powis Square promise to dissolve. Note also that this space is presented as culturally barren in comparison with the furnishings, murals and paintings of Turner's house – the painting on the wall of Tony's bedroom is 'low brow', mass reproduction. Chas's bedroom, seen during the opening sex scene with Dana (Ann Sidney) and the fight with Joey Maddocks (Anthony Valentine), is a space of masculinist, homophobic aggression and style – the sharp-edged furnishings and orderliness indicating what Peter Wollen refers to as that 'armour of masculinity' with which Chas denies his own 'femaleness'.[44] The *mise en scène* of Harry Flowers's bedroom might be described as gangster kitsch. Like Chas, Flowers's suggested homosexuality is associated with violence. As MacCabe observes, the film appears to propose the Freudian thesis of the 'fundamental centrality of homosexuality, but as a component of heterosexuality'.[45] In this respect the gang's 'office' is crucial as it signals a violent homoeroticism that is expressed through the signs of a sadistic culture of power which is recognisably patrician/Old English – the painting, leather seats, oak-paneling and cigars – and through the evidence of a more contemporary interest in the hardened male, working-class body, visible in the body-building magazines and bullets that are kept in Flowers's desk draw. In the Memo from Turner scene, this same space – stripped of its contents – contains the collapsed, naked bodies of the gang members, locked in fetal positions suggestive both of violent death and post-coital exhaustion and intoxication.

It is in contrast to these various spaces of working-class intimacy – Tony's, Chas's and Harry's – that Turner's bedrooms/dressing rooms/music rooms/bathrooms acquire their peculiar impact. These are countercultural spaces of sex/gender transformation and orientalism in which 'class status and background' are unclear.[46] 81 Powis Square is constructed in terms of a countercultural chronotope that is marked by its 'liminoid' and heterotopic qualities – that is to say, it possesses qualities of transformation and difference which define its relationship to the utopian dream of exceeding the limitations of sex, gender, nation and class.[47] The London location of the house is itself significant, as Wollen points out – it pushes the focus of *Performance*'s 'modernist' art film predecessors, such as *The Servant* (1963), *Repulsion* (1965) and *Blow-Up* (1967), northwards from Chelsea/South Kensington to an area 'just off Portobello Road, then seen as a crumbling crime-ridden ghetto'.[48] In this way *Performance* anticipated 'Jarman's *Jubilee* and such later Notting Hill films as *Crystal Gazing* ... or Hanif Kureishi's *London Kills Me*. Unexpected elements of *Performance* can also be found in Greenaway's *The Cook, The Thief, His Wife and Her Lover*.'[49] Wollen wrote this before the appearance of the 'fairy-tale' London films of the late 1990s that we looked at in Chapter 2. These films were to superimpose an exclusive, west London idyll over the social heterogeneity of an area of London that is fleetingly visible in the background of those shots in *Performance* which were gathered around the exterior of the 81 Powis Square/Lowndes Square.[50]

The omission of *Withnail and I* from Wollen's list of post-*Performance* London films is interesting as the later film appears to offer an account of the collapse of the countercultural bohemianism that both he and MacCabe celebrate.[51] Moreover, *Withnail and I* makes apparent something which can already be seen in the configuration of *Performance*'s countercultural chronotope – something that the nostalgic, participant memories of Wollen and MacCabe fail to fully develop.[52] Hill's work is useful here – he points out that 81 Powis Square is not only a space in which identities can be transformed but also a space that is peculiarly disconnected. 'The separateness and otherness of the household is evident in the lack of connections between its inhabitants and the outside world ... the inhabitants do not interact with anyone else. This is evident too by the way in which they are depicted as possessing their own, alternative, conceptions of space and time.'[53] This separation and disconnection is linked, through the pastoral motif in the film, to a certain narcissistic apoliticism. The house's walled garden is an extension to the orientalist fantasies woven by Turner and Pherber – the former reads a passage from *The Adventures of Marco Polo* in which Asani Sabbar is described as building a fortified garden paradise – fantasies which can be understood in relation to what Wollen describes as the film's 'hippie pastoral'.[54] Certainly the 'garden idyll' of 81 Powis Square is recognisably part of the counterculture's critique of modernity; however, as Hill puts it:

> In place of active participation in the politics and development of the alter-native society, the inhabitants' energies are directed towards the narcissistic pleasures of drug use ... These preoccupations mirror the real counterculture, where the pursuit of these pleasures, imaginary utopias and isolation from mainstream society fuelled the assessment of many that the development of the counterculture into a significant and lasting political force, able to achieve substantive objectives, was impossible.[55]

There is then what Hill calls a 'premonitory vision' of the fading of the post-1968 counterculture to be found in *Performance*.[56] This sense of eclipse, detectable in the film's brooding 'end of an era' atmosphere, is identified, in Hill's reading, as internal to the counterculture whereas in MacCabe's account there is a tendency to displace this problem outwards onto 'Old England'.

Despite its usefulness in supplementing the interpretations of the film made by Wollen and MacCabe, Hill's discussion of *Performance*'s representation of countercultural disengagement – the 'inertia and withdrawal' of 81 Powis Square in relation to any development of an 'alternative society' – might itself be taken further.[57] In opening up the 1960s pastoral utopianism carried in theme of the garden, Hill draws on early modern references, including Andrew Marvell's poem 'The Garden'. Likewise, on the strength of the way that America is used in the film as an image of freedom, he refers to a European conception of the 'New World as a garden idyll' which stretches back to the sixteenth century and earlier.[58] The problem with these contextualising references is that they fail to register a complex, Atlantic history of capitalism and class struggle. Thus, Hill's quote from 'The Garden' – 'Society is all but rude,/To this delicious solitude' – is used to support the assertion that 'The garden has repeatedly been situated ... as separate from and in some senses outside of the rest of society.'[59] Whilst this is undoubtedly true, what needs to be added is that the separateness of the garden, especially in English culture, is related to forces which inextricably draw it back into the social. Marvell's poem, for example, cannot be fully appreciated without taking account of the social struggles of the era in which he was writing – as Christopher Hill puts it, the problems which appear in Marvell's various idyllic gardens are the problems encountered by 'an individual in an age of revolutionary change'.[60] (I will argue in Chapter 7, in a discussion of Jarman's *Jubilee*, that the pastoralism of the early modern English garden needs to be thought about in terms of the development of capitalism in the colonies and at home.)

Having considered the utopian elements of *Performance*'s countercultural pastoral, Hill subjects its *orientalising* aspects to scrutiny in terms of 'broader and longer-running ... associations' by which he means to refer to the 'Hippy trail' linking up London with Morocco and Afghanistan.[61] He then goes on to claim that 'This trail can be configured as a supply route for 81 Powis Square, interpreted in terms that translate and restage Said's assessment of the reliance of Mansfield Park upon an Antiguan sugar plantation in Austen's novel.'[62] Edward Said's reading of Jane Austen's novel in the context of 'imperial practices of exploitation and plunder' is one which was foregrounded in the film adaptation of the book, *Mansfield Park* (1999).[63] However, as Moretti points out, there is a debate amongst historians as to whether or not the colonies played an '*indispensable* role in British economic life'.[64] He disputes Said's reading of the novel and argues that the fortunes which appear in the nineteenth-century English novel from the direction of the colonies, function to sever the 'wealth of the elite' from the "multitude of the labouring poor" of contemporary England', thus concealing the class struggle this wealth necessitated.[65] Why make these points? Certainly not to erase the significant, if not 'indispensable' role played by colonial slavery and exploitation in the development of the British capitalist class.[66] The intention is to draw attention to other 'broader and longer-running associations' that Hill's account of the significance of 81 Powis Square misses. Thus, in what follows I will argue that alongside the countercultural chronotope of sex/gender transformation and idyllic social isolation, another space is present, one which suggests the experience of a working class that extends beyond national boundaries and which appears aligned, like Chas in flight, towards a wider Atlantic world. This space is registered in MacCabe's text; however, his reading of it is mainly restricted to Cammell's unshot, alternative ending in which Chas/Turner makes it to America.[67]

A good place to begin an analysis of the presence of this space in the film is with a character who goes missing in Hill's analysis – Noel, the black tenant of Turner's basement. Despite the fact that the link between Noel and Chas is coincidental – Chas overhears that Noel, a musician, is going to Liverpool for a job and moves into his flat – the exchange of places that ensues is an important one and it points to something that lies beyond the countercultural chronotope whose disconnected lassitude Hill so accurately analyses. The importance of Noel is that he helps to give shape to this world outside 81 Powis Square. This effect can be explored if we look at the key, Paddington station scene. Chas, on the run after killing Joey, is in one of the station cafés waiting for a train to take him to a relative in Barnstable, Devon, where he intends to hide. (Shortly before arriving at Paddington, Chas has been talking to his mother on the phone – from her accent it seems that she is Irish, a point which I will return to.) Whilst Chas is waiting, Noel arrives and greets his mother, who is white. This fact is in itself notable. It suggests a transgression – one that goes uncommented on by MacCabe, who is principally concerned with sex/gender transformations – of a key racialised boundary separating 'white' women and 'black' men. At this point then – on the run from the police and abandoned by the Flowers' gang who liken him to a sick 'dog' – Chas finds safety in what he overhears of the conversation between Noel and his mother. Narratologically, Noel's significance in this scene approximates to what Vladimir Propp referred to as the functions of the 'helper' and 'donor'.[68] That is to say, Noel makes it clear that he is leaving 'all' his 'sounds' and his 'whole life' in the basement, and that the arrangement he has with Turner – whose status and relationship to Noel as 'landlord'/property owner is emphasised – is that his room shall be sublet to someone 'who has respect for another person's life', i.e. Noel's. The style of the uncredited actor's performance in this scene is important. His voice is projected in a way that fails to observe the decorum of the 'private conversation' and it therefore makes what he has to say available to everyone within earshot. His side of the conversation is a general invitation to listen – it acquires its distinctiveness partly by the way it is contrasted to his mother's style of address which is contained, intimate and at times close to inaudible. In other words, in his role as helper/donor, Noel provides Chas with assistance – conceal-ment from the 'filth' and the 'firm'. Chas uses the information he gathers from this conversation to set up the possibility of an escape – and in return he pays Noel's debt of £41 back rent, money that the latter had promised Turner out of the payment he is to receive from his 'gig' in Liverpool. There is then an exchange effected between Noel and Chas, and the narrative presents it as one which is mutually sustaining. Furthermore, the narrative suggests that both their lives are orientated towards America. That is to say, Noel re-routes Chas away from Devon and back to London and his basement flat – from where Chas will seek to get to America – whilst Noel himself makes his way to Liverpool which is, historically, an Atlantic port. (It is also, of course, a city with important links to Ireland.) During their conversation, Noel and his mother are seated beneath a large painting of what looks like an ocean-going ship. Finally, as Chas takes possession of Noel's room we notice a small photograph of Dr Martin Luther King above the bed – drawn attention to by Pherber's gesture of ripping down the photo immediately beneath it. 'Black', 'white', male, female, Irish, American, English. A transatlantic web of transportation links, familial experiences, cultural exchanges and radical politics suddenly opens up within which the basement of 81 Powis Square sits, now no longer simply just an annex to a countercultural pastoral.[69] But what kind of world is this – that is to say, what, in comparison to the other worlds depicted in the film, are the characteristics of its social interactions?

To help to frame an answer to this question we need to return to the scene in the Paddington railway station café. As Chas sits in the café there are two moments, intercut with the arrival of Noel, that reprise a motif that has run throughout the first half of the film. The first involves the café waitress who brings Chas's order to him. She appears suddenly and is shot in slow motion as she looks directly into the camera. She has first been seen, indistinctly, behind the café counter's glass screen – the camera zooms out from her onto Chas who is then left in the foreground of the shot. This cinematographic device is used in other scenes to isolate and then pull into an enlarged frame, peripheral figures. Take for instance the shot of a black mechanic in the car hire garage that Chas and the gang visit – once again, there is a zoom out to a re-establishing shot which puts the black worker in the background of the frame, foregrounding Chas's gang.

It is this motif then – the delineation of a look which is peripheral to the action, often belonging to marginalised and/or working figures, suggesting 'documentary' style glimpses of a world beyond the fiction – which is developed and intensified in the café scene.[70] There is a quality to the waitress's look which is solicitous. This impression is reinforced by the corporealising effect of slow motion which exaggerates the way she bends towards the camera – her eyes down as she places the tray – and then catches and extends the moment when she looks up again, directly into the camera. The shot can be read as Chas's point of view; however, it suggests less his control of the visual world and more his visibility. But to whom? This question immediately poses itself with the second looker to catch Chas – a smiling girl outside the window of the café who is cradling a cat and, again, looking directly at the camera. Her gestures are similar in their air of open attentiveness to those of the waitress. Whilst the girl is silent, the waitress, in the shot that follows her slow motion glances, returns to being a 'waitress' and speaks. As she continues to lean in, towards Chas, she mixes a request for the price of the sandwich with a working-class endearment, calling Chas 'love'. Similarly, note Noel's opening greeting to his mother who has been looking after some of his sound equipment whilst she waits for him – Noel: 'Hello Ma, thanks Ma, you're a darling.' Note also the editing together of two close-ups, one showing Noel and his mother stroking one another's hands and the other, a shot of Chas's hand stroking the fabric of the sleeve of his coat and thereby, in the matching of the action, creating a sense of an impossible reciprocity and inclusion between the three of them across the cut.

Chas betrays only a minimal acknowledgement of the waitress, turning away from her as she leans towards him – presumably to protect his disguise. Equally, he offers no clear acknowledgement of the smiling girl. It is as if these peripheral figures, who are both inside and outside the fiction – part of an overtly emphasised background – create with their looks, a sense of another world which is interested in, even has a claim on, the world of the narrative. The last of such looks which Chas will receive is from a first-floor window overlooking 81 Powis Square as he stands at the door waiting for Pherber to let him in. Again, the look belongs to a black watcher whose status as the last witness from 'outside' the world of Turner and Flowers is fateful as Chas will not reappear from this world. There is an unthreatening curiosity to all these looks which receives a peculiar emphasis from the fact that Chas is on the run and therefore, at this time, his visibility is narratively charged. Ordinarily, to glance at the marked man is to be a danger to him – here this is not the case. By contrast, when Chas walks out of 81 Powis Square at the end of the film, it is in front of Flowers' watching 'men' who are there only to ensure he does not escape. (There are none of the bystanders – both black and white – who occupy the dilapidated spaces of the square and act as witnesses to his arrival.) There is a passage in MacCabe's book which, in the context of a discussion of the politics of the film, raises some of these issues:

> But *Performance*'s politics have nothing to do with the epiphenomena of parties and governments and everything to do with the realities of class exploitation. England is represented as a country enthralled to a vicious and cynical ruling class. The lawyer and the gangster are, despite differences of language and social class, ultimately united in their common exploitation of a people only glimpsed on streets and offices ... The only area which lies outside this control is the house at 81 Powis Square, the locus of the sex and drugs and music which has the potential to transform the society.[71]

This is an important passage – it both moves towards and away from the argument being built here. That is to say, it recognises how the film, on its edges, generates a sense of a working class which is more diverse than the one represented by the Flowers gang. However, there is also that distracted focus on Old England that we have already examined, along with its counterbalance, the countercultural 81 Powis Square. Note also how MacCabe describes this other world as being 'glimpsed'. This is only partly accurate – it is true that its existence remains beyond the explicit focus of interest in the film; however, its presence is not passive. As I have argued, it remains apart and *looks in* as much as it is *looked at*. For MacCabe, 81 Powis Square, with its ability to 'transform society', is the only hope for Chas. But this is to fail to pursue his own sense of the exception constituted by this heterogeneous working class whose presence surrounds Chas in these scenes, even if the latter does not recognise it or is effectively cut-off from it by his fugitive status. Indeed, this disconnection only intensifies our sense of the peculiar and significant status of this other 'outside' or alternative 'hidy-hole' whose existence comes to our attention through a relay of curious and even solicitous looks.

Finally, an exclusively countercultural understanding of Powis Square can also be seen in Hill's essay which, as I have already pointed out, omits Noel from its discussion altogether. Thus, despite proposing a more critical view of the 'hippie pastoral' than that presented by MacCabe, Hill effectively substitutes Pherber for Noel in the basement. Here is his description of Chas's arrival: 'It is to the cellar that Pherber leads Chas when he arrives. This is the room that has just been vacated and that Chas is hoping to rent.'[72] It is Noel who 'leads' Chas to the basement and it is Pherber who follows him into the space as he makes his claim on it – a claim which is based on a pretended understanding with Noel. Also, it is possible to read that space, as I have done, in ways which are more culturally specific than Hill suggests – as Noel warns us and Turner accepts, it still contains Noel's 'life'. As well as emphasising an air of bohemian solitude, 81 Powis Square belongs to another imaginative geography, or indeed another 'geo-narrative system'[73] that stretches out into a wider proletarian world, one which opens up in the brief interval between what Wollen describes as the film's two halves – the gangster movie of the first (the world of Harry Flowers) and the 'hippie pastoral' of the second (the world of Turner).[74]

WITHNAIL AND I AND THE END OF THE 1960s

It is instructive to compare *Performance* with a film treating the same era but made later when the utopianism of the 1960s moment had vanished.[75] *Withnail and I* makes comment on the passing of the 1960s and is coloured by what is, for the time it was made, a characteristic view of the working class. It is heavy with an atmosphere of countercultural decline and defeat which it explores through the personal relationships and experiences of its principal characters – Marwood (Paul McGann) and Withnail (Richard E. Grant) – as they emerge out of the bohemian class mixing of the era with different prospects. A relationship of farcical repetition seems to exist between the two films. In terms of sexual politics, *Performance*'s androgyny, deconstructed genders and liberated sexuality becomes, in the later film, the panic-stricken affirmation of heterosexuality and exaggerated disgust at social difference. The sinister vision of Old England's class system in *Performance* becomes a source of elite and plebeian grotesquerie in *Withnail and I*, as the bohemian class mixing of the 1960s falters and is replaced, at the end of the film, by a new, socially 'decontaminated' aestheticism. In *Withnail and I, Performance*'s countercultural pastoralism confronts a farcical English 'heritage' pastoralism. The countercultural heterotopia of *Performance* reappears as a dystopia in the later film. Crucially, *Withnail and I* contains no sense of the charismatic working class evoked in *Performance* by the casting of Johnny Shannon and the acting of James Fox. The class dynamic is concerned not with a mix in which the proletariat and countercultural bohemians threaten Old England. Instead, it traces a process of middle-class disengagement from revolutionary politics and the re-establishment of a traditional English class landscape.

The narrative of *Withnail and I* is structured around the experience of Marwood, the 'I' of the film's title. Marwood and Withnail share a bohemian Camden town flat or a 1960s 'heterotopia' which has degenerated into a

Figure 8 *Withnail and I.* Courtesy of Equator Films

heterodystopia. As the era ends, the informality of its communal ethos alters and
we experience the flat through the appalled reactions of Marwood to incursions
of threatening heterogeneity – rats as big as dogs in his kitchen, thieving hippie
drug dealers in his bed and 'huge spades' in his bath. Thus, all we see of this
lapsed utopian 'other space' is the flat aftermath of bohemianism, registered in
the *mise en scène* through a combination of domestic squalor and 1960s retro-
connoisseurship. A similar but less immediate impression of lost utopia is provided
by Monty's (Richard Griffiths) desolate Lake District cottage to which Marwood
and Withnail escape when Camden becomes unbearable. This decayed, pastoral
utopia belongs to an earlier social formation – an elite, sexually transgressive
Oxbridge associated with Evelyn Waugh's melancholy evocation of the interwar,
upper-class dandies or 'children of the sun' whose lives have been chronicled by
Martin Green.[76] Green's image of the culture of this elite brotherhood of dandies
is one which foreshadows the 1960s Chelsea set's transgressive mix of bohemian
'society' elements and London *low-life*. (It is perhaps not entirely coincidental
that Monty lives in Chelsea.) Monty's relative, Withnail, is recognisably an upper-
class bohemian – it is interesting that his name carries a graphically undetectable
phonetic encoding, an identifying characteristic of the hieratic nomenclature that
marks the apex of the English class system.[77]

Like the Camden that Marwood and Withnail flee from, the Lake District idyll
is also presented in a state of deflated abandonment – the party props are dust
covered and Monty's gay lyricism has, with age, turned into a cover for priapic

opportunism. Also, like London, this is a space full of danger for the middle-class Marwood – Withnail, with typical upper-class nonchalance, offers him up as sexual bait for Monty. Thus, this film gives us a recognisable representation of the middle class – the protagonist as blank cipher literalised here as the anti-eponym of the title[78] – seeking to extricate itself from a colourful tableaux of English class types (the rural and urban plebs and the effete upper classes).[79] Of particular interest is the representation of the urban proletariat in the opening scenes in which Marwood, as narrator, casts an appalled eye over the inhabitants of the Wanker's Cafe. Tabloid newspaper headlines and 'greasy spoon' decor metonymically establish a sense of working-class credulity and ugliness. The *mise en scène* is accurately described in the directions of Bruce Robinson's screenplay. 'The café is a hovel. Grease and fumes and ketchup bottles with blackened foreskins. Some horrible faces in here. Marwood watches an old woman eating – her fried-egg sandwich ruptures. Loathing and fascination. Loathing wins it and he turns away.'[80] This middle-class view on working-class grotesquerie is also evident in the pub scene that follows shortly after Marwood's nausea in the Wanker's Café. Again, this scene is provided with a frank gloss by Robinson: 'Only two women in here and they look like men. Faces like rotten beetroots … Everybody here has one thing in common. They come in here to get drunk. It's a horrible place. Shit-coloured formica. Carpet like the surface of a road. The atmosphere is rank with smoke and Irish accent.'[81] As a representation of the 1960s then, this film cannot even begin to imagine the sense of revolutionary possibility located in the 'energy' of the working class that MacCabe detects in *Performance*.

Towards the end of the film there are two scenes which when taken together construct an implicit argument about the trajectory of the middle class from the 1960s to the 1980s. The first is a kind of valedictory saturnalia in which Withnail and Marwood encounter the domestic 'invaders' already mentioned – the hippie Danny (Ralph Brown) and Presuming Ed (Eddie Tagoe). This scene combines two lines of action: the smoking of a giant joint and Marwood's discovery that he has been offered a lead role in a repertory company production outside London. It therefore acts not only to set in motion the conclusion of the friend-ship between Withnail and Marwood, but also to signal, allegorically, the end of the countercultural licence of 1960s London. The effects of the drug induce a panic in Marwood which Danny points out is simultaneously political and personal. Marwood demands another drug to counter the effects of the first one and refuses Danny's advice of getting higher on the original joint. That this advice is not simply hippie pharmacology is made clear when Danny likens Marwood's situation – and implicitly that of the counterculture generally – to that of someone caught in the dilemma of holding on to a rising balloon. This comically impossible situation conveys a serious point about the abandonment of revolutionary struggle. To say no to more of the drug, argues Danny, is a 'polit-ical' decision – it is to opt out of that struggle.[82] This idea of countercultural failure is expressed aphoristically in a remark attributed to Presuming Ed which echoes the Rolling Stones and at the same time evokes liberation struggles of the era, 'We [the counterculture] have failed to paint it [the 'greatest decade' in human history] black.' At the same time, the comic image of the rising balloon indicates the problem of the disparity between the counterculture's pretensions and the necessary endurance demanded of those involved in revolutionary struggles.[83] The image suggests either, cynically, that revolution is a matter of timing your escape (ensuring that you don't hold on beyond the point at which you can still fall safely to the ground) or tragi-farcically that it requires self-defeating determination (if you do hold on longer than you should, then all you have left to do is to carry on holding on in the knowledge that your grip will eventually loosen and you will fall anyway). In other words, this image suggests a perspective in which revolutionary activity is neither a pressingly felt need nor even necessarily desirable. Interestingly in this respect, Wood, following an observation by Alan Sinfield, has argued that the presumption of a relationship between 1960s countercultural radicalism and revolutionary politics is based on a misrecognition. Sinfield argues that many 1960s radicals were 'closet Keynesians'.[84] In other words, as Wood puts it, 'the revolutionary rhetoric of many people was not really about revolution or socialism. It was about delivery on the promises of 1945.'[85] Thus, the radical project of the 1960s might best be understood not so much as an attempt to abolish capitalism but rather as a desire to promote a form of welfare capitalism or social democracy which would 'include excluded groups'.[86] The 'revolutionary' qualities of the experiences of this generation were 'less to do with the scope of their transformative objectives' and more to do with the opposition they came up against in seeking to realise their 'limited objectives'.[87]

Indeed there is a feeling of 'limits' experienced and new directions taken in the final scenes of the film. An elliptical cut takes us from the disintegrated saturnalia – Presuming Ed's bass chanting, Withnail's high-pitched, maniacally stoned cackling, and Danny's wasted, affectless drone providing the sonic disorder that Marwood must remove himself from – to the now determined sobriety of Marwood as he packs his suitcase in preparation for his departure from the house. What is notable about this scene is the character's fastidiousness, seen in his fresh and conservatively styled hair, his snappy hat and the addition of a copy of J.K. Huysmans *À Rebours* to his suitcase.[88] As Kevin Jackson observes, Marwood's 'look' is reminiscent of 'the go-getting City style of 1986' – the removal of his 'curly locks' is, we assume, 'a self-conscious premonition of Thatcherism'.[89] The *mise en scène* of his departure is organised as a sequence of decontaminating gestures – the addition of Huysmans's novel indicating the insistence of an aestheticised distancing from the heterogeneity/squalor of countercultural bohemianism. The film's placement of the character fits with Callinicos's comments on the journey of the new middle classes from 1960s radicalism to the 1980s obsession with style and the 'aesthetics of existence'.[90] Callinicos argues that postmodernism represents a specific generation's experience of political disillusionment after the defeats of counterculture and an 'aspiration to a consumption-oriented lifestyle'[91] in which there develops a 'narcissistic obsession with the body, both and male and female, less as an object of desire than – when disciplined by diet and exercise into a certain shape – as an index of youth, health, energy, mobility'.[92]

Withnail and I takes this moment of stylistic reinvention back to the end of the 1960s and associates it with the distress of personal/political betrayal. The end of the film is uneasy about endorsing Marwood's escape and the implication that the 1960s can be reduced to an individually negotiated rite of passage, one that is successfully accomplished in the case of the narrator, but stumbled over by Withnail. Marwood is removed from the final shots both visually and as a voice-over, and the scene is left to Withnail who delivers his final performance to the caged animals at Regents Park Zoo. On a personal level the significance of this scene from Shakespeare's *Hamlet* has been prepared for by Monty's comments about the disillusionment that strikes an actor when it becomes apparent that they will 'never play the Dane' – Withnail has reached this point. But the speech is also an expression of the apocalyptic nihilism, well recognised in the 1980s, which will become a feature of this generation as it moves beyond the hopes of the 1960s.

CHAPTER 6

The Problem of England: Aesthetics of the Everyday

Ideas of Englishness and heritage culture; histories of class struggle; the myths of neo-liberal capitalism; images of the 'underclass' milieu; the relationship of London to the promises of urban modernity, and the politics of aesthetic projects designed to transform the alienated, dilapidated everyday world – all these subjects find a place in the most recent films of Patrick Keiller. The emphasis in this chapter will be mainly on *Robinson in Space* and *The Dilapidated Dwelling* (2002), which both move decisively beyond framing the failures of English modernity in terms of the theses of Nairn and Anderson whose influence is clear, as we have seen, in the earlier *London*.

PARADOXES OF A CULTURE OF CAPITALISM

Robinson in Space is an experimental, fictionalised, picaresque documentary which acts as a sequel to Keiller's earlier and first 35mm, feature-length film, *London*.[1] Both films contain the same two unseen characters, Robinson and an unnamed narrator. The relationship between these two men is delicately poised – they are ex-lovers and friends. Having resumed their friendship and working partnership after a break following the conclusion of their study of London, they mount seven journeys of 'investigation' that take the 'problem of England' as their subject matter. The national space they explore is overlain with a national narrative which, in the words of the narrator, is the 'result of a particularly English form of capitalism'. This 'form', whose origins, we are told, go back to the time of Defoe and the Glorious Revolution of 1688, is described by Keiller – playfully adopting the persona of Robinson in an interview – as 'the usual "gentlemanly capitalism" stuff, you know, public schools, the City, bad food, bad sex'.[2] 'Gentlemanly capitalism' represents the dominance of the City of London over the national economy and a consequent prioritisation of short-term, speculative investment and the neglect of manufacturing. These aspects of the national economy are held to have been endorsed and protected by a pre-modern state which has, historically, been closely aligned with the City.

Needless to say, such arguments have been at the heart of the Nairn–Anderson theses.[3]

Gentlemanly capitalism then is at the root of the 'problem of England' that Robinson's employers, an advertising agency, have sent him to investigate. It is the summer of 1995, and one can imagine that employers such as these have sensed, like Robinson, the atmosphere of political change. More than this, in the dog days of a Thatcherism ignominiously shrunk to the dimensions of a Majorism which has itself begun to listlessly simulate 'modernisation', this advertising agency has 'heard' of Robinson's earlier project on London and is doubtless attracted to the diagnosis of English cultural and political backwardness it contains.[4] From the start we fear that their interest in this material is unlikely to be the same as that motivating the revolutionary *manqué* Robinson. Their engagement of Robinson suggests that his sensibility and political imagination are eminently exploitable. That is to say, his investment in the idea that cultural and political anachronisms are to blame for the protracted history of failed British modernisation might easily generate work for an industry or even a political party committed to the proposition that a modern culture, identified with a creatively or stylishly rebranded national 'image', could possibly pull off the magic trick of reversing the disfiguring ugliness of what the narrator in *London* calls 'dirty old Blighty'.[5]

Regardless of the true motivations of his employers, which remain, ultimately, obscure, the development of Robinson's research in *Robinson in Space* leads to a revision of the initial premise of a slowly declining English economy dragged under by an anachronistic culture. The duo wander across the country noting, with meticulous care, details of the national-economic infrastructure and the culture of everyday life until they are sacked, not surprisingly, by their employers. The story begins with a sacking – at the start of the film we discover that Robinson has been recently dismissed from his part-time university teaching job in London – and it ends with one. But in between, an unfamiliar and challenging image of the national economy and culture is fabricated through a deconstruction of the 'bourgeois paradigm'. Recall that according to the latter, historical progress assumes the exclusive form of bourgeois, capitalist modernity. When viewed from such a perspective, the representation of capitalism in *Robinson in Space* appears dominated by the figure of paradox. Thus, Robinson's roaming takes him into an English countryside in which pastoral iconography, conceived of in the bourgeois paradigm as an index of a pre-modern past, ceases to signify an immemorial idyll. Instead, what we discover in this landscape is the evidence of vigorous and sinister capitalist enterprise. Among the images of stately homes and open countryside, Robinson and the narrator turn up the 'windowless sheds of the *logistics* industry – new prisons, agribusiness, UK and US military bases, mysterious research and training centres' along with 'the proliferation of new fencing of various types', 'cameras' and 'security guards'.[6] Only indirectly visible in its effects, capitalism features as a *creepy* and 'cruel' social form made manifest through an arrogantly marked-out and aggressively defended terrain of private property.[7] This partially obscured landscape suggests the appearance of a 'new Gothic genre', one in which powerful private and state organisations acquire the attributes of tyrannical social orders of the past.[8] But rather than arbitrarily imposing a 'gothic' appearance on a new rural space, Keiller manages to suggest that this oppressive and sinister atmosphere belongs to a continuous tradition – that of the English *culture of improvement*.[9] This impression is achieved through the attention given to the indications of possession and exclusion in the landscape – fences, walls, gates. Such features are used to recall the discourse and ruthless practice of capitalist profitability that originated in the seventeenth-century English countryside. The activity of 'improving' landlords involved extinguishing the customary claims of the landless to the commons. A new definition of property was being elaborated as these landlords claimed the common land through enclosure.[10] Property was henceforth not just private but for the exclusive use of the owner, and the sense of 'making better' carried by the word 'improvement' could not be separated from the effect of making the lives of the dispossessed worse.[11]

The history of this dispossession is the memory space that Keiller supplies for the cruel, 'new space' of the contemporary rural scene.[12] For example, the Charborough Park sequence opens with a long shot of picturesque parkland, a drive and surrounding statuary casting long afternoon shadows. However, the

Figure 9 *Robinson in Space* – Tilbury. Courtesy of the BFI

commentary alerts us to the connection between the estate and the wealth generated from the slave trade. The following shot and the narrator's comment- ary recall the transported Tolpuddle Martyrs and remind us of the connection between the Enclosure Acts in Dorset and the 'degradation and starvation' of the proletariat of which George Loveless spoke.[13] (The process of enclosure prevented the rural proletariat from supplementing their starvation wages with the resources of the commons.) This sequence then offers a contextualisation of the iconography of English pastoralism. Images of the pastoral picturesque do not signify a timeless Old England. Rather, we might view them as the effacement of the scars of a very busy history. As the narrator puts it, quoting Sherlock Holmes, a 'dreadful record of sin' is concealed by the 'smiling and beautiful countryside'.

Robinson in Space's destabilisation of the bourgeois paradigm is to be found not only in the combinations of image and voice-over but also in the mute details of shot composition. Thus, from time to time, Keiller combines, in the same shot, English pastoral vistas with unfamiliar industrial intrusions. This is done according to a technique which might be described as a kind of witty, 'misfit' composition. Conventionally distinct orders of time and space are combined in the same frame – for example, a shot of the Knauf factory at Ridham has as its foreground a pastoral landscape whilst the background is dominated by the futuristic structures of the factory. Conversely, a shot of the village Leigh-upon- Mendip has a foreground that is dominated by the vertiginously sliced hillsides that form the Halecombe quarry. The village is in the background, but because of the compression of the perception of depth in the shot, it appears to be perched on top of the quarry itself. In another example, a long shot of a ship at Tilbury whose framing excludes the port, creates the impression that the ship's prow is pushing through the Thames's adjacent fields. In ways such as these the opposition between a pre-modern, English, rural order and a modern, industrial, authentically capitalist one, is quietly but insistently questioned.

In so far as *Robinson in Space* rejects the idea that 'pastoral retreatism'[14] has adversely affected English social development, it distances itself from what W.D. Rubinstein calls the 'cultural critique' of British economic decline.[15] Recall that the 'cultural critique' holds that an archaic English culture, rooted in a peculiar class structure dominated by an aristocratic hegemony, is to be linked to the twentieth-century decline of the national economy. In conversation with Patrick Wright, Keiller cites with approval Wood's rebuttal of that variety of the cultural critique formulated by Nairn and Anderson, according to which Britain is the victim of a 'peculiar capitalism' rather than simply 'peculiarly capitalist'.[16] If 'peculiar capitalism' designates a divergence from the path of capitalist modernity then, by contrast, 'peculiarly capitalist' suggests less the temporal exoticism of the English class system, detached as it seems from the forward moving forces of capitalist enterprise, and instead demands that one makes an effort to gather together in the same frame what are, in the context of the bourgeois paradigm, the historically opposed phenomena of capitalism and Englishness.[17]

Just as important as the dismantlement of the long-standing idea of a *peculiar English* capitalism is the assault on more contemporary conceptions of capitalism and associated images of class. Thus, *Robinson in Space* disables the bases of the neo-liberal discourse of the 'underclass'. Keiller's approach to the milieu of the 'underclass' is to switch attention away from suppositions of working-class moral weakness and to attend instead to the systemic features of capitalism, including its dependence on processes of class struggle and its frequently destructive relationship with the social environment. Charles Murray, that pioneer of 'underclass' theory, cites Middlesbrough as a location in which an 'underclass' has developed.[18] Coincidentally, some of Robinson and the narrator's most important general discoveries about the state of the national economy are confirmed on Teesside. That is to say, they establish that this is an area where the contradiction between a declining social and urban infrastructure and a thriving capitalist system is at its clearest. Thus, there are successful manufacturing industries in the region, particularly in intermediate products (for example chemicals and capital goods) and in steel production.[19] Shots of the chemical production site at Wilton and the dockside cranes and coal deposits of the Tees are accompanied by the narrator's references to the buoyancy of the industrial sector in the area. Generally then, in the sections of the film dealing with the north-east, the iconography of industrialism ceases to signify economic decline and instead is associated with successful capitalist enterprise. However, whilst the narrator briskly stacks up the abstract indices of economic success, he also reminds us of the conditions and effects of that success - high levels of unemployment in industries with automated plant; unregulated labour markets; the highest prison population in Europe, and urban dilapidation. Furthermore, these circumstances are not restricted to the north-east. Urban dilapidation is also visible in the images provided of the north-west (Liverpool), and the south (Reading). In this way, a thriving British economy is linked to ugliness and deprivation rather than to the alluring aesthetics of the consumer culture with which neo-liberalism capitalism prefers to associate itself.[20] The sequence on Teesside ends with a shot of prison construction which helps to place crime - one of the defining features of 'underclass' existence for Murray - in the context of the deleterious social impact of 'modernisation' on the local industries since the 1960s.[21] This is a representation of capitalism in which it is seen to involve inescapable social conflict.

A similar emphasis on struggle is to be found in the film's representations of science and technology. Robinson's obsession with the *buckminsterfullerene* focuses these issues. This carbon molecule was discovered partly by British scientists working unsupported by state or industry and, as the narrator informs us, the patents for its exploitation are all held abroad. The fate of the molecule seems then to epitomise the anatomy of anti-industrial British backwardness suggested by the cultural critique. But this sense of obstructed national economic glory tends to restrict our understanding of the dynamic of capitalism. The implication is that if not for the combined shortsightedness of state and industry,

British scientists would deliver us directly into the lap of a millennial, Promised Land of a thriving capitalist economy. Such scenarios present technological change as an autonomous scientific and technical process and disguise the struggles that inseparably accompany technological development. Keiller brings these struggles to our attention through the reproduction of the spherical, geodesic form of the buckminsterfullerene molecule in various objects featured in the landscape throughout the journeys. Take for instance the shape of the camp set up by the ecological group 'The Land is Ours' that is featured following the first mention of buckminsterfullerenes.[22] These protestors are squatting on land near the site of the Diggers' occupation of the commons at St George's Hill in 1649.[23] They therefore establish a link with those who struggled to resist the capitalist enclosure of the commons and the spread of the exclusive rights of private property during the English revolution.[24] Technological futures, the ones glimpsed through the new molecule, are bound up, through this visual figure, with a tradition of struggle that is far from exhausted.

AESTHETICS OF RESISTANCE

Keiller's representation of class involves breaking with some of the most enduring styles of English social realist, documentary film-making. Some have argued that this tradition tends towards a belief in the unproblematic visibility of the socio-economic system.[25] By contrast, *Robinson in Space* suggests that capitalism is not transparent and legible. Indeed, the film takes as its very subject matter what it confesses to be the 'problem' of the relationship between capitalism and English society. The device of using two unseen characters – one unnamed, the other unheard, and both acting like spies – gestures towards the conventions of documentary omniscience; however, at the same time the film locates the perspective of Robinson and the narrator in a landscape marked by unequal power relations and class struggle, with all the disadvantages this suggests. This effect is achieved through a variety of stylistic means. Cinematographically, both *London* and *Robinson in Space* are marked by the repetitive use of immobile camera and long shots which inflect social realist documentary panopticism with a *heritage pictorialism*. According to Higson, the latter, long a feature of the British heritage film, consists of self-consciously composed long shots and long takes designed to frame heritage properties.[26] He has argued that such shots exceed the narrative requirements of the depiction of character point of view and that they establish a public gaze which has heritage spectacle as its object.[27] The construction of such a gaze is compatible with the phenomenon, noted by anti-heritage critics in heritage culture generally, whereby the private property of an elite class (the 'spectacle of one class' as Higson puts it)[28] becomes the pseudo-public national *heritage treasure* of everyone.[29]

The cinematography in the Robinson films appears to mimic this 'studied', 'self-conscious' pictorialist style; however, the kind of gaze it creates is distinctive and entirely opposed to the one ascribed by Higson to the heritage film.[30] The presence of Keiller's fictional witnesses creates an uncomfortable and ambiguous viewing position around both films' carefully composed shots of pastoral and urban heritage. The spectator's awareness of the unseen narrator and his companion endows each image with the potential to act as a point-of-view shot – framings often include obstructions that are consistent with the type of fictional look being suggested. For instance the house at West Green built by Henry 'Hangman' Hawley is shot from the far side of the road running past the barred gate to the obelisk that salutes neo-liberal capitalism. Designed by neo-classical architect Quinlan Terry and built by Alistair, Lord McAlpine, former treasurer to the Conservative party, the obelisk celebrates the latter's avoidance of 'tax gatherers'. Our view of this monument is partly obscured by the branches of overhanging trees – thus creating the impression that Robinson and the narrator are at least partly concealed. A shot showing Windsor Castle, whose attached royal estate blocks the Thames path, gives us a view over the perimeter wall which fills the bottom half of the frame leaving the distant perspective of the castle in the top half of the frame. The impression created is of a suspended, illicit 'peering' over the obstruction.

Such shots imply that we are surveying private not public property and that we are doing so from a space that it is specifically inhabited and vulnerable. In this way the secure, taken for granted public space that acts as the precondition of a public gaze acquires an unfamiliar presence – that of a contested space only brought into existence by the efforts of invisible trespassers. These implied situations of clandestine observation and the enforcement and maintenance of private property activate off-screen space and generate the insistent sensation of narrative suspense. Something might happen at any moment to Robinson and the narrator – detection, eviction, arrest, harassment. Heritage spectacle, the putative heartland of the immobile English class system, becomes then a living site of struggle rather than the encrustation of anachronism.

This *view from the outside* delivered by Keiller's cinematographic style is a key aspect of his representation of the relationship of heritage spectacle to class struggle and capitalism, and it can be further elaborated upon by reference to the work of Robert Hewison and Raymond Williams. To return to the example of the West Green House obelisk, it is interesting to note that this heritage property appears in Hewison's book as an emblem of what he finds detestable in heritage culture – that 'deep cultural convulsion that manifests itself most clearly in our obsession with the past'.[31] However, it is not the convergence of Hewison's anti-heritage critique and Robinson's project that captures the attention here. Any such convergence is ultimately misleading as Robinson's discoveries cannot be contained within the parameters of the cultural critique guiding Hewison.[32] Rather, what is notable is the photograph included in Hewison's book which shows the obelisk from the opposite angle to the one given to us in Keiller's film.[33] The camera position in Hewison's photograph is immediately behind a statue looking down the avenue, past the monument to the gate and road, with the wooded area in which we might imagine a concealed Robinson and the narrator, rising up in the foreshortened background. This is an arresting image when juxtaposed with Keiller's film, as it makes clear the director's avoidance of the view from the *inside looking out* – there is only one such shot in *Robinson in Space* and that is from a terrace at Cliveden. The inclusion of this shot is linked by the narrator to Garibaldi who is supposed to have commented on the views from Cliveden down the river.

Turning now to Williams, in a passage in *The City and the Country*, written at a time when heritage culture did not yet have the controversial prominence it was to acquire in the 1980s, he discusses the pastoral landscapes of the 'great' house and attempts, by staging a drama of vision, to make us see its position in the landscape in a particular way.[34] First he asks us to alter the direction of our look so that it includes the 'land' as well as the 'stones and furniture'.[35] This redirected look is one that can be taken 'from any point'.[36] That is to say, it is not a look which is premised on a particular vantage point, such as the privileged position we might imagine the owner of the land might adopt; however, equally, as it is a look that can be taken at any point it implies a landscape whose essential

Figure 10 *Robinson in Space* – West Green House. Courtesy of the BFI

characteristics are everywhere visible and therefore a landscape in which there is no cover. A particular kind of history is the object of this look. Williams: 'Think it [the land] through as labour and see how long and systematic the exploitation and seizure must have been to rear that many houses, on that scale.'[37] The look must turn from house to land and to the meagre evidence of the lives of those whose labour was exploited (subjected to 'robbery and fraud') in order to build up the 'great' houses.[38] What Williams ask us to note, insistently, is the 'barbarous disproportion of scale' that these monuments to agrarian capitalism represent. That is to say:

> What these 'great' houses do is to break the scale, by an act of will corresponding to their real and systematic exploitation of others. For look at the sites, the facades, the defining avenues and walls, the great iron gates and the guardian lodges. These were chosen for more than the effect from the inside out; where so many admirers, too many of them writers, have stood and shared the view, finding its prospect delightful. They were chosen, also, you now see, for the other effect, from the outside looking in: a visible stamping of power, of displayed wealth and command: a social disproportion which was meant to impress and overawe.[39]

For Williams, this spectacle, which casts a 'shadow' on the viewer, is only mitigated by the 'partial' public 'reclamation' of the 'great house' as hospital or agricultural college.[40] He adds, in a passage that reads almost like a straight gloss on *Robinson in Space*, that such 'welcome signs' have by no means removed the evidence of 'the old kinds of power' still visible in the 'surviving exploiters and in their modern relations – the corporation country-house, the industrial seat, the ruling-class school ... the explicit forms of the long class-society'.[41] Keiller then, like Williams, asks us to adjust our look – to take it from the *outside*, within the 'shadow' of 'the long class-society' and the 'system' that has nurtured it from the sixteenth century to the present.

Any discussion of the cinematography in the Robinson films needs to consider their cultivation of *photogenie*. The latter originated in Impressionist film theory and was embraced by surrealists such as Louis Aragon. Keiller has adopted the latter's account of the décor of the 'cinematic marvelous'[42] to define *photogenie* thus: 'To endow with a poetic value that which does not yet possess it, to wilfully restrict the field of vision so as to intensify expression: these are two properties that help make cinematic *décor* the adequate setting of modern beauty.'[43] These two 'properties' of *photogenie* have guided Keiller's film aesthetic from his earliest photographic experiments. The first – the endowment of 'poetic value' on that which is lacking it – suggests the cultivation of a particular subjectivity which sets out to heroically embrace the world and to find the marvelous in the conventionally mundane. Keiller calls this an 'inclusive, poetic subjectivity'.[44] On this level Keiller's Robinson films are reverential in their tenacious hold, both in the image and the voice-over, to the everyday. If the cinematographic style is superficially rather staid, the hoped for effect remains one of transformation. As Keiller has said in interview on the making of *London*:

> But the whole point of making the film is rather optimistic in that the idea is to make everybody value the place. It is to say: LOOK. London has no decent postcards. The imagery of London is debauched by the monarchy and tourism: the 'glamour of backwardness'. And the purpose of making the film is not to say all these things that everybody knows ... but to make anew, to rediscover, to reconstruct it and to reveal it as a place which might be in the wrong hands but is not irredeemable ... Obviously it is a reconstruction and it is subjective – in that sense it's not a documentary, it's a sort of polemic for the necessity of continually re-imagining our surroundings.[45]

The second property mentioned by Aragon – the wilful restriction of the 'field of vision so as to intensify expression' – has a particularly destabilising effect on conventional presuppositions about the nature of the documentary film image as a representation. For Keiller, this restriction of the field is actually a general property of 'film space'.[46] In other words, because film space is of necessity constructed out of a view which is 'very narrow compared with experience of actual, three-dimensional space', it always involves a process of 'imaginary extension' from the screen.[47] Film space for Keiller is 'always a fiction, even when the film is a documentary'.[48] This sensitivity to the frame and the potential properties of off-screen space are clearly behind his ability to evoke the implied, unseen drama of the Robinson films.

Keiller's stylistic choices throughout his film-making career have been designed to exploit this transformative, fictionalising, *photogenic* quality that for him is inherent in the medium. The long-held and enigmatically framed still images of the Robinson films; the unexpected juxtapositions on image and soundtrack; the use of hyperreal fine-grain colour film stock – these techniques all assist in generating the transformations Keiller is seeking.[49] Indeed, in as much as the Robinson films seek to induce states of affective transformation, they fit with what Bill Nichols calls the 'performative documentary' of the 1980s and 1990s.[50] Like the 'performative documentary', Keiller's films aim to 'stress subjective aspects of a classically objective discourse', and to test the boundaries separating the documentary from the 'experimental, personal and political, essay and report'.[51] However, what ultimately sets apart the documentary form developed in the Robinson films is that, unlike Nichols's performative form, these films do not incur a loss of 'referential emphasis' or refuse to be explicit or to 'explain or summarise'.[52] Keiller's films *do* seek to name and explain 'overarching conceptual categories' – in the case of *Robinson in Space*, those of capitalism and *Englishness*.[53] This complex approach to film-making is perhaps then best described as one in which elements of the performative documentary co-habit with a more expository method.[54] Indeed, as we shall see, his last project to date, *The Dilapidated Dwelling*, is a more conventional, made for television documentary in which the expository drive – one which sets 'problems' and seeks 'solutions' – predominates over the poetic.[55]

Keiller's own writings are an invaluable resource for further insights into the ways in which his film-making has been influenced by the tradition of altered subjectivity found in European modernism. For instance, in an article written in 1982 he notes the effects on the photographic image of townscape and landscape of the evacuation of human presence.[56] As an example of this effect he cites Atget's photographs of deserted Paris streets and quotes Walter Benjamin's observations on them – that they appear to be establishing evidence from the scene of a crime and that 'With Atget, photographs become standard evidence for historical occurrences, and acquire a hidden political significance.' [57] As Keiller says, these images create the 'sense that anything could happen' in his deserted spaces.[58] The Robinson films are clearly influenced by this style of photographic practice – for instance, the scenarios implied by the cinematography we have already described are suggestive of a staked-out crime scene. One might take as further examples the eerie, evacuated City of London sequence in *London*, and the sense of imminent but endlessly postponed human arrival in the rural scenes in *Robinson in Space*. In the 1982 article Keiller continues these observations with a reference to Georges Bataille's comment that the siting of architectural monuments often coincides with crime scenes – crime here is to be understood in the sense of the bloody antagonisms and conflicts that have attended the history of class struggle.[59] Keiller makes this inference clear by asking us to consider the history of Trafalgar Square in London.[60] In *Robinson in Space* the technique of creating the impression of crime scenes with 'hidden political significance' can be seen in the way that landed estates and monuments are endowed with an aura of theft, expropriation and oppression that the clandestine activities of Robinson and the narrator memorialise. Examples would include: West Green House (built by Culloden cavalry commander General Henry 'Hangman' Hawley, a reputedly bastard son of the House of Hanover); St George's Hill (site of an ongoing battle over the 'commons') and Charborough Park (built and sustained on the proceeds of the interconnected activities of the enclosure of the English commons and New World slavery). The 'gothic', aristocratic face of a rapacious elite present in some of these examples is matched, as we have seen, by a rural presence which is more contemporary and anonymous but just as vigorous in the pursuit of the fruits of private property.

In sum, social space in the Robinson films – urban and rural – is both overcast by the shadows of 'the long class-society', and alive with intimations of the revolutionary transformation of everyday life. In this way Keiller insistently crosses the utopian with the apocalyptic. Thus, in *Robinson in Space*, Robinson's pursuit of utopia is mixed with an atmosphere of threat that is created through the science fiction theme of extraterrestrial invasion – see for instance the high-tech industries and gated communities in the Thames Valley sequences. The soundtrack uses an otherworldly, eerie musical motif from *A Matter of Life and Death* (1946) – a motif which in its original context conveyed the contention of cosmic forces over the life and future of a World War II airman. Powell and Pressburger's allegory of the hopes for a renewed post-war Britain is, as Ian Christie remarks, remobilised in *Robinson in Space* 'to bear witness for a nation once again unsure of its identity and future'.[61] The film ends in the north-west, around Blackpool and Sellafield. Blackpool is a recognised site of what Keiller calls the 'carnivalisation of everyday life' – one which he speculates might have been of interest to a surrealist like Aragon.[62] Sellafield, on the other hand, is linked to the theme of a cosmic struggle over the very stuff of life – the nuclear reactor's dome picking up on the complex associations of the buckminsterfullerene.

THE PROBLEM OF THE EVERYDAY

For a full account of Keiller's utopianism we need to return to that key concept – the everyday – which is central to the Robinson films and at the same time lodged at the heart of the radical aesthetic traditions of the European avant-gardes of the twentieth century.[63] Within the latter, the everyday constitutes the terrain on which a dialectical struggle between alienation and liberation is played out – as Anne Kaplan and Kristin Ross explain: 'It is in the midst of the utterly ordinary, in the space where the dominant relations of production are tirelessly and relentlessly produced, that we must look for utopian and political aspirations to crystallise.'[64] As a potentially liberating concept the 'everyday' was deployed by the 'modernist avant-gardes' in the manner of a 'euphoric' embrace of modernity.[65] Keiller is fond of quoting Roman Jakobson on this: 'Nowadays, the department-store mirror monstrosity and the village inn's tiny fly-bespattered window are considered to be of equal poetic worth. And just about anything can come flying out of them... No nook or cranny, no activity, no landscape, or thought stands outside the pale of poetic subject matter.'[66] Jakobson's observations are interesting if read in the light of Bakhtin's description of the idyll of the family novel as the celebration of enfolded, inward looking social spaces. The nooks and crannies sought out by the modernist avant-gardes are available within a landscape of modernity which is open. However, the serendipities of *littleness* in *Notting Hill* are, by definition, the exclusive experiences of the owners of a privatised public space – take the example of the park bench inscription. The idyllic category of littleness lies outside that relationship to the everyday and the ordinary captured by the modernist dialectic in which, to quote the opening address of *Robinson in Space*, the routinised, reified 'dead weight of things' confronts the possibility of its own miraculous liberation.[67] The same might be said of the experiences shaped by the urban pastoral. The latter grounds a middle-class view of the irredeemable, changeless, undialectical everyday of a degraded working-class world.

The difference between a representation of an everyday world which remains connected to revolutionary desires – as found, for instance, in the Robinson films – and a representation of the everyday which is closer to the apolitical voyeurism afforded by the spectacle of the 'underclass' in the urban pastoral, can be appreciated if we consider the work of photographer and film-maker Richard Billingham.[68] In an appreciative essay on Billingham, Michael Tarantino comments, with reference to the artist's film of his own family members, *Fishtank* (1998), that 'the fishtank is an artificially constructed space, one which is built to keep the inhabitants inside and to facilitate the viewing of them from outside'.[69] The film's title succinctly captures the role that the 'underclass' plays in the urban pastoral with its emphasis on a secure containment that promises an unobstructed, exotic class spectacle. As Stallabrass remarks, the film and the earlier collection of photographs featuring the same subject, *Ray's a Laugh* (1996), present Billingham's family as a 'lumpen' 'underclass' who appear to 'subsist on welfare and home brew'.[70] It is the 'stasis' of this spectacle of 'violence and degradation' which captures Stallabrass's attention.[71] These are images of subjects whose lives appear to be 'without the possibility of change'.[72] Furthermore, Billingham refuses to contextualise his subject matter. Tarantino defends this refusal to politicise the poverty on show in the photographic work; however, his conception of the scope of any such politicisation remains restricted to a dismissed liberalism. As he puts it: 'The project of photographing this family is by no means a liberal justification or plea for understanding ... [it] ... offers no apologies for that subject matter, nor for the foibles of its subjects. There is a difference between a poverty of surroundings and a poverty of life. The latter is nowhere in evidence.'[73] One sees here what Stallabrass views as a characteristic disparagement of a politicised aesthetic in this generation of British artists.[74] Tarantino's limited conception of the political in terms of a 'liberal justification or a plea for understanding' is problematic. That is to say, this proper suspicion for containing the images in a tacitly moralising and patronising liberal framework appears to lead him into an alternative position in which the 'underclass' theory of Charles Murray pushes itself forward, by default, as providing the relevant distinctions with which to judge the work. Thus, Tarantino sets up an opposition between 'poverty of surroundings' and 'poverty of life' and claims that Billingham's work maps the former but avoids the latter. The defensiveness of this argument is in itself a capitulation to well-established reactionary positions on poverty. That is to say, by defending these images as representations of lives that have not surrendered their intrinsic humanity in the face of material impoverishment (these are images of people who 'just seem to get on with it') the argument reproduces Murray's definition of the 'underclass'. As Murray says, it is not 'condition' that is critical in identifying the 'underclass', it is 'behaviour'.[75] In other words, it is the degree to which people living in poverty remain capable of retaining their 'respectability' that distinguishes them from the 'underclass'. In an era in which the New Right has relentlessly politicised poverty – both in revisiting theories of the 'unrespectable' working class and in pursuing social policies whose effect is to increase social inequality – an apolitical approach to the subject can only with difficulty present itself as neutral. Indeed, it is ironic that for Tarantino, the perceived threat to the integrity of the images comes from the liberal and not the conservative when it is the latter who is the unrecognised source of the recognised danger - that the images will be judged as providing evidence of an 'underclass' 'poverty of life'.

It is important to distinguish this everyday of the urban pastoral from the tradition of critical thought on the quotidian that runs through Dadaist and surrealist culture, the post-war writings of Henri Lefebvre and the activities of the situationists in the 1960s – all of which represent key sources of inspiration for Keiller. As Kristin Ross argues, this tradition loses its radical edge after 1968:

> The literature devoted to rethinking the notion of the everyday after 1968 reflected a sensibility disabused of what came to be seen as the naiveté of hope for social transformation… Writers like Michel de Certeau, in his *L'Invention du quotidian* (1980), in effect 'reinvented' the quotidian. Their new, more contentedly phenomenological quotidian dispensed with Lefebvre's emphasis on critique or transformation, and instead celebrated the homey practices – cooking, hobbies, strolling – of life as it is lived in the here and now by individuals intent on escaping the rationalist grids of modern administration.[76]

It is against the background of this slackening of the 'hope for social transformation' that the drama of Robinson's escapades in both films takes shape. Robinson maintains a commitment to the utopian possibilities lurking in the present; however, he finds this commitment hard to maintain. The familiar rhythm of both films is an oscillating movement that takes him from delirious optimism to lethargic pessimism and back. He seems constantly on the verge of both a breakthrough and a breakdown. The breakthrough sought is a way beyond the alienated 'dead weight' of everyday reality – thus the films track his experimentation in the techniques of the modernist defamiliarisation of that reality. However, this project is an 'exhausting' one which raises many issues concerning the relationship between politics and art.[77] For instance, there is what might be called the problem of an *English everyday*. If the French post-war concept of the everyday was dominated by an image of Americanised mass culture and consumption that fitted the state-led process of accelerated modernisation then by contrast the English everyday was and remains, according to Robinson, dominated by the poverty of its consumer culture and the disabling distance between the state and processes of modernisation.[78] This is England as 'dirty old Blighty', 'uneducated, economically backward, bizarre, a catalogue of modern miseries, with its fake traditions, its Irish wars, its militarism and secrecy, its silly old judges, its hatred of intellectuals, its ill health and bad food, its sexual repression, its hypocrisy and racism, and its indolence. It's so exotic, so homemade.' This opening to *London* should be compared with the opening to *Robinson in Space* – the complaint in the latter about the malign force which reverses efforts of imaginative transformation is in part explained in this list of English shortcomings from the earlier film.[79] The image of *Blighty* is one which evokes the English 'miseries' reviled by Nairn and Anderson – as I have argued, in *Robinson in Space* Keiller subjects these and related aspects of Englishness to greater scrutiny. However, what is striking about this opening to *London* is that it manages to suggest both loathing and affection or an enchanted ambivalence which is clear in Paul Scofield's delivery of the voice-over as it slows down to a contemplative sigh when he reaches the word 'indolence'. The everyday here is both contaminated by the forces of reaction and is a source of perverse comfort – the very terms of failure are so rich in a peculiar national quality that the implication is that they become, for the English, a compensatory form of domestic exoticism.

This difference between the experience of capitalist modernity in France and in England is important in terms of the politics of the everyday. That is to say, it appears that in the English context the everyday is already, in part, aestheticised and therefore less amenable to tactics of resistance that rely on cultivating such sensibilities. By contrast there is a conflation in the French context of modernity, capitalism and rationality against which the concept of the quotidian acquires its attractiveness and significance. This opposition supports a politics such as that advocated by Certeau[80] – a politics which depends upon a Weberian account of the historical process of rationalisation and that, as Wood argues assimilates 'the various meanings of reason and rationality, so that the instrumental rationality of capitalism is by definition related to reason in its Enlightenment meaning'.[81] From such a perspective a project emerges that contests a capitalist modernity that is uncritically identified with the Enlightenment project and which takes the side of 'passion, non-logicality and the imaginary' against the oppressive forces of bureaucratic, technocratic and panoptical domination.[82]

Robinson's investigations in *Robinson in Space*, as we have seen, discover a successful economy matched with dilapidation and chaos. Thus, the film draws attention to the fact that in the English context capitalism cannot be confined to an orderly image of itself – the 'pristine culture of capitalism' reveals no evidence of the rationalist telos ascribed to capitalism in the French case. Instead of Cartesian rationalism and notions of rational planning, English capitalism has been associated with an adherence to the belief in the hit and miss of the 'invisible hand' of the market; a destructive ideology of the 'improvement' of property rather than humanity, and philosophical empiricism.

Anthony Easthope's study of a distinctively English discursive formation of empiricism is useful here.[83] He contrasts English and French culture in the following way:

Just as the repressive rationalism of France breeds a counter-discourse of extremity, violence and irrationalism, from de Sade to Rimbaud to Lautremont to the Surrealists, so the English preoccupation with fact generates its converse in a special kind of consciously playful, seemingly harmless but excessive fictionalising and white magic (both the founding fathers, Hobbes and Locke, admit the pleasures of fancy so long as they are contained in subordination to fact).[84]

He also points out that: 'Among the binary oppositions which strive to maintain the Western tradition Derrida includes seriousness/play. For the English tradition more appropriate terms would be "serious/silly".'[85] The Robinson films aspire to *playfulness* and reflect the admiration which Robinson has for European traditions of cultural experimentation and innovation associated with the influence of the modernist avant-gardes. However, Robinson's escapades also frequently evoke, as critics have observed, the atmosphere of whimsical English *silliness*.[86] The dispiriting thing about such silliness or 'nonsense' is that despite its ability to take empiricist discourse to extremes, it remains dependent on its norms.[87] Silliness does not represent a departure from what is referred to in *London* as the 'malady of home' – indeed it might be viewed as a connoisseurship of Englishness masquerading as disaffection.

Change then remains desired in the Robinson films; however, the means of bringing it about seem elusive or unavailable. Robinson's predicament gives emphasis to the problematic status of the everyday as a resource that not only inspires but saps the energies required to sustain such hopes. In this respect one of the most striking things about both films is the affective dissonance they generate around the protagonists. The mood in both films passes quickly through a medley of conflicting emotional tones – including melancholy, boredom, lethargy, aesthetic *frisson*, anxiety, mania, obscure utopian longings, fear, depression and silliness. But more than simply registering the dialectical nature of the everyday, Keiller is aware, especially in the work which has followed *Robinson in Space*, that a contemporary politics of the everyday not only faces the seductions of an English empiricist myopia but also those of a postmodern populism. Interestingly, both influences converge in the idea of the *homely*. As we have seen, Ross's account of Certeau's reinvention of the concept of the everyday – the form adopted in postmodern populisms – uses the word 'homey'. Similarly, the narrator's word to sum up the pull of the English everyday is the related 'home-made'. The common meanings shared by the two uses celebrate a creativity that is cut off from questions of systemic change. In the English case the *everyday* denies the existence of a vantage point from which the systemic aspects of capitalism can be assessed. Likewise, postmodernism is strongly influenced by the belief that the *everyday* offers an alternative to spurious, totalising perspectives on culture and society. As Michael E. Gardiner puts it, the concern with a complete transformation of society, still in evidence in the activities of the situationists, has shifted to a concern with 'the exploration of transient moments of creativity and subversive tactics within the parameters of the existing system'.[88]

Keiller has commented recently on the way in which the contemporary fashion for psychogeography appears connected to this recognisably postmodern condition of creativity within reduced horizons.[89] Citing the situationists he makes the point that the radical subjectivity espoused by the movement and embodied in the practice of *la dérive* was not originally viewed as 'an end in itself'; rather it was considered to be a prelude to making changes in the fabric of everyday life.[90] (In *The Dilapidated Dwelling* Keiller discusses Constant's *New Babylon* project.) To return then to the problem of the relationship of the political to the aesthetic raised by the concept of the everyday, the issue here seems to be the ambiguous status of these techniques of imaginative transformation. If in *London* the task Robinson sets himself is to 'poeticise' his deprivation, by the time of *Robinson in Space* such activities have themselves become associated with an abiding sense of political frustration: 'Perhaps poeticizing the everyday is something we have to do when we long for change, but cannot attain it.'[91]

The motivation for Robinson's poeticisation of his world originates in a political antagonism which is exacerbated by the urban and rural landscapes of neo-liberalism – landscapes which are associated in the film with the qualities of ugliness, sadism and dilapidation. This political antagonism has a class dimension which Keiller describes in the following way: 'To some extent, *London* took the deprivation of its protagonist Robinson, a disenfranchised, would-be intellectual *petit-bourgeois* – like thousands of others in London and other places, mostly connected with higher-education – and made it into some sort of shared experience. This is something that generally raises the spirits, a problem shared, and so on.'[92] However, the narrative of the film suggests Robinson's isolation as much as it does any collective belonging. Robinson and the narrator move in a world in which the institutions and organisations of class consciousness are attenuated or ineffectual and they depend on individual solutions to common problems.[93] In the light of this situation the danger with Robinson's strategy of sustaining the hope for change through the cultivation of a radical subjectivity is that such activity can become little more than a means of rendering bearable the actual acceptance of diminished expectations. Keiller evokes this dilemma in the following way when looking back at his own experiences of the 1980s – in the following quote he is discussing how, in an era of political reaction, he found a perverse comfort provided by a good view over London from his flat: 'As we felt ourselves losing ground, both politically and economically, our sense of loss was partly mollified by observing these visible changes in the detail of the landscape as spectators at some sporting event might watch the opposition winning. We might not like the way things were going, but at least we had a good view.'[94] In such extreme states of alienation the human world disappears into the natural one – Keiller describes his experience of seeing the city landscape from his flat as 'a very slow but visible movement of self-organising matter'.⁹⁵ Undoubtedly this sense of the possibilities of life being reduced to a passive observation of forces beyond one's control is one which is supported by a situation in which even 'phenomena like the fluctuations of the stock market have become part of "nature"'.⁹⁶ Keiller is arguing that the success conservative, neo-liberal governments have had in identifying their policies with the 'natural' laws of capitalism can be fully appreciated if one considers the irony that whilst their political opponents have challenged them on their record of presiding over an era of social decay, these same opponents have left unaddressed the more fundamental issue of whether or not 'successful' capitalism can ever be divorced from its destructive social effects. Keiller sums up this problem in a way which puts into question the distinction between economic 'decline' and 'successful enterprise':

> People whose everyday experience is of decayed surroundings, pollution, cash-starved public services, job insecurity, part-time employment, or freelancing tend to forget about the United Kingdom's wealth. We have been inclined to think we are living at a time of economic decline, to regret the loss of the visible manufacturing economy, and to lower our expectations. We dismiss the [Conservative] government's claims that the United Kingdom is 'the most successful enterprise economy in Europe' but are more inclined to accept that there might be less money for schools and hospitals…⁹⁷

Capitalist wealth produces social decline. If neo-liberal political competence is challenged – if, for instance, one disputes its claims to economic success – whilst at the same time the fundamental laws of the capitalist market are left unquestioned, then the 'problem' of the social will remain. The proposition that a fundamental acceptance of capitalism has taken hold, and that it restrains the kinds of social regeneration that the political successors to the Tories, New Labour, explicitly endorse, is one which *The Dilapidated Dwelling* addresses.

The difference between a defeated *aestheticisation of the social* (Robinson in *London*) and a *politicisation of the social* (Robinson in *Robinson in Space*) lies in the movement away from the myths about capitalism which were able to survive even in a vigorously anti-Tory political culture. The distance travelled between these two positions can be measured in Keiller's reflection on the genesis and outcome of the Robinson films. The following quote addresses the sense of despair which was common on the left in the 1980s – a despair out of which the film *London* emerged: 'In the UK, the subjective transformation of landscape seems to offer the individual a way to oppose the poverty of everyday surroundings. As individuals, we can't rebuild the public transport system, or re-empower local democracy, but we can poeticise our relationship with their dilapidation.'⁹⁸ Compare this – with the pathos of its individualising perspective – to the conclusions drawn by Keiller at the end of an essay systematising the discoveries about capitalism and neo-liberalism to be found in *Robinson in Space*:

'There *seems* to be no reason why the United Kingdom cannot afford a minimum wage, increased expenditure on welfare and education, incentives for industrial investment, environmental improvements, reempowered local government, and other attributes of a progressive industrial democracy.'[99] The desired spheres of action clearly overlap – what is different is the judgment regarding the possibilities of successful intervention in these areas. The italicisation of 'seems' indicates, however, a further complication. The vision of equality and improving conditions of life aimed at here can only achieve a limited realisation within a capitalist system. There are then good reasons why the spirit as opposed to the hollow letter of such hopes, articulated on the eve of the New Labour victory of 1997, will struggle to be realised without an appreciation that they require not just the parliamentary defeat of the New Right, but a full understanding of the obstructive powers of the capitalist marketplace. Of course, this is precisely what the ideology of New Labour forbids.

These reflections bring us directly to the concerns of *The Dilapidated Dwelling* which is also focused, quite precisely, on the question of the systemic logic of capitalist markets. A television documentary, it was made with the intention, in part, of influencing government policies towards housing.[100] It retains some of the features of the Robinson films, including the journey/investigation format and a minimal fictional frame; however, these aspects are less pronounced than they are in the earlier films. Keiller describes *The Dilapidated Dwelling* as a 'comparatively straightforward television documentary' which he originally conceived as a 'piece of architectural research'.[101] It contains a combination of archival footage and interviews with experts – many academic – linked together by a narration which circles around an investigation into the state and prospects of residential dwellings ('old space'). With the 'disempowerment of local government' and the continuing reliance on market provision, there has been an increase in this space's dilapidation.[102] This process of neglect is for Keiller barely mitigated by the allure of virtual, digital environments or by the development of 'new', corporate space. Residential housing in the UK is, as the narrator (Tilda Swinton) informs us, 'the oldest and most dilapidated in western Europe'. This immediately raises the possibility of revisiting one of the central themes of the Robinson films – that is to say, the question of the relationship of Englishness to processes of decline might act as an explanation for Britain's uniquely aging and neglected residential housing stock. However, the idea that such a phenomenon might be the result of a 'backwards capitalism' is not one which is given the credence it might have been given by Robinson in *London* – the process of political analysis that these three films cumulatively represent would make such an interpretation unconvincing. Ellen Meiksins Wood is one of the interviewees in the film, and she offers a vigorous rebuttal of the Nairn–Anderson account of English backwardness – as she puts it: 'I would argue that Britain is what it is not because it is an inadequately developed capitalism or a case of arrested development but precisely because it is the most capitalist culture in Europe.' The housing market is then another example of the 'pristine culture of capitalism'. Wood goes on to support her thesis with the specific example of the Arts and Craft movement which she argues was a self-conscious 'political project' undertaken in a context in which the traditions of craftsmanship were long gone – driven out by the capitalist market. The narrator goes on to record the irony that the English Arts and Craft project went on to provide the model for the twentieth-century speculative builder. What dominates then in the history of residential building in Britain is the capitalist market – a laissez-faire system which has produced 'unsophisticated and over-priced' buildings which are 'amateurish and artlessly made' and which cannot be properly maintained as builders 'don't have the skills, the materials or the time'.[103]

The film argues that these problems resist solutions framed in terms of markets. Historically, the only modest successes that have been achieved have been through the initiatives taken outside markets – the efforts of civic bodies such as the London County Council and charitable organisations such as the Peabody Trust are given as examples. In the case of the Millennium Village on the Greenwich peninsula, the narrator informs us how the innovations of the architects (Hunt Thompson) including 'flexible interior lay outs, energy efficiency and a mix of tenures among neighbours' were abandoned by the developers. As the narrator puts it, gently but not without a sense of ironic understatement: 'It is very difficult to develop better housing in a market economy.' In his written work, Keiller has been less circumspect in setting out what he believes to be New Labour's dilemma concerning housing: 'Labour's belief in finding an accommodation with the market seems to preclude a revival of public-sector house building on anything like its former scale, but the history of house building suggests that the market will never be able to modernise *dwelling* on its own, and Labour is committed to modernisation.'[104]

The conclusion to the narrator's final report makes it clear that the subject of this documentary – *housing* – is also to be understood in that word's most general and basic sense as the activity and possibility of human *dwelling*: 'In the west we have become used to seeing benefits in an economic reality defined by markets. But at the moment there is one product that the market doesn't produce. It is the one that everybody wants.' These remarks bring us back to the themes/idiom of the Robinson films, but with a difference. The longing for change returns but now it is clearer what stands in the way. Keiller had said in *London* that Robinson is poor not because he lacks money but because 'everything he wants is unobtainable'.[105] There is a similar sense here that the exploration of a fundamental experience of human life – dwelling – has identified irreconcilable differences between the expectations and desires associated with that experience and those that can be accommodated by the 'market'.

We can further develop these thoughts on the vicissitudes of progressive politics in the face of the determining powers of the capitalist market if we refer to one of Keiller's most recent reconsiderations of *London*.[106] A decade after shooting finished he returns to that aspect of the film that looked at the hopeful cosmopolitanism of the metropolis. As the narrator and Robinson navigated London in 1992 they brought to our attention Divali at Southall; the Atlantic pub in Brixton which enabled Robinson to 'mention the arrival of post-war emigrants from Jamaica on the *SS Empire Windrush*'; the Notting Hill Carnival, and the Ridley Road market in Hackney. This leads Keiller to reconsider the paradox pointed out in the film by Robinson – the conjunction of what might be called London's enduring *festival of cosmopolitanism* on the one hand and the lastingly 'unsociable' and 'reactionary' aspects to the city on the other.[107] In examining this paradox the film had proposed, as a possible explanation, the idea that London is marked by some 'absence' – one explaining the possibilities for 'incoming cultures to establish themselves' and one which simultaneously 'limits the extent to which London's diverse cultures experience each other'.[108] I have argued elsewhere that the further elucidation of this 'absence' might lie in Wood's thesis of a 'pristine culture of capitalism'.[109] Keiller seems in part to agree: 'If the everyday experience of London in the early 1990s really was characterised by some more or less definable sense of *absence*, combined with an apparent comparative openness to incoming cultures, perhaps this had something to do with London's, or the UK's economy.'[110] Thus, historically London has exerted what Wood points out is the pull of the first *capitalist, capital city* and this fact might help to explain its shortcomings as an urban space – shortcomings such as a 'civic void' and the preponderance of private space, which have restricted the possibilities available to the incoming, culturally heterogeneous workforce that the capital needs to constantly suck up to function.[111] The comic-tragic predicament of a metropolis which increasingly cannot house its own workforce is the latest manifestation of this problem.

Having established this retrospective clarification of some of the key issues that the film raised, Keiller seeks to assess the ways in which the situation might have changed in the intervening decade. Urban space remains dilapidated – the market still dominates here, as we have seen in *The Dilapidated Dwelling* – and continues to display 'the general seediness' that Wood claims is, historically, a hallmark of British urban culture under the impact of the 'commodifcation of all social goods'.[112] However, what does seem to have changed is the emergence of 'a previously absent "burgherdom", whose aim is to make urban experience in London more like that of a certain kind of European city.'[113] What is Keiller's assessment of this belated burgherdom – a 'white, well-heeled middle or even ruling (if not exactly upper) class'? [114] He suggests that it might represent 'a commitment to the kind of public and other spaces in which London's potential to become a genuinely cosmopolitan city might be realised'.[115] However, this 'commitment' is immediately qualified. This new culture of public space (the project of 'regeneration') is parasitic on the older spaces of cosmopolitan London – it is a force for gentrification and thus exclusion by means of the market, whatever its good intentions.[116] But more than this, Keiller appears to doubt that this vision

Figure 11 *London*. Courtesy of the BFI

of a regenerated London can really be accurately described as European after all: 'The pavement cafes of post-1994 London seem to have arrived, not from Europe, but via North America. The evolution of London's population, too, increasingly polarised between extremes of rich and poor, more closely resembles that of North American cities than anything in Europe.'[117] What Keiller is describing here provides a useful context in which to put the fairy tale London films that I looked at in Chapter 2. Recall also Wayne's argument that such films were examples of the dominance of British cinema's 'Atlanticist paradigm'.[118] That is to say, films such as *Notting Hill*, produced within the economic dominance of the American film industry, have been marked by representations that reduce the 'diversity and complexity of life' as lived in London – the multiculturalism that Robinson celebrated in *London*.[119] The Atlantic pub sign, spotted in the Brixton of Keiller's *London* in 1992 and reproduced as a still to accompany his retrospective essay, stands as a reminder of this different and subordinate international culture which nevertheless persists in London.

CHAPTER 7

Peculiar Capitalism: Occult Heritage

Derek Jarman's *Jubilee* (1978) is poised between the failing moment of post-war social democracy and the emergent moment of New Right political and economic neo-liberalism. Like many British films made in the following decades, it creates the impression of recording terminal visions of the working class, urban space and traditions of national identity, in particular those associated with Englishness.[1] The penultimate scene of the film puts the remnants of Bod's (Jenny Runacre) gang in a Dorset country house that, as Tony Peake puts it, represents 'the very worst of Little England, a place whose inhabitants are so dozy that Hitler can retire there unnoticed'.[2] This politically ominous image of an imploding English class system, its 'country house' apex overrun by a collection of 'lumpenproletariat low-life', can be contrasted with the images of *déclassement* generated in the politically optimistic 1960s.[3] By the time of *Jubilee* such optimism had long passed and Jarman's subsequent work often evokes what might be called a *post-apocalyptic saturnalia* in which the defeat of post-war dreams of social reconstruction and the rise of the New Right are responded to with anger and despair, along with displays of sensual abandonment that do not signify – as in traditional chiliasm – the imminence of utopia, but on the contrary seem to be coloured by this atmosphere of demoralisation. *The Last of England* (1987) is an example of such 'inverted millennarianism'.[4] It is also, like *Jubilee*, full of images of urban dereliction, violence and criminality. It is this iconography of decline that we have seen Smith label 'garbage culture' and Stallabrass identify as the raw material for a contemporary 'urban pastoral'.

What of Jarman's imaginative resistance to this 'apocalyptic degeneration of England in the late 20th century'?[5] In this chapter I will be looking at *occult heritage* as one form in which such resistance takes shape, not just in Jarman's *Jubilee* and *The Last of England*, but also in Chris Petit and Iain Sinclair's *London Orbital*. What is occult heritage? At its simplest it represents valuable but neglected resources of the past. These resources represent an *occult* heritage in the sense that they are hidden or obscured by official heritage culture. They might also be perceived to be in danger of disappearing. As experimental film-makers, loosely united by their interest in poeticised or fictionalised documentary and their opposition to political and economic neo-liberalism, Jarman, Sinclair and Petit have a particular relationship to the past that might be captured by this idea of occult heritage. Thus, Jarman's response to what he believes to be the national emergencies of the late 1970s and 1980s is to hold onto images of dissident or marginalised Englishness from the Renaissance to the English romantics, and to use these images as a means of resisting the philistinism and brutality of his own time. If the apocalyptic mood often dominates in Jarman's work, then Petit and Sinclair's *London Orbital* sets out to confront the dangers of the false millennium of New Labour's repackaging of economic neo-liberalism. Their objective is to reconnect with a more recent past, that of the post-war period of reconstruction, along with earlier twentieth-century traditions of progressive metropolitanism 'trashed' by the sham modernisation of both the Tories and New Labour.

Jarman, Sinclair and Petit are then film-makers who ally themselves with endangered 'inheritances' which they view as offering counter-memories that might sustain the hope for cultural and social resistance and transformation. For his part, Jarman's use of the past produces a 'prophetic' posture which he associates with English visionaries such as William Blake and the Renaissance magus and courtier to Elizabeth I, John Dee. The prophetic form of films like *The Last of England* is, as we will see, indissociably bound up with issues of power and struggle. Petit and Sinclair extract a secret or lost past through arcane, modernist inspired traditions and rituals, in particular those associated with psychogeography. As Phil Baker argues, in its contemporary forms, urban psychogeography or the 'gnosis of place' seeks to open up, through rituals of exploration, interconnected sites, sensations and memories in the city fabric which have been by-passed by the 'market forces' which are turning London, for instance, into a 'Tourist spectacle'.[6]

In this way, for Jarman, Sinclair and Petit, the desire to memorialise an oc-culted past is joined to a creative activity whose politics are associated with the esoteric, marginal, visionary and magical. Here then is a second layer to 'occult heritage'. When Sinclair charges Margaret Thatcher with introducing 'occultism' into British political life he places himself under the obligation to produce counter-conjurations or 'extraordinary projects' to resist her 'demonic possession'.[7] *London Orbital* is clearly constructed as such a project, although its target is just as much New Labour as it is the Tories. Likewise, in *Jubilee*, the esoterically coded visions of Dee are intended as a means of resisting the de-structive forces hatching within a moribund social democracy. But this strategy of joining of culture and politics through 'magic' has, since Jarman shot *Jubilee*, been shadowed by the development of contemporary ideologies of capitalism which, it has been argued, have increasingly taken on the trappings of the occult. In order to illustrate this complex convergence of a politically engaged poetic of occult heritage with ideologies of neo-liberal capitalism, I will look at the work of Peter Ackroyd which carries significant intertextual links with that of Sinclair. Ackroyd's writings demonstrate how occult heritage can be absorbed into a celebration of capitalism and lose its redemptive dimensions. I will then consider whether or not Sinclair and Petit's use of the figures of the occult in *London*

Orbital results in an overwhelming and debilitating sense of the power of the dominant social order. In Jarman's case the issues are different – here what needs to be considered is whether or not his conceptualisation of an occult or visionary heritage is too restricted in terms of class and nation. However, at the same time, I will try to show how the prophetic form of *The Last of England*, and the buried historical and class resonances of *Jubilee*, can take us beyond these restrictions. To argue this case I will take what is both an obvious and at the same time easily overlooked detail – the title of Jarman's film, 'Jubilee' – in order to bring past and present together in what Walter Benjamin called a 'constellation' or 'dialectical image'.[8] As we know, for Benjamin, a redemptive attitude to the past was best served by a combativeness in which such arresting montages worked to invigorate resistance.[9] It is for this reason then that the chapter and the book end with *Jubilee* as the film can help to place our current, attenuated image of class politics in more vital, inspiring historical frameworks.

LONDON ORBITAL

Petit's and Sinclair's film is an adaptation of Sinclair's book *London Orbital: A Walk around the M25*. Both projects mount an investigation of London from the unfamiliar perspective of its own orbital motorway. The film is an experimental documentary combining digital and film media, and resembles a visionary road movie. It is narrated by the film-makers themselves. The book is related to Sinclair's previous psychogeographic explorations of London – explorations whose objective, whether in novelistic or journalistic form, appears to be to resist the conditions of the neo-liberal present, including the impact on London of property speculation; urban redevelopment and gentrification; the 'occult logic of "market forces"', and official heritage culture.[10] This resistance most frequently takes the form of an excavation of the 'alienated and recalcitrant' evidence of London history.[11] It has long been recognised that Sinclair's writings have had a significant influence on Peter Ackroyd whose own prolific output represents, according to Phil Baker, the mainstreaming of contemporary psychogeography.[12] Establishing the similarities and differences between Sinclair and Ackroyd will assist us in acquiring a clearer sense of the specific qualities of the former's work and also help in analyzing the film *London Orbital*.

As Patrick Wright has observed, Ackroyd's early fiction was indebted to what were then relatively unknown works by Sinclair such as *Lud Heat* in which the latter developed a 'scavenging poetic' designed to open up the history of struggle, failure and 'unfinished business' ghosting the increasingly ruined hopes of post-war planning.[13] For Wright, Sinclair's literary use of the occult to figure the relationship of past and present is subject to a 'beguiling simplification' in Ackroyd's hands.[14] Thus, Sinclair's politics as 'laureate' of the failure of the welfare state are of little interest to Ackroyd whose visions of the London past merge painlessly with a triumphant present.[15] Worse, seeking out obscure local history in the manner pioneered by Sinclair and given a mainstream profile by Ackroyd has become recognised as a prelude to the gentrification of previously neglected corners of London. Indeed, in the book *London Orbital*, Sinclair makes an analogy between Ackroyd and Dracula – missing from the film – according to which the vampire, with his maps and timetables and interest in the London property market, is the 'original psychogeographer'.[16]

A good place to explore Ackroyd's interest in occult heritage or 'visionary' culture is his 1993 television lecture entitled: 'London Luminaries and Cockney Visionaries'.[17] Here he identifies a tradition which includes, amongst others, William Hogarth, William Blake, J.M.W. Turner, Charles Dickens, Angela Carter, Iain Sinclair and Michael Moorcock. What unifies these figures is their visionary sensitivity to the 'sacred' dimensions of the metropolis.[18] They are all able to 'hear the music of the stones, to glimpse the spiritual in the local and the actual, to render tangible things the material of intangible allegory'.[19] In seeking to address the question of what it is that has provoked these visions, Ackroyd gives us formulations such as the following: 'For many thousands of years – literally thousands – it [London] has been a city of commerce and trade. It has attracted the poor and then crushed them in its progress since, as the old prayer of the London alchemist puts it: "it is the city of gold, it is the city of fire, it is the city of death".'[20] The combination of commerce and the occult here is typical of Ackroyd's representation of the London out of which his visionary moment emerges. In this quote he appears to register the relations of exploitation that London grew fat on; however, as an *attractor* of the poor, the metropolis ceases to embody the grim logic of the capitalist labour market and becomes instead a magnet of *opportunity*. The alchemical metaphor in which the bedazzled poor are 'crushed' and yet redeemed suggests that that opportunity creates waste, but it is waste that may, through the mediation of the desires and energies of the adept, be transformed. Such images are systematically developed in Ackroyd's texts and they build up a poetically layered representation of the history of London as a *market*. For instance in his book *London: The Biography*, the 'ancient trackways of England' are shown to be aligned with London's 'modern thoroughfares', thus becoming a kind of occult network doubling the contemporary city.[21] Within this network Ackroyd identifies monuments such as the 'London Stone', an alleged relic of 'legendary London'.[22] Among the different explanations of its significance, he draws attention to the hypothesis that it represented a marker or Roman milestone and that over the centuries it has stood as a 'guardian spirit' watching over passing traffic.[23] At the same time, it is associated with the philosopher's stone, the alchemical key to the transmutation of base metals into gold.[24] In this way, the London Stone condenses the fundamental meanings associated with Wood's 'commercialisation model' of capitalism – it helps to mythically embellish an image of London as a visionary city of wealth in which capitalism is *movement*, *circulation*, *traffic* and the value generated through such means out of the most apparently unpromising material.[25] This is not Wood's original, *capitalist* capital city. London here is the golden phoenix which rises out its own devastation – the ultimate booster's fantasy. Needless to say, capitalism as a system of social relationships marked by exploitation and the compulsions of economic necessity disappears in all this.

In comparison with Ackroyd's mythic metanarrative of 'Golden' London, Sinclair's occult mapping of London – what he calls 'dark heritage' – opens up a troubled relationship between present and past rather than a reassuring one.[26] A by no means exhaustive list of the diverse strands that run through Sinclair's poetic of the occult would include the 'visionary' wanderings of William Blake; the psychogeography of the situationists; the radical antiquarianism of 1960s counterculture; the mystical folklore of Old England; post-war, British neo-romanticism; and the literary traditions of nineteenth-century Gothic romanticism. By adapting such imaginative influences, he seeks to establish political positions on the present – typically, splenetic anti-Thatcherism and later anti-Blairism. He is particularly concerned to distance himself from the heritage industry which he views as a compact between the neo-liberal state and capitalist enterprise to pacify and erase the awkward past. Discussing London dockside redevelopment in the context of the Millennium Dome fiasco, he notes how historically resonant urban sites seem to be of interest only in as much as they reflect the 'acceptable glories' of conventional national history – '... the knighting of Sir Franics Drake and Sir Francis Chichester, visits by Samuel Pepys, location work for the latest Jane Austen ...'[27] Before such heritage spectacle 'the dark history of the Greenwich marshes, a decayed industrial wilderness, is brutally elided'.[28] Occult heritage culture, in Sinclair's case at least, has its face set against the hollow retro-styling of millennial neo-liberalism.

But what of Sinclair's film work? We can follow the intersection of radical politics and occult heritage in his collaborations with Chris Petit. *The Cardinal and the Corpse* (1993), for instance, features Alan Moore whose graphic novels have explored what Stewart Home has dubbed the 'Occult Establishment' – or rather, Old England as a malignant force of oppression. Moore's *From Hell* can be read as a popularisation of themes in Sinclair's *White Chapell: Scarlet Tracings* and *Lud Heat* in the way that it combines an interest in E.O. Gordon and John Michell's theories of sacred geometry with conspiracies which implicate Queen Victoria, Prince Albert and the Masons in the infamous Whitechapel/Jack the Ripper murders of 1888.[29] Allen Hughes and Albert Hughes' adaptation *From Hell* (2002) conveys these aspects of the book. As Sinclair himself puts it in a review of the film: 'The pitch is republican – with Queen Victoria, stripped of her Dench-heritage charm, as a marble puppet issuing death threats that must be carried out by a cabal of aristocrats, civil servants and surgeons ...The underclass only exist as victims.'[30] Home appears in *The Falconer* (1998) and talks on the subject of occult rituals and a hidden, sinister power struggle whose culminating, bloody act, to be staged at the Millennium Dome, appears to involve the House of Windsor.[31] His 'paranoid poetic', evidenced in squibs, manifestos and pulp fiction, conjures up 'psychic war' or what Sinclair refers to as the 'revenge of the disenfranchised'.[32] Whatever its iconoclastic and parodic force, this use of the tropes of occult heritage risks sustaining the entrancing, fatal glamour of the monarchical/aristocratic apex of the English class system. The consequence of this is that the more mundane sources of the historic power and longevity of the English capitalist class are rendered less perceptible. Thus, the thrill of implicating the ruling classes in *secret histories* can absorb political energies and distract from what is an even more arduous task of disclosure – giving substance to what Wood calls the *non-history* of capitalism and its paradoxical relationship to the English class system.[33] As we have seen, Wood argues that it is the early establishment of the social relations of capitalist production working within the fossilised shell of the *ancien régime* that needs to be grasped if the confidence, strength and adaptability of the English ruling class are to be understood. (This argument summarises the 'paradoxical relationship' referred to above.) Secret histories, in this context, seem to reinvigorate what Nairn calls the 'caste' qualities of the English class system rather than assisting in their dismantlement.[34]

Petit and Sinclair do distance themselves from a politics focused on Gothic Old England. In *The Cardinal and the Corpse* it is clear that the employment of the geomantic trope of the 'ley line' in the subplot involving Moore works as a parody of contemporary urban-occultism. Such magical figures are primarily of use to Sinclair in providing formal structures to organise his political antagonisms. This is particularly the case in the film and book *London Orbital*, which draws attention to what neo-liberalism tries to forget through what Sinclair, as narrator, calls its logic of 'deletion, exploitation and subterfuge'. If the millenarianism of neo-liberal utopianism is amnesiac – Sinclair makes the cultural vacuity of the celebratory Dome at Greenwich stand in for this commodified blankness – then the painful endurance test of the walk around the periphery of the space colonised by this destructive force is intended to recall those who are being for-gotten. The chain of the deleted includes the former inmates of the old London asylums whose medical records Sinclair witnesses being burnt in skips as former hospitals are developed into residential property sites. In both the film and the book, these asylums are imagined as haunting the motorway 'like abandoned forts' or 'black mandalas of madness'.[35] Here the invocation of occult heritage is largely an impassioned 'rant' against neo-liberal capitalism which foregrounds the theme of struggle missing in Ackroyd. The image of the *orbital* circulation of capital, painlessly creating value as it proceeds, is confronted with an image of the painful circulation of counter-memories.

Roger Luckhurst's discussion of what he calls the contemporary literature of 'Occult London' adds to our picture of the political inspiration behind much occult heritage.[36] At the same time, his arguments also provide a useful starting point for any attempt to assess the politics of *London Orbital*. He gathers together evidence of a flourishing 'occult imagination' of London in a range of writers, including Aidan Dunn, Stewart Home, Geoff Nicholson, China Miéville, Ackroyd, Sinclair and Christopher Fowler.[37] Setting himself the task of accounting for the way in which the streets of the capital are overrun, in the output of these writers, by esoteric fantasies of conspiracies and secrets ghosting the every-day, he proposes the following explanation. A contemporary London Gothic starts to emerge after 1986 when the Greater London Council was abolished by an imperious executive, bloated with the absolute powers that Her Majesty's government has in the British parliamentary system. Thatcher's anti-democratic glamour conjures up the nightmare of a tyrannical past in the heart of London – this is Thatcher as a New Right Dracula.[38] In *London Orbital*, Petit and Sinclair also liken Thatcher to Dracula; however, their film suggests additional, un-recognised sources for the fascination induced by the labyrinthine structures of occult heritage – sources lying beyond the problem of a metropolitan democratic deficit. My analysis will concentrate on the film's condensed central figure which brings together Dracula, Thatcher and the road itself – this is what Sinclair calls the 'blood metaphor'. The opening sequence includes video footage from 1988 of Thatcher cutting the ribbon to open the road, an act which gives Dracula 'new grazing grounds'. In a general sense the idea is to suggest the entrapment of the population of London within the M25 perimeter as a kind of defenceless blood-bank for the unappeasable appetites of the vampiric undead. Sinclair's conceit is that the road and its cardinal quadrants represent the chambers of the heart, and that that heart belongs to Dracula. The counterbalance to Dracula is the 'hospital' which represents the redemptive and commemorative side of Sinclair and Petit's interest in the road – the hospital is where blood is given/donated rather than taken. Of particular note is the closing of Harefield Hospital under New Labour, an act which permits the exploitation of more valuable real estate. If Harefield – a hospital specialising in heart surgery – represents the past of a social democratic welfare state, then Carfax, the main London residence of Dracula and the place where Esso have their oil depots for the South East, represents its neo-liberal present. Historically, the donation of blood has worked as an image of an altruistic social which welfare policies have sought to harness. Dracula/Esso signals the replacement of freely given blood by a poisonous, planetary commodity, oil.

Sinclair's contribution to the film is to challenge this vampiric sapping of the welfare state under neo-liberal regimes. In this respect the opening is significant – Sinclair's first words are: 'My London had been trashed, balkanised. I'd stayed too long in one place. I'd seen sixties tower blocks rise and I'd seen them tumble.' The life cycle of the tower block – doomed icon of post-war modernity – is captured by editing together recent tape-footage of high-explosive demolitions with Sinclair's own film archive of images from his family's past in the same Hackney locations.[39] This montage of images of 1960s utopianism and late 1990s neo-liberal, millennial apocalypticism has an intensity similar to that achieved in Jarman's *The Last of England*. That is to say, uncommented on 'home movie' images of Anna Sinclair, when edited with images of urban destruction, can

be compared to the imagery taken from Derek Jarman's father's movies of the
Jarman family that his son insets into the agitated montages of 1980s Thatcherite
wastelands of the earlier film.[40] In both cases there is an intense sense of loss. In
London Orbital note the haunting quality of the extreme close-ups and tracking
shots of Anna Sinclair as she walks through different urban spaces. Because of
their subject matter and their filmic qualities – colour fading, scratching and
other traces of degeneration – they offer representations of the precious, fragile
processes of memory that are posed against what Sinclair calls the 'trashed
history' of the present which *London Orbital* associates, figurally, with the digital
medium and by extension, with the road.[41]

It is also interesting that the film sequences do not conform to the formal
conventions of the home movie. Anna Sinclair rarely looks towards the camera,
even when she is framed in close-up. The effect is to suggest the enactment of
a private fiction in a 'real' public, urban environment – which in turn implies
a comfortable co-existence of the film-makers and their world. Film memories
lay claim to a public rather than a *balkanised* space. Film images take us to a
hospitable, locatable and subsequently trashed space of the past, one in which
cultural experimentation was felt to be an option. But for now, Sinclair is left with
a 'stark' choice between the digital age and older models of redemptive cultural
practice. As he says, he has to choose between opting for the activity of a 'digital
mudlark, rummaging through exhausted footage for retrievable images' on the
one hand, and a circumnavigation of the M25 on foot, on the other.[42]

Trudging in a wide arc around London, primed with the sense of a political
burden whose expression demands of him rituals of exorcism, Sinclair adopts
the persona of vampire hunter. Later on in the film, Petit will suggest a further
basis for the poetic analogy binding vampirism, the digital, Thatcher and the road
when he discusses the difficulty that *London Orbital* presented in the editing
stage – a difficulty he puts down to a combination of the subject matter and the
medium. The 'ceaseless, undramatic motion' of the road fails to offer, at any given
point, a reason for the cut and, at the same time, the digital camera, because of its
ability to 'shoot anything', reinforces the incompatibility between the stream of
digital images and the 'edited time' of cinema. When discussing this 'ubiquitous'
and 'accommodating' nature of the digital medium Petit mentions the lack of
'emulsion shadows' and the 'flat' 'anti-image' it produces. The M25 and digital
vision are perfectly matched then – it is the electronic surveillance cameras
that line the road and that are never turned off and whose results are real-time,
undiscriminating *anti-images*, that are able to do justice to the motorway's
peculiar qualities.

These thoughts on the 'anti-image' are applied to Thatcher when Petit tells us
that the precise location of the opening of the road is unmarked. Just as digital
tape resists the filmic 'cut', so Thatcher's actions, in opening the road, release
an energy that cannot be shaped or given form in established ways. Sinclair's
response to the news that Thatcher's moment with the scissors is recorded but

Figure 12 *London Orbital*. Courtesy of Illumination Films

not locatable, is to refer us back to Dracula. By opening the road, Thatcher gives the vampire his river crossing and seals him inside a magic circle from which he can no longer be excluded. As Petit points out later when discussing the suburban visions of J.G. Ballard, Thatcher's iconic gesture marks an 'end' not a 'beginning', in the sense that it does not symbolically inaugurate a 'future' which would be recognisable within cultures of metropolitan modernity, but instead, signifies the defeat of such dreams of modernity. A defeat which, as the vampirism/digitality/ driving figure suggests, will be hard to present in the 'cinematic' form of an 'image'. The eternity of the circular road, the immortality of the vampire and the illimitable qualities of the digital vision – here is the victory of an energy which can no longer be located, distanced, excluded or even imaged. (In the light of this, it is interesting that the examples of ritual exorcism that the film proposes for the road are enacted in the forms of older media, like the visionary excursion; the postcard warning; the transfixing still photograph; the ancestral book; Laurence 'Renchi' Bicknell's healing paintings; Rachel Lichtenstein's archival labours; or indeed Sinclair's own precious, scratchy 8mm memories.) At the same time that Petit is telling us about Dracula's triumph, Thatcher can be heard on the soundtrack, congratulating Pinochet for bringing 'democracy' to Chile. In terms of the possibilities for a progressive, counter-politics of the 'occult', there appears to be a fatal condensation of signs here. Pinochet, Thatcher and George W. Bush with his family business link to the Esso storage facility back at Carfax abbey, all of them 'vampire lovers' as Sinclair puts it. Out of this gothic/occult vision of London there emerges a strong sense of disempowerment in the face of an officially empowered, 'criminal' cabal that is stripping and trashing what is of social value with supernatural impunity. In this respect, *London Orbital* evokes precisely what Luckhurst warns against – the helpless seduction of a theatre of occult power in which conjuration and counter-conjuration endlessly circle one another.

Ironically perhaps, it might be possible to suggest an explanation for this sense of political intimidation with the help of the London chronology published in Ackroyd's metropolitan 'biography'. The entry under the year 1986 carries more separate pieces of information than any other in that decade – the entry reads as follows:

> 1986   Completion of the M25 ringway; abolition of the GLC; the 'big bang' in the Stock Exchange.[43]

The convergence of these three events provides a wider context within which to put the preceding analysis of *London Orbital*. Petit, Sinclair and Luckhurst cover the first two – but what of the opening up of the financial markets? One of the most striking implications of the cosmogonic metaphor – 'big bang' – is that it lends deregulated, neo-liberal capitalism an origin beyond which there is little point in going. It is then a particularly apt image for totalising pretensions of neo-liberal economics which can be picked up even in a film as resistant to the politics of New Right as *London Orbital*. We can pursue this argument further if we return once again to the film's use of the Dracula figure. Franco Moretti offers a useful reading of Stoker's fiction with the help of Marx's unravelling of the vampire metaphor.[44] As Marx puts it, capital is 'dead labour which vampire-like, lives only by sucking living labour, and lives the more, the more labour it sucks'.[45] This voraciousness is, as Moretti puts it '... impelled towards a continuous growth, an unlimited expansion ... accumulation is inherent in his [Dracula's] nature ... His nature forces him to struggle to be unlimited, to subjugate the whole of society. For this reason, one cannot "co-exist" with the vampire. One must either succumb or kill him.'[46] The same quality of unlimited expansion attaches itself to Ackroyd's vision of London. Ackroyd is unable to grasp capitalism as a delimited, historically specific social system – the final sentences of his 'biography' of London are interesting in this respect as they can be read as expressing an involuntary confirmation of the vampiric, totalising logic of that system: 'It [London] contains every wish or word ever spoken, every action or gesture ever made, every harsh or noble statement ever expressed. It is illimitable. It is Infinite London.'[47] The capitalist's struggle 'to be unlimited' is how Moretti describes the curse afflicting Dracula. Stoker imagines vampiricism as an 'an ever-widening circle' of victims – which is how Sinclair imagines the M25. Ackroyd's use of the figure of limitlessness is intended to express his admiration for London in the terms of Blake's visionary, inclusive poetic, but given the inhuman qualities he admits London possesses, this blessing is just as much an unconscious tribute to a city whose existence remains vampiric.

Note Moretti's stress on the stark choice the vampire metaphor of capitalism poses –'succumb or kill'. It might be argued that within the contemporary occult imagination of London, capitalism's challenge cannot be presented in this way. But why not – the sense of the extremity of the situation is clear enough? An answer might lie in the inversely proportional relationship between the awe for a *supernaturalised* neo-liberal capital, and a corresponding dismissal of the potential of the labour that for Marx remained the ultimate source on which the vampirism of capitalism depended. The occult imagination then is marked by its dim apprehension of an *indefatigable, untranscendable, neo-liberal capitalism* and its clear belief in the *political negligibility of the proletariat*. It is the latter which ultimately leaves *London Orbital* hostage to the former. On the one hand Dracula, on the other an 'ever-widening circle of victims'.

Clearly this argument requires us to address the representation of the working class in the film, and we can begin to do this with the help of the soundtrack. The visual complexity of the film is matched by an acoustic density which is suggestive of the mingling of past (Thatcher's voice) and present (electronic noise and the ambient sounds of the road's 'acoustic footprint', including short, edited extracts from radio phone-in programmes listened to by drivers such as Petit). The radio clips recur throughout the film and need to be considered in terms of the contrast they create with the voice-overs of the two narrators. Petit and Sinclair's voices carry the cultural authority of the English middle-class accent whereas the radio voices are predominantly working class and lack such authority and prestige. But this difference in the class positioning of the voices in the film is not just a matter of accent – it also involves the difference between the form of the radio *talk-show* and the *film-essay*. Thus, whilst the talk-show extracts ostensibly address many of the issues considered by Petit and Sinclair – such as the experience of driving on the road – they do so in a form which is designed to elicit exaggerated and bluntly expressed *opinion*. The suggestion is that the cognitive and poetic value of these fragmented statements is low, especially in comparison with the statements generated within the film-essay format. The talk-show clips are difficult to follow because they have been edited to emphasise their status as confrontational, repetitive, ambient chatter; however, when they do become distinctly audible in the mix, they tend to suggest frustrating and un-illuminating exchanges. (For instance: 'are you completely mad?';'just build the damn thing';'unbelievable';'complete and utter nightmare'.) Such fragments typically involve the proposal of a simple solution to the problem of the M25 – rebuilding, extending – which is then reinforced by an expression of conviction. This creates a very different impression to that made by Petit and Sinclair's erudite and sensitive philosophising on the road. As film-essay, *London Orbital* places the working-class dialogue on the radio as going nowhere, or rather it suggests it is *going around in circles*.

In one scene the radio talk-show is used as transitional device that moves us from literary, journalistic and poetic discourses to a sociological/political excursus on drug and criminal cultures in Essex. This transitional sequence is interesting for what it reveals about the role of these working-class voices. As Petit concludes his voice-over with a reference to the fact that one of the names for the drug Ecstasy is M25, a talk-show exchange follows him and we hear someone suggesting that the road needs two extra lanes. At the same time, the image track shows a high-angle shot from a motorway bridge with the cars beneath passing in slow motion. At the moment when each succeeding car reaches the bridge there is a brief freeze-frame on the front seats which reveals the posture of the driver and passenger. The soundtrack meanwhile samples a phrase – 'totally out of order' – which is clearly spoken in working-class intonations and represents an idiom that is associated with the radio talk-show form. The final freeze-frame from the bridge shows us a car in which the driver has both hands off the steering wheel and his mouth agape. It is a striking image, difficult to interpret; however, an approximate range of the meanings it evokes can at least be determined by the context. The soundtrack is an important part of this context – the sampled phrase is mixed with the repetitive beat of a musical theme and then used over the following sequence which edits together surveillance footage of Essex gangster Bernard O'Mahoney – writer of the book *So This is Ecstasy* – and Margaret Thatcher opening the M25.[48] A split screen is used to show us, on one side, O'Mahoney captured on CCTV footage, brandishing a knife in a fight with another man and, on the other, the scissors in Thatcher's hands that she has used to cut the ribbon. The voice-over tells us that O'Mahoney worked on the building of the M25 and that, like other Essex criminals, he took advantage of the improved access that the road gave from Essex out into other parts of the country.

What emerges from these images and sounds is, in part, a quite familiar representation of the working class. The word *Essex* is a key political signifier in contemporary British culture, and it is used here to hold in place these signs of working-class violence and criminality. As a symbolic location, Essex stands for a post-industrial, *Thatcherite* working class. In the general election of 1992, it was one parliamentary constituency in Essex – Basildon – that stood, metonymically, for the thesis of a 'permanently Tory' south-eastern, working class.[49] This is a working class described by Sinclair in the book: 'The M25 was exposed as a class barrier... Chaps from Plaistow headed for Essex. Why not? Villians and cabbies. Getting away from: litter, sink schools, compulsory ethnicity. The motorway opened the whole thing up, rave culture, warehouse clubs (with girly names), cashmomey. Sacks of it.'[50] It is not just the alliance between Thatcher and Pinochet which the film brings to our attention then, but also an alliance between a politically regressive working class and the New Right. It is interesting that in the opening title sequence, the identifiable sounds are, in turn, a barking dog, Thatcher and a fragment from a radio talk-show from which the words 'nightmare' and 'Essex' reverberate shortly before the start of Sinclair's opening words – 'My London had been trashed'.

Finally, to return to the disturbing image of the driver, it is also possible to read the opposition in the film between driving and walking in terms of class. The film depicts the M25 motorist – inert, slumped, mouth agape, one flicking a 'V' sign to the camera – as the 'undead' that Sinclair warns Petit he risks becoming if he drives the road. In contrast, the walker-artists such as Laurence Bicknell, and of course Sinclair himself, are engaged in 'projects of restitution' – projects which are designed as M25 circuit-breakers. Note also that the link between the road and the retail parks – Bluewater, Thurrock, Lakeside – suggests another commonplace image of the post-industrial working class, one in which its political potential is supposedly compromised by its poor consumer choices. At Bluewater, towards the end of the film, echoes of Thatcher's voice return on the soundtrack whilst Petit complains of trashy American culture and the 'retail undead', and Sinclair warns that this retail park is full of 'zombies' serviced by 'punishment-colony androids'. Bluewater is a 'retail swamp' for the post-industrial working class; it is a landscape which awaits its apocalyptic destruction by fundamentalist terrorists.

JUBILEE, THE LAST OF ENGLAND AND THE VISIONARY ATLANTIC

Derek Jarman was fascinated by a visionary tradition which he frequently located within the framework of the English Renaissance. In *Jubilee* – a film he referred to as a 'dream vision' – this interest is attached to Elizabeth's courtier and alchemist John Dee. As Michael O'Pray puts it, in the sequences involving Elizabeth I and John Dee 'the beauty of poetry, mysticism and cosmological wisdom is contrasted with the violent banality and apocalyptic degeneration of England in the late 20th century'.[51] However, whereas in *Jubilee* Dee and Elizabeth signify a nostalgia for an Elizabethan golden age – see for instance the film's lyrical ending in which the Queen and Dee make their way along the cliff's edge at Winspit, passing into the dusk – in *The Last of England* Jarman cultivates visionary personae more closely allied to Blake's conception of the artist. As O'Pray argues, Blake, as a 'radical visionary', is an 'important figure in understanding Jarman'. He adds that *The Last of England* is perhaps the clearest expression of Jarman's 'Blakean spirit'.[52] I would like to develop these observations in order to argue that the specific form in which this affinity manifests itself in Jarman's film-making is around the figure of the *prophetic artist*. Blake's work belongs to a 'Protestant prophetic tradition' and is, consequently, steeped in the eschatological rhetoric of apocalypse and millennium.[53] This tradition, forced underground and out into a wider Atlantic world after the defeat of the radical left in the English Revolution, is an intensely politicised one.[54] It is interesting, therefore, that, when asked what *The Last of England* was about, Jarman used the idiom of this struggle in quoting Oliver Cromwell: 'For the day of vengeance is in my heart and the year of my redeemer is come…And I will tread down the people in mine anger, and make them drunk in my fury.'[55] Cromwell's words were spoken in 1654, well after the decisive rightwards turn of the Revolution of 1649. Nevertheless, this quote shows Jarman summoning a mood of committed struggle in response to Thatcherism. The film registers a shift away from the 'apoliticism and anarchism' of Jarman's punk period, towards a sustained and angry engagement with his political adversaries.[56] In this respect Blake is an apt tutelary figure as his poetry is exemplary in its depiction of the necessity of constantly renewed struggle. (Los, Blake's mythological alter ego and figure for the prophetic artist, commits himself to unceasing labours in his determination to bear witness to a lost utopian, 'Atlantean' civilisation.) Indeed, when Jarman describes himself as 'a pivot around which to weave the scattered threads of British culture' he seems close to the conception of the prophet-bard that attracted Blake in his illuminated, epic poems.[57] Like Blake, Jarman considered himself under the obligation to keep alive a vision of liberty in times of trouble.

The textual resources of prophecy, as Blake used them, constitute what Jon Mee, citing Robert Lowth, calls an aesthetic of 'obscurity'. This aesthetic is to be understood in terms of the hortatory rather than predictive function of prophecy. That is to say, its objective is to galvanise the oppressed.[58] It achieves its effects through inspired, portentous, complex and often 'disjunctive' narratives which use the 'parabolic style' of the Old Testament, with its techniques of 'bold ellipsis' and 'violent, hyperbolic imagery'.[59] Hill's reading of the film suggests some overlaps with this prophetic tradition. As he points out, its 'state of the nation' argument is one in which stable, conventional political allegory and insight are ultimately exceeded through an 'aesthetic density' (montage editing, charged performances, cinematographic intensities) which communicate through 'moods, attitudes, and feelings' such as those evoked in the apocalyptic register of Tilda Swinton's dancing 'curse' of the 'patriots'.[60] Despite the mood of desperation, the film is not then purely pessimistic. It is just as much Jarman's rallying cry of prophetic ire at a moment of danger – a moment when, as he saw it, a neo-liberal political order threatened to irrecoverably poison Englishness with philistinism, homophobia, greed, racism and xenophobia. Even if *The Last of England* projects 'terminal visions' of England, these visions remain pregnant with the atmosphere of imminent and continuing convulsion. What Mee says of Blake might be applied to the effect achieved in the film: 'The denouements of all Blake's prophetic narratives present an apocalyptic process which opens out rather than marks the end of history.'[61] Thus, Tilda Swinton's dance could be interpreted as the enactment of a *prophetical frenzy* which concentrates the film's apocalyptic atmosphere into an implacable act of resistance. Furthermore,

Figure 13 *The Last of England* – The Bride's dance. © Photographed by Mike Laye/image-access.net

it seems at least likely, given Jarman's knowledge of Blake, that on one level, Swinton's character allegorically evokes the biblical figure of Jerusalem. As Mee points out, Jerusalem personified as the bride of God is a recurrent motif in the Bible. Equally common is 'the representation of the desolate Jerusalem as a grieving widow or lamenting woman'.[62] In the millenarian context in which Blake worked, the association of a desolate Jerusalem with England might, for instance, represent a prophecy of the national destruction that was felt to threaten as a result of the counter-revolutionary wars of the time.[63] For Jarman, Swinton's performance as the desolate bride/Jerusalem clearly represents his gut fears about what an uncontested Thatcherism might mean for the nation.

However, the traditions of dissent and struggle which Jarman associated himself with can be approached with different emphases. Lawrence Driscoll, for instance, persuasively argues that he consciously allied himself to a tradition of patriotic, Romantic, middle-class dissidence and anti-industrialism – 'the British tradition'[64] – that has enshrined the cultural ideals of 'beauty, elegance and sensitivity' against the philistinism and greed of a culturally impoverished, utilitarian middle class.[65] Those aspects of *Jubilee* which evoke what Steven Dillon calls 'the idyllic retreat to the past', specifically the scenes featuring Dee and Elizabeth, would fit with this aspect of Jarman's sense of his own work.[66] It is also clear that Jarman felt that his allegiance to this tradition was not understood or appreciated in the

Figure 14 *Jubilee* – Punk Britannia. © Whaley-Malin Production Ltd.
Photograph by Jean-Marc Prouveur

punk milieu in which *Jubilee* took shape. He distanced himself from punk whilst
using its sarcastic iconoclasm to assault those Old English institutions such as the
Church and the modern 'royal family' which he loathed. In this respect the film's
title is interesting as it opens up the cultural and class resonances of punk in a
way which exceed Jarman's own sense of the movement. On the most immediate
level 'jubilee' makes reference to 1977, the year of Elizabeth II's 'silver' jubilee

celebrations. It was precisely the dignity of this celebration that the Sex Pistols attacked with their song 'God Save the Queen'. Jarman's punk use of 'jubilee' is thus set against what David Cannadine refers to as Old England's shamelessly 'invented', 'ornamentalist' traditions of empire and class. The ritual of the 'jubilee' has had a pre-eminent place in such traditions from the late nineteenth century on.[67] However, there remains another meaning to 'jubilee' which takes us well beyond the 'ornamentalism' of Old England. To understand this meaning we need to return to the tradition of prophecy within which Mee places Blake's work. When we do so, 'jubilee' doubles back on itself, signifying not the celebration of Old England but its prophetic denunciation. What then is this other meaning to jubilee? Peter Linebaugh: 'Jubilee is an Old Testament legal practice of land redistribution, debt cancellation, slave manumission, and year-long sabbath.'[68] He goes on: 'In modern history the notion has provided a powerful constellation of ideas for those opposing enclosure of common or waste land into private property in Britain and for those opposing slavery on the plantations in the America and the Caribbean.'[69] There is then a 'hidden' historical conflict within the word. It compresses the senses of *English ornamentalism* and *revolutionary Atlanticism* and is therefore a useful miniaturisation of the relationship between the English class system and class struggle which I have drawn attention to in various places in this book. The Atlantic proletariat, as we have seen, is figured by Linebaugh and Rediker as a hydra. This mobile, multi-ethnic class was not 'unified culturally'; however, it was 'self-active' and 'creative' in formulating, disseminating and nurturing revolutionary traditions, and the 'Atlantic Jubilee' is a key example of this.[70]

Romantic, middle-class dissidence is, from this perspective, too restrictive in terms of both nation (it transposes an intercontinental tradition of anti-capitalism and anti-imperialism into a narrowly English tradition) and class (in its depiction of a lonely, heroic middle-class fraction that is solely responsible for the guardianship of cultural value and political progress). A middle-class, dissident 'traditionalism', exclusively focused on what it considers to be the Thatcherite appropriation of Englishness – for instance, an official, heritage culture, 'public school/*Chariots of Fire* version' of Blake – is in danger of missing the complexity of another Blake.[71] This other Blake was, as Mee points out, closer in his sources of inspiration to a 'culture of vulgar enthusiasm'[72] than he was to the 'respectable rationalist discourse' of the middle-class reformers of the time.[73] As Mee says: 'The prophetic platform, expressing social grievances and utopian visions in terms of the biblical paradigms of Babylonian oppression and millenarian expectation, was in fact one long established in the rhetorical resources of the popular culture by the time Blake wrote.'[74] Furthermore, the fetch of Blake's imagination, especially from 1791 to 1794, was Atlantean. As Linebaugh and Rediker point out, for this Blake 'freedom was not merely English'.[75]

The problem of the relationship between Englishness and these larger conflicts of empire can be found elsewhere in the details of Jarman's work – for instance in his self-identification with the figure of the gardener. Driscoll makes the point that for Jarman, resistance to the grasping materialism and 'commercialisation' he associated with Thatcherism drew strength from a neo-romantic, utopian vision of the British countryside and the prospect of a modest retreat into English horticulture.[76] However, ironically, gardening is deeply implicated in the intertwined histories of capitalism and empire. There is a clear link between the apparently unexceptional, mundane activity of cultivating land and the history and ideology of capitalist forms of private property.[77] As Patricia Seed argues, within the ambit of the European colonial project, England was unique in its emphasis on gardening as a *ceremony of possession* – she refers to the English as 'tantalised by the garden'.[78] Failure to 'improve' the land, to cultivate or garden, was seen as justification for the brutal dispossession of the native.

To return to *Jubilee*'s punk influences, it is possible to show how, as a culture of protest against post-war welfare capitalism, punk was, in various ways, also linked to an expanded history of working-class struggle. It has long been noted that one of the cultural and political influences behind some of the bands was situationism.[79] Macolm McLaren, the manager of the Sex Pistols, was influenced by the activities of a loose affiliation of individuals who comprised an English section of the situationists and whose activities were based in London. McLaren's television documentary *The Ghosts of Oxford Street* (1991) represents the culmination of an incomplete student film project which stretched back to 1969.[80] It was inspired by Guy Debord's situationist critique of consumer society. Here again the history of a picaresque and motley proletariat elliptically emerges – the West London situationist cell (King Mob) with whom McLaren was familiar at this time were referencing the Gordon Riots of 1780 in their chosen name. The original film – of which little original footage remains – was not simply a situationist attack on the 'society of the spectacle' peddled by Oxford Street department stores, it was also, in its various written forms at least, cognizant of the road's significance for the topography of class struggle in eighteenth-century London.[81] Thus the Gordon Riots of 1780 are interpreted by McLaren and collaborator Jamie Reid as more than just an irrational outburst of anti-Catholicism – as their explanation of the events in their treatment makes clear, class struggle is the point of their interest: 'The middle-class started it against the Catholics. Then hundreds of shopkeepers, carpenters, servants, soldiers and sailors rushed into the streets. There were only a few Catholic houses to smash. So they started to smash all the rich houses. The middle classes did not want anything to do with this.'[82] This account, whilst simplified for the purposes of dramatic contrast and conflict, is nevertheless close in outline to the judgment of George Rudé who was one of the few historians to have deemed the actions of the rioters worthy of serious scrutiny at the time that McLaren and Reid conceived and planned their film.[83] A later treatment describes the project thus:

From Tyburn at the gallows to the Gordon Riots and Barnaby Rudge to Nash and the rebuilding of street, from its dangerous curves to a wide and perfectly straight highway, so an army could swiftly move down it without fear of ambush. For a new bourgeois to parade down it, to the invention of a cul-de-sac, and the doorman to trap and catch thieves on it. The coming of the department store and crowd control. The politics of boredom, and the fact that more Mars bars are sold on Oxford Street than anywhere else in the world. This is a journey in 24 hours of a life on Oxford Street.[84]

These notes reveal how the film sought to link literature, architecture, urban planning, the judicial system, consumer society and everyday life to class struggle – it was therefore 'totalising' in its ambitions. Furthermore, McLaren and Reid had isolated a key site in the history of class struggle with which to structure their film – Tyburn.[85] In Blake's mythopoetic system, this place of execution is associated with the London Stone.[86] This 'stone' condensed an epic struggle. On the one hand, Blake imagined it as a Druidical sacrificial altar or symbol of Empire, presided over by a 'Polypus of Death'.[87] On the other hand, he saw it as a remnant of a ruined Atlantean civilisation of liberty.[88] Blake's Polypus can, then, be thought of as a mythological antagonist to Linebaugh and Rediker's Atlantic hydra. Tyburn and the prison that fed it – Newgate to the east – also preoccupied Lord George Gordon, alleged instigator of the Gordon Riots.[89] In his discussion of Lord George Gordon's career after 1780, Douglas Hay makes the point that the former's prophetical 'vision' of social justice involved him struggling against a bloody criminal code which demanded capital punishment and transportation for theft.[90] Hay argues that Gordon's vision was close to that of Thomas Spence for whom the idea of jubilee appeared as an 'image of revolution in property and society and human nature'.[91]

Many of these intertwined historical allusions are carried over into the post-Sex Pistols film, *The Great Rock and Roll Swindle* (1980) and McLaren's *The Ghosts of Oxford Street*. Both films contain references to Tyburn and the Gordon Riots. Early on in the former, effigies of the Sex Pistols are taken across the river to the Tyburn gallows. In the later film, it is the Manchester band The Happy Mondays who are hung there. As the self-styled 'Situationist Spiv'[92] making 'cash from chaos', McLaren may well have resembled the sinister entrepreneur Borgia Ginz (Jack Birkett) in Jarman's *Jubilee*.[93] However, this should not distract us from recognising that the imaginative framework McLaren provided for the Sex Pistols, in both his promotional activities and the film projects which pre-date and post-date the punk phenomenon, is steeped in a history which helps to give greater precision in locating the influences and allegiances of a figure such as Blake – a figure, who in Driscoll's account at least, Jarman claimed for a much more limited, high cultural, middle-class pantheon.

The year that McLaren finally brought his Oxford Street film to the public – 1991 – was also the year that Linebaugh published *The London Hanged* and that Isaac Julien released *Young Soul Rebels*. Julien's film was an attempt to revisit 1977 in order to contest the 'chauvinism' of the Royal Silver Jubilee and to rescue the memory of national *counter-narratives* carried within 'black popular culture' of the time.[94] As he points out, whilst the 'obvious opposition'[95] of punk to traditional narratives of Englishness was then and is now, clearly visible, the oppositional status of 'black working-class youth cultures', particularly those linked to soul and disco, has been neglected and obscured.[96] Crucially, such cultural forms are linked to a 'wider black diaspora'.[97] In 1977, soul offered a 'fluid space', one which transgressed the 'rigidities of sex and race' and was capable of inspiring utopian forms of cultural and political experimentation and resistance.[98] Whilst it would be foolish to pretend that the political divisions noted by Julien between punk, the 'conventional left' and soul, were not real and disabling, nevertheless in challenging the rigidities and restrictions of race, sexuality, nation and gender, the 'jubilee' memorialised in *Young Soul Rebels* is clearly part of that buried culture of 'jubilee' whose traces Linebaugh was, at the same time, excavating in his history of working-class London.[99]

Linebaugh concludes the chapter on the Gordon Riots in his social history of Tyburn with Blake's engraving 'Albion Rose'. There has long been speculation that Blake participated in the delivery of Newgate[100] and Linebaugh interprets the image and appended lines in terms of the 'traditional English apocalyptic myth' embodied in Milton's *Samson Agonistes*.[101] As the lines make clear, this *traditional English* myth is intended to have international resonances:

Albion rose from where he labour'd at the Mill
with Slaves
Giving himself for the Nations he danc'd the dance
of Eternal Death.[102]

Epilogue: 'And then what?'

In many places in this book attention has been directed towards the question of the influence of ideologies of neo-liberalism on the representation of class across a range of different types of film. Examples have been sought from mainstream, art house and experimental sources, and I have covered romantic comedies, heritage films, social realist dramas of working-class defeat, poetic documentaries, visionary road movies and, stylish, postmodern 'youth' films. The figures I have found most useful in describing the ideological impact of this era of capitalist triumphalism are those drawn from the register of the occult. If the London fairy tale films of Working Title represent a benign, idyllic representation of this socially corrosive form of capitalism, then Petit and Sinclair evoke its malefic, socially vampiric face. The root of the 'magic' of neo-liberal capitalism depends on the belief, in a post-cold war world, in the inevitable, post-historic, post-political *reality* of capitalism. Capital, not labour, is viewed as the exclusive origin of social wealth.[1] This is a form of extreme alienation through which capitalism becomes thoroughly naturalised and mythified. The reach of this ideology is correspondingly extensive. For instance, in the case of *London Orbital* we saw film-makers who are unmistakably opposed to the neo-liberalism of the New Right reproducing its ideological kernel: irresistible capitalism/politically finished proletariat. Exploring this relationship between neo-liberalism and the working class elsewhere in the book, I argued that the colonisation of heretofore neglected areas of life was figured, in a key post-industrial elegy like *The Full Monty*, as 'entertainment'. Neo-liberal capitalism seems to demand the complete exposure of labour to its priorities of 'flexibility' – that is to say, labour is required to engage with capital outside the regulative, welfarist activities of the state or trades union, and to submit to unceasing demands which require constantly renewed, agile and exhausting responses. Jobs are not only 'not for life', they are not *for* the 'working class' at all. In this respect we saw how *Dockers* cannot help foregrounding the ways in which ideologies of neo-liberalism have turned traditional left politics, in as much as they are based on this category of the 'worker', into unimaginable acts of defiance.

Dockers is largely, if not entirely, an unexceptional example of the tradition of British social realism. Exploring the relationships of different aesthetic forms to the culture of neo-liberalism has been an important part of the ground covered by this book. If *Dockers* stands out in its adherence to the tradition of social realism, then it is not alone. Although I have not considered his work here, Ken Loach's films from the 1990s, including *Riff-Raff* (1990), *Raining Stones* (1994), *Ladybird, Ladybird* (1996), *My Name is Joe* (1998) and *The Navigators*, have used the combined naturalistic and melodramatic forms and styles of this tradition to present us with images of the remorselessly constricting socio-economic forces of our present moment. For instance, in *The Navigators*, a union representative of a newly privatised railway maintenance company is the last worker left after his boss has finished systematically pushing the older labour force into a dangerous, casualised job-market. Alone, playing a game of chess with himself, he finds himself in checkmate – as he puts it: 'whatever move you make you lose'. Loach has tended to relocate the need that presents itself in these films for structural challenges rather than the epiphenomenal alterations of the capitalist system to an elsewhere beyond the nation. Thus, socialist revolution – a hopelessly outmoded political concept within a culture hegemonised by neo-liberal capitalism – features in his account of the Spanish Civil War, *Land and Freedom* (1995), and in the Nicaragua of *Carla's Song* (1996).

Loach's political pessimism includes the prospects for any social democratic, cross-class solidarity in the face of neo-liberalism's impact on the most vulnerable sections of the working class. *Ladybird, Ladybird* and *My Name is Joe* both demonstrate how working-class dilemmas tend not to be amenable to the solutions offered by middle-class, professional intermediaries associated with the welfare state. However, the determinist pessimism of a film like *My Name is Joe* needs to be seen as a response to the moralising prejudices and class antagonisms fostered by the illusions of unconstrained individual choice that have flourished under neo-liberal political regimes – illusions which support the ideology behind that paragon of poor choices, the 'underclass'. Mike Leigh's films, like Loach's, are also generally seen as part of the British socialist realist tradition, and have, in recent years, sought to capture and contest the logic of neo-liberal social damage. With Leigh the focus has tended to be on the domestic enclosure of class realities. Despite the destructive nihilism of *Naked* (1993), there is a clear sense in films such as *High Hopes* (1988) and *All or Nothing* (2001) that the regenerative possibilities of working-class 'mutuality' and endurance remain, despite the deformations on society, culture and self wrought by neo-liberal regimes.[2]

If these directors have not received space in this book, this is not because their work has been judged irrelevant. On the contrary, as the brief observations above should make clear, their films would fit with the themes and issues raised in Chapter 3. Indeed, there are many other directors whose work I might have also included here, such as Bill Douglas, Alan Clarke, Peter Watkins, Terence Davies, Lynne Ramsay, Michael Winterbottom, Andrew Kotting, Gillies Mackinnon, Peter Mullan, Isaac Julien and Pawel Pawlikowski. Such omissions have been determined by matters of space, as well as by the decision to avoid an auteur-style 'survey' of the field in favour of a selection of films which might enable my themes of the representation of class and capitalism to emerge most clearly. But there is another, equally important reason behind these omissions. That is to say, as Judith Williamson points out, there is a common assumption that when we see 'class' and film brought together we immediately assume it is exclusively the 'working class' who are being referred to. As she says: 'Lots of films are about upper-and middle-class people, but we don't tend to see those as "about" class in the same way.'[3] Class is rooted in encompassing social relationships and experiences. A critical perspective that brings together class and capitalism, and which is focused on the wide view of class relationships should, hopefully, find as much to say about a film like *Notting Hill* as about *Dockers*.

But my neglect of the stalwarts of British social realism is not just a result of my desire to catch an inclusive and socially dynamic image of class in British cinema within the covers of a relatively short book. I have also been concerned to look at the politics that might be ascribed to departures from social realist forms and styles. Thus, in the case of *Trainspotting*, I argued that the aesthetic of 'black magic realism', in as much as it works to deconstruct the opposition between realism and fantasy, is predicated on a particular relationship between the middle class and the working class. This relationship suggests, as we saw, a distinctive middle-class political and cultural outlook. In the psychogeographic, occult heritage of Sinclair and Petit, neo-liberal capitalism is a subjugating force which no collective class antagonist, especially not the post-industrial working class, could ever hope to contain. The postmodern ironies of 'slacking' produce a characteristically convoluted, 'redemptive' magical narrative form in *Late Night Shopping* – an invisible hand separates out 'slacker' from 'working class', protecting the former, crushing the latter. *Sliding Doors* also mobilises, rather awkwardly, a redemptive, 'fairy-tale' narrative form which rescues Helen from proletarianisation. Interestingly, there are links between the slacker sensibility of *Late Night Shopping* and the sensibility displayed by Keiller's fictional hero, Robinson. The point of overlap seems to reside in the project to explore the powers of a subjective transformation of the oppressive, everyday world of neo-liberalism, with its McJobs and its 'dilapidated' social realm. This sensibility – one which is hyper-alert to irony, style and the fleeting, miraculous moments of beauty in a degraded world – has origins in the radical aesthetic traditions of the historical, European avant-gardes. It is, of course, also behind psychogeographic attempts, such as those found in Sinclair and Petit's work, to resist and transform the 'hyper-capitalised banalisation' and alienation of the cityscape.[4] Keiller's Robinson films recognise the ways in which such aesthetics of resistance may end up reproducing the invasive ideologies of neo-liberal capitalism. That is to say, such forms of subjective transformation can lead to a tacit acceptance of the shrunken dimensions of neo-liberal social and political horizons – what might be called, following Keiller's suggestion, the *poeticisation of defeat*. Keiller's complex aesthetic – with its subjective, transformative, poeticising aspects and its simultaneously tenacious referential-realist dimension – is not exactly captured by the categories of the *performative* or *expository* documentary. However, what seems clear is that Keiller's formal choices appear to emerge, as we have seen, out of his systematic engagement with the structuring myths of neo-liberal capitalism, the dilemmas of contemporary, liberal-left politics and the 'problem' of Old Englishness. As Joe Brooker argues, from the evidence provided by the 'vigour, originality and political charge' of the Robinson films, the realist project in British cinema is far from 'washed up'.[5]

Finally, let us return once again to the problem of Englishness and class. Here I argued that the English class system separates class and capitalism. We looked at the implications of this in the critical reception of *Performance*, particularly in reference to a *carceral* model of class. We also saw – in the discussions of the heritage film and the romantic comedies of Working Title – how the stabilities of the English culture of class seem to place us beyond capitalism's ceaseless turmoil. This is an impression which fits with Wood's account of the ideological achievement of the English 'pristine culture of capitalism'. But if this culture has a long history so too does the working class. It is in relation to such longer historical class narratives that the London/Atlantic dimension of the book takes on a particular significance. This theme, clearest in the discussions of *South West 9* and *Jubilee*, has sought to emphasise how traditions of Englishness remain implicated, even in their most hallowed forms, in wider, intercontinental forms of class struggle. The relatively recent recovery of these historical frameworks helps to provide answers to the key question, posed by Freddy in *South West 9*. Recall that I interpreted this question – 'How did we end up like this, all of us?' – as a demand that we try to attend to the consequences of a historically unfolding, socially determining process of 'capitalist imperialism' still deeply relevant to early-twenty-first-century Britain. It is a question then which is related to the one that Robinson is prompted to ask in *London* – by what means is the multicultural promise of London undermined and contained? The answer that emerges out of Keiller's three most recent films is clear – the problem does not lie in some kind of defective English modernity, but rather is buried in the *peculiarly capitalist* national past and present. The subject of Freddy's question – the 'we' and 'us' – is inclusive. However, this is not a question that one can easily imagine William and Anna asking themselves as they sit in their idyllic garden, at the still, hushed centre of a privileged world which lacks the categories of connection and cause, rhyme and reason. It is a question, however, that necessarily accompanies the processes by which the working class has been and continues to be, made, unmade and remade.

Notes

PREFACE

1. Ellen Meiksins Wood, *The Pristine Culture of Capitalism: A Historical Essay on Old Regimes and Modern States* (London: Verso, 1991).
2. Ibid., p. 38.
3. Ibid., pp. 1–19.
4. Benedict Anderson, *Imagined Communities: Reflections on the Origin and Spread of Nationalism* (London: Verso, 1983).
5. Sleeve notes, *Gosford Park*, DVD, USA Films, 2001.
6. See James Walvin, *Fruits of Empire: Exotic Produce and British Taste, 1660–1800*, (London: Macmillan, 1997).
7. See Bryan D. Palmer, *Cultures of Darkness: Night Travels in the Histories of Transgression* (New York: Monthly Review Press, 2000).
8. Roger Scruton, *England: An Elegy* (London: Pimlico, 2001).
9. Linda Colley, *Britons: Forging the Nation, 1707–1837* (London: Pimlico, 1992).
10. Scruton, *England*, p. 4.
11. David Cannadine, *Ornamentalism: How the British Saw Their Empire* (London: Penguin, 2001).
12. Andrew Higson, *English Heritage, English Cinema: Costume Drama Since 1980* (Oxford: Oxford University Press, 2003) p. 84.
13. Claire Monk, 'Sexuality and the Heritage', *Sight and Sound* (October 1995), pp. 33–4.
14. See Paul Gilroy, *After Empire: Melancholia or Convivial Culture?* (London: Routledge, 2004).
15. See Ellen Meiksins Wood, *The Retreat from Class: A New 'True' Socialism* (London: Verso, 1986), p. 113.
16. Robert Murphy, 'Citylife: Urban Fairy-tales in Late 90s British Cinema', in Robert Murphy (ed.), *The British Cinema Book*, 2nd Edition (London: BFI, 2001), p. 296.
17. Mike Wayne, *Marxism and Media Studies: Key Concepts and Contemporary Trends* (London: Pluto, 2003), p. 70.
18. Ellen Meiksins Wood, *The Origin of Capitalism: A Longer View* (London: Verso, 2002).

19. Wood, *The Pristine Culture of Capitalism*, pp. 1–19.
20. Wood, *The Origin of Capitalism*, pp. 11–33.
21. Ellen Meiksins Wood, *Democracy Against Capitalism* (Cambridge: Cambridge University Press, 1995).
22. See Paul Smith, *Millennial Dreams: Contemporary Culture and Capital in the North* (London: Verso, 1997) and Jean Comaroff and John L. Comaroff, (eds), *Millennial Capitalism and the Culture of Neo-liberalism* (Durham: Duke University Press, 2001).
23. Jean Comarrof and John L. Comarrof, 'Millennial Capitalism: First Thoughts on a Second Coming', in Comaroff and Comaroff , *Millennial Capitalism* p. 4.

INTRODUCTION
BRITISH CINEMA AND CLASS: PASTORAL VISIONS

1. Wood, *Democracy Against Capitalism*, p. 76.
2. Ibid., p. 76.
3. Wayne, *Marxism and Media Studies*, p. 9.
4. See Wood, *Democracy Against Capitalism*, pp. 19–48.
5. See Gary Day, *Class* (London: Routledge, 2001), p. 13.
6. Raymond Williams, *Keywords: A Vocabulary of Culture and Society* (London: Fontana, 1990), pp. 65–6.
7. Ibid., p. 66.
8. David Cannadine, *Class in Britain* (New Haven: Yale University Press, 1998).
9. Ibid., p. 19.
10. Ibid., pp. 19–20.
11. Ibid., p. 22.
12. Ibid., p. 22.
13. Ibid., pp. 15–16.
14. Ibid., p. 12.
15. This argument is indebted to the work of those historians who have been referred to as the British Marxist Historians. See Harvey J. Kaye, *The British Marxist Historians: An Introductory Analysis* (London: Macmillan, 1995) p. 3.
16. Cannadine, *Class in Britain*, p. 24.
17. E.P. Thompson, 'Eighteenth-Century English Society: Class Struggle without Class?' *Social History*, 3 (May 1978), pp. 133–65.
18. See Wood, *Democracy Against Capitalism*, pp. 76–107.
19. See Harvey J. Kaye, *The Education of Desire: Marxists and the Writing of History* (London: Routledge, 1992), p. 63.

20. Colin Barker, 'Some Reflections on Two Books by Ellen Wood', *Historical Materialism*, 1 (1997), p. 45.

21. Ibid., p. 45.

22. Cannadine, *Class in Britain*, pp. 8-15.

23. For a list of Nairn and Anderson's relevant articles from the *New Left Review* see Wood, *The Pristine Culture of Capitalism*, p. 178. See also, Tom Nairn, *The Break-Up of Britain* (London: Verso, 1981); Tom Nairn, *The Enchanted Glass: Britain and its Monarchy* (London: Vintage, 1994); Tom Nairn, *After Britain: New Labour and the Return of Scotland* (London: Granta, 2000); and Tom Nairn, *Pariah: Misfortunes of the British Kingdom* (London: Verso, 2002).

24. See Perry Anderson, *English Questions* (London: Verso, 1992) p. 17. The original essay was entitled 'Origins of the Present Crisis' and was published in *New Left Review*, 23 (January/February 1964), pp. 26-53.

25. Nairn, *The Enchanted Glass*, p. 239

26. Wood, *The Pristine Culture of Capitalism*, p. 32.

27. Ibid., p. 32.

28. See Nairn, *The Enchanted Glass*, pp. 260-68.

29. Wood, *The Pristine Culture of Capitalism*, pp. 31-8.

30. Ibid., pp. 36-8.

31. Ibid., p. 37.

32. Ibid., pp. 34-7.

33. Ibid., p. 37.

34. Ibid., pp. 37-8.

35. Ibid., pp. 2-19.

36. Ibid., p. 2.

37. Ibid., pp. 1-19.

38. Ibid., p. 2.

39. On 'heritage spectacle' as a regressive vision of upper-class Englishness, see Andrew Higson, 'Re-presenting the National Past: Nostalgia and Pastiche in the Heritage Film', in Lester Friedman (ed.), *British Cinema and Thatcherism: Fires Were Started* (Minneapolis and London: University of Minnesota Press and UCL Press, 1993), p. 119.

40. Raymond Williams, *The Country and the City* (St Albans: Paladin, 1975), p. 53.

41. Andrew Higson, *Waving the Flag: Constructing a National Cinema in Britain* (Clarendon Press: Oxford, 1995), p. 171.

42. Ibid., p. 274.

43. Ibid., p. 274.

44. Ibid., pp. 44-5.

45. Ibid., p. 44.

46. Terry Eagleton, *Against the Grain: Essays 1975-1985* (London: Verso, 1986), pp. 149-50.

47. Sue Harper, *Picturing the Past: The Rise and Fall of the British Costume Film* (London: BFI, 1994). On British popular genres see also Marcia Landy, *British Genres: Cinema and Society, 1930–1960* (Princeton: Princeton University Press, 1991).

48. Harper, *Picturing the Past*, p. 183.

49. Ibid., p. 5.

50. Ibid., p. 26 and p. 182. See also Nairn's account of what he calls an English 'folklore from above' in Nairn, *The Enchanted Glass*, pp. 174–89.

51. Harper, *Picturing the Past*, p. 38.

52. Ibid., p. 38.

53. Ibid., p. 51.

54. Ibid., p. 2.

55. Ibid., p. 3.

56. See for instance the images of the revolutionary French mob in Ralph Thomas's adaptation of Charles Dickens's *The Tale of Two Cities* (1958). Dickens's *The Tale of Two Cities* (1859) is one of the key Pimpernel literary intertexts.

57. Terry Eagleton, *The Ideology of the Aesthetic* (Oxford: Blackwell, 1990), pp. 31–69.

58. Ibid., p. 43.

59. Colley, *Britons*, p. 149.

60. Ibid., p. 164.

61. Ibid., p. 189.

62. Ibid., p. 187.

63. Harper, *Picturing the Past*, p. 26. See Baroness Orczy, *The Scarlet Pimpernel* (New York: Signet Classics, 2000).

64. E.P. Thompson, *Polemics and Persons: Historical Essays* (London: Merlin Press, 1994), p. 332.

65. John Stevenson and Chris Cook, *Britain in the Depression: Society and Politics 1929–1939*, 2nd Edition (London: Longman, 1994), p. 268.

66. Higson, *Waving the Flag*, p. 27.

67. Ibid., pp. 256–8.

68. Ibid., p. 181.

69. Ibid., p. 238.

70. David Mellor, 'Sketch for an Historical Portrait of Humphrey Jennings', in Mary-Lou Jennings (ed.), *Humphrey Jennings: Film-maker, Painter, Poet* (London: BFI, 1982), p. 67.

71. Higson, *Waving the Flag*, p. 269.

72. Ibid., p. 268.

73. Robert Murphy, *Realism and Tinsel: Cinema and Society in Britain, 1939–1948* (London: Routledge, 1989), pp. 146–67.

74. Peter Wollen, 'Riff-Raff Realism', *Sight and Sound* (April 1998), p. 19.

75. Ibid., p. 19. See also, Sarah Street, *British National Cinema* (London: Routledge, 1997), p. 68.

76. Jose Harris, 'Tradition and Transformation: Society and Civil Society in Britain, 1945-2001', in Kathleen Burk (ed.), *The British Isles since 1945* (Oxford: Oxford University Press, 2003), p. 96.

77. Higson, *Waving the Flag*, p. 269. See also John Hill, *Sex, Class and Realism: British Cinema, 1956-1963*, (London: BFI, 1986), pp. 136-43.

78. See John Hill, *British Cinema in the 1980s: Issues and Themes* (Oxford: Clarendon Press, 1999), p. 166.

79. John Hill, 'Failure and Utopianism: Representations of the Working Class in British Cinema of the 1990s', in Robert Murphy (ed.), *British Cinema of the 90s* (London: BFI, 2000), p. 184.

80. Julia Hallam, 'Film, Class, and National Identity: Re-imagining Communities in the Age of Devolution', in Justine Ashby and Andrew Higson (eds), *British Cinema: Past and Present* (London: Routledge, 2000), p. 267.

81. Julian Stallabrass, *High Art Lite* (London: Verso, 2000).

82. Ibid., p. 236. See also John Brewer, *The Pleasures of the Imagination: English Culture in the Eighteenth Century* (London: Harper Collins, 1997), p. 53.

83. Stallabrass, *High Art Lite*, p. 253.

84. Ibid., p. 214.

85. Ibid., p. 253.

86. Ibid., p. 246.

87. See Steve Chibnall, 'Travels in Ladland: The British Gangster Film Cycle, 1998-2001', in Robert Murphy (ed.), *The British Cinema Book*, pp. 281-91.

88. Ibid., p. 284.

89. Stallabrass, *High Art Lite* pp. 247-8 .

90. Higson, *Waving the Flag*, p. 182. See also Samantha Lay, *British Social Realism: From Documentary to Brit Grit* (London: Wallflower, 2002), p. 41.

91. Stallabrass, *High Art Lite*, p. 238.

92. Iain Sinclair, *Dark Lanthorns: David Rodinsky as Pyschogeographer* (Uppingham: Goldmark, 1999), p. 41.

93. See Iain Sinclair, *Lights Out for the Territory: 9 Excursions in the Secret History of London* (London: Granta, 1997), p. 301.

94. James Donald, *Imagining the Modern City* (London: Athlone, 1999), pp. 184-5.

95. Higson, *Waving the Flag*, p. 273.

96. John Hill, 'British Cinema as National Cinema: Production, Audience and Representation', in Robert Murphy (ed.), *The British Cinema Book*, p. 211.

97. Stuart Hall, 'The Question of Cultural Identity', in Stuart Hall, David Held and Tony McGrew (eds), *Modernity and its Futures* (Polity: Cambridge, 1992), p. 309.

98. Ibid., p. 310.

99. Ibid., p. 310.
100. Slavoj Žižek, 'Over the Rainbow', *London Review of Books*, Vol. 26 No. 21 (4th November 2004), p. 20.
101. Ibid., p. 20.
102. Ibid., p. 20.
103. Ibid., p. 20.
104. In 1990 Norman Tebbit questioned the national status of black and Asian Britons who favoured overseas cricket teams over English ones. In the early 1990s John Major associated Britain with village cricket and warm beer.
105. Moya Luckett, 'Image and Nation in 1990s British Cinema', in Robert Murphy (ed.), *British Cinema of the 90s*, p. 96
106. Mike Wayne, *The Politics of Contemporary European Cinema: Histories, Borders, Diasporas* (Bristol: Intellect, 2002), pp. 119–38.
107. Ibid., pp. 120–3 and p. 132.
108. Ibid., p. 128.
109. See Hill, *British Cinema in the 1980s*, pp. 205–40.
110. Chibnall, 'Travels', p. 285.
111. Ibid., p. 283.
112. Ibid., p. 285.
113. Wayne, *The Politics*, p. 120.
114. Pamela Church Gibson, 'Imaginary Landscapes, Jumbled Topographies: Cinematic London', in Joe Kerr and Andrew Gibson (eds), *London: From Punk to Blair* (London: Reaktion, 2003), p. 366.
115. Chibnall, 'Travels', p. 284.
116. Cora Kaplan, 'The Death of the Working-Class Hero', *New Formations*, 52 (Spring 2004), p. 101.
117. Hill, *British Cinema in the 1980s*, p. 215.
118. Ibid., p. 205.
119. *South West 9*, DVD, Prism Leisure, 2002.
120. Wayne, *The Politics*, p. 132.
121. For Paul Gilroy 'conviviality' is used to refer to: 'the processes of cohabitation and interaction that have made multiculture an ordinary feature of social life in Britain's urban areas...'. See Gilroy, *After Empire*, p. xi.
122. M. Gillespire, quoted in Wayne, *The Politics*, p. 121.
123. Smith, *Millennial Dreams,* p. 14.
124. Comaroff and Comaroff, *Millennial Capitalism*, p. 2.
125. Ibid., p. 5.
126. Ibid., p. 3.
127. Wood, *The Origin of Capitalism*, p. 28.
128. Ibid., p. 28.
129. Ibid., p. 7.

130. Nairn, *The Enchanted Glass*, p. 240. For Nairn, the Palace of Westminster symbolises the 'baroquely gilded hegemony' of the City's 'early' or commercial capital. See Nairn, *The Enchanted Glass*, p. 241.

131. Tony Blair quoted in Stephen Driver and Luke Martell, 'Blair and "Britishness"', in David Morley and Kevin Robins (eds), *British Cultural Studies* (Oxford: Oxford University Press, 2001), p. 462.

132. Colley, *Britons*, pp. 374–5.

133. Susan Bassnett, 'Afterword' in Morley and Robins (eds), *British Cultural Studies*, p. 501.

134. On the contemporaneity of the eighteenth century see John Brewer's documentary film *Sense and Sensation: English Culture in the Eighteenth Century* (2002).

135. See Kevin Robins, 'To London: The City Beyond the Nation', in Morley and Robins (eds), *British Cultural Studies*, p. 485.

136. Colley, *Britons*, pp. 15–17.

137. Ibid., p. 5.

138. Thompson, *Polemics and Persons*, p. 323.

139. Ibid., p. 323.

140. Ibid., p. 323

141. Peter Linebaugh and Marcus Rediker, *The Many-Headed Hydra: Sailors, Slaves, Commoners and the Hidden History of the Revolutionary Atlantic* (London: Verso, 2000), p. 332.

142. Ibid., pp. 332–3.

143. Ibid., p. 2–7.

144. Ibid., p. 36–7.

145. Ibid., p. 2.

146. See Ellen Meiksins Wood, *Empire of Capital*, (London: Verso, 2003), pp. 73–117.

CHAPTER 1
THE UPPER CLASSES: THE HERITAGE FILM

1. Higson, *English Heritage*, pp. 9–45.

2. Higson, *Waving The Flag*, pp. 26–97.

3. Higson, *English Heritage*, pp. 9–45.

4. Ibid., p. 262.

5. Sheldon Hall, 'The Wrong Sort of Cinema: Refashioning the Heritage Film Debate', in Murphy (ed.), *The British Cinema Book*, pp. 192–3

6. Andrew Higson, 'Heritage Cinema and Television', in Morley and Robins (eds), *British Cultural Studies*, p. 252.

7. Ibid., p. 252.

8. Higson, *English Heritage*, p. 28.

9. Ibid., p. 6 and p. 26.

10. Higson, 'Heritage, Cinema and Television', p. 253.

11. Higson, 'Re-presenting the National Past', p. 115.

12. Higson, *English Heritage*, pp. 56–63.

13. See Claire Monk 'The British Heritage-Film Debate Revisited', in Claire Monk and Amy Sargeant (eds), *British Historical Cinema* (London: Routledge, 2002), pp. 177–80.

14. Higson, *English Heritage*, p. 12.

15. Ibid., pp. 46–7.

16. Ibid., p. 12.

17. Ibid., pp. 37–42.

18. Ibid., p. 72.

19. See Claire Monk, 'The British "Heritage Film" and its Critics', *Critical Survey*, 7 (2) (1995), p. 120.

20. See Pam Cook, 'Neither Here nor There: National Identity in Gainsborough Costume Drama', in Andrew Higson (ed.), *Dissolving Views: Key Writings on British Cinema* (London: Cassell, 1996), p. 51–65.

21. Higson, *English Heritage*, p. 75.

22. Hall, 'The Wrong Sort', pp. 196–7.

23. Monk, 'The British Heritage-Film Debate Revisited', pp. 187–91.

24. Ibid., p. 187.

25. See Patrick Wright, *On Living in an Old Country* (London: Verso, 1985) and Robert Hewison, *The Heritage Industry: Britain in a Climate of Decline* (London: Methuen, 1987). It is important to recognise the differences between Wright and Hewison. The former has a more nuanced sense of the cultural politics of heritage than is often recognised. See for instance 'Sneering at the Theme Parks: An Encounter with the Heritage Industry', Patrick Wright in conversation with Tim Putnam, in *Block* 15 (1989), pp. 48–55.

26. Norman Stone, 'Through a Lens Darkly', *Sunday Times*, 10 January 1988. Reprinted in Kobena Mercer (ed.), *Black Film, British Cinema* (London: ICA, 1988), pp. 22–4.

27. Ibid., pp. 22–3.

28. See Cairns Craig, 'Rooms without a View', in Ginette Vincendeau (ed.), *Film/Literature/Heritage: A Sight and Sound Reader* (London: BFI, 2001), pp. 3–6, and Higson, 'Re-presenting the National Past', pp. 109–29.

29. Monk, 'The British Heritage-Film Debate Revisited', pp. 189–90

30. Ibid., p. 188.

31. Ibid., p. 190.

32. Ibid., p. 188.

33. Ibid., p. 190.

34. W.D. Rubinstein, *Capitalism, Culture and Decline in Britain, 1750–1990* (London: Routledge, 1993), pp. 1–3. See also, Paul Dave, 'Representations of

Capitalism, History and Nation in the Work of Patrick Keiller', in Ashby and Higson (eds), *British Cinema*, pp. 341–4.

35. Stuart Hall quoted in Alex Callinicos, 'Exception or Symptom: The British World Crisis and the World System', *New Left Review* 169 (May/June 1988), p. 97.

36. On the political culture associated with Charter 88, see Anthony Barnett (ed.), *Power and the Throne* (London: Vintage, 1994).

37. The Thatcher government sought to sponsor the 'heritage industry' in the National Heritage Acts of 1980 and 1983.

38. Nairn, *The Enchanted Glass*, p. 367.

39. See John Corner and Sylvia Harvey, 'Mediating Tradition and Modernity: The Heritage/Enterprise Couplet', in John Corner and Sylvia Harvey (eds), *Enterprise and Heritage: Crosscurrents of National Culture* (London: Routledge, 1991), pp. 45–75.

40. Alison Light, 'Englishness', *Sight and Sound* (July 1991), p. 63.

41. Hill, *British Cinema in the 1980s*, p. 27. Also, Higson, *English Heritage*, pp. 77–80.

42. Hill, *British Cinema in the 1980s*, pp. 20–81.

43. Ibid., p. 27.

44. Ibid., pp. 26–7.

45. Ibid., pp. 26–7.

46. Ibid., p. 27.

47. Ibid., p. 87.

48. Ibid., p. 91.

49. Ibid., p. 85.

50. Higson, *English Heritage*, p. 72.

51. Wood, *Democracy Against Capitalism*, p. 261.

52. Tom Nairn, 'Ukania Under Blair', *New Left Review*, 1 (January/February 2000), pp. 87–8. The House of Lords, the unelected 'second chamber' of Parliament, was used by Thatcher to prop up her controversial legislative programme.

53. Susan Watkins, 'A Weightless Hegemony: New Labour's Role in the Neoliberal Order', *New Left Review*, 25 (January/February 2004), p. 10.

54. Paul Dave, 'Heritage Cinema and the Bourgeois Paradigm', *New Left Review*, 224 (July/August 1997), pp. 111–26.

55. Hill, *British Cinema in the 1980s*, p .91.

56. Wayne, *The Politics*, pp. 52–6.

57. Pamela Church Gibson, 'Fewer Weddings and More Funerals: Changes in the Heritage Film', in Robert Murphy (ed.), *British Cinema of the 90s*, p. 117. In her nuanced reading of the contemporary costume film, Julianne Pidduck explores the 'class critique' to be found in *Jude, Gosford Park, Angels and Insects, The Remains of the Day* and *Sister My Sister* (1994). In particular, she draws attention to the way these films bring into the cycle a sense of

class struggle which encompasses not only an aspiring middle class but also, and unusually, a painfully labouring working class. See Julianne Pidduck, *Contemporary Costume Film: Space, Place and the Past* (London: BFI, 2004), p. 137.

58. Ibid., p. 119.
59. Kara McKechnie, 'Taking Liberties with the Monarch: The Royal Bio-Pic in the 1990s', in Monk and Sargeant (eds), *British Historical Cinema*, p. 221.
60. On George III see Colley, *Britons*, pp. 195–236. On Victoria see David Cannadine, 'The Context, Performance and Meaning of Ritual: the British Monarchy and the "Invention of Tradition" c.1820–1977', in E. Hobsbawm and T. Ranger (eds), *The Invention of Tradition* (Cambridge: Cambridge University Press, 1992), pp. 101–64.
61. Philip Kemp, *Sight and Sound* (December 1999), p. 59.
62. On nineteenth-century popular politics and the Tichborne case see Rohan McWilliam, *Popular Politics in Nineteenth-Century England* (London: Routledge, 1998), pp. 67–70.
63. Richard Johnson, 'Barrington Moore, Perry Anderson and English Social Development', in Stuart Hall, Dorothy Hobson, Andrew Lowe and Paul Willis (eds), *Culture, Media, Language: Working Papers in Cultural Studies*, 1972–1979 (London: Routledge, 1980), p. 61.
64. Ibid., p. 66.
65. Ibid., p. 66.
66. Ibid., p. 66.
67. Wood, *The Pristine Culture of Capitalism*, p. 37.
68. Ibid., p. 38.
69. Wood, *Democracy Against Capitalism*, pp. 28–31.
70. Francis Mulhern, 'Britain After Nairn', *New Left Review*, 5 (September/ October 2000), pp. 56–7.
71. See Higson, *English Heritage*, p. 32.
72. Monk, 'Sexuality and the Heritage', p. 33.
73. Ibid., p. 33.
74. Church Gibson, 'Fewer Weddings', p. 123.
75. Ibid., p. 122.
76. Luckett, 'Image and Nation', p. 90.
77. Wayne, *The Politics*, p. 52.
78. New Labour renamed the Department of National Heritage as the Department of Culture, Media and Sport, 'as a symbol that we mean to look forward not back'. See David Morley and Kevin Robins, 'Culture, Heritage, Tradition: Introduction', in Morley and Robins (eds), *British Cultural Studies*, p. 176.
79. Monk, 'Sexuality and the Heritage', pp. 33–4.
80. Monk, 'The British Heritage-Film Debate Revisited', p. 193
81. Ibid., p. 193.
82. Ibid., p. 193.
83. Ibid., p. 192.

84. Monk, 'Sexuality and the Heritage', p. 34.
85. Church Gibson, 'Imaginary Landscapes', p. 364.
86. Tom Paulin, *The Faber Book of Political Verse* (London: Faber & Faber, 1986), p. 15.
87. See William Raban's *MM* (2002) in which the Millennium Dome and Canary Wharf are figured as alien presences.

CHAPTER 2
THE MIDDLE CLASSES: FAIRY TALES AND IDYLLS

1. Many of these romantic comedies, including *Four Weddings and a Funeral*, *Notting Hill*, both Bridget Jones films, *About a Boy*, *Love Actually* and *Wimbledon*, were produced by Working Title, a fact to which I will return later.
2. Murphy, 'Citylife', pp. 296–300. Murphy excludes *Fever Pitch*, *Maybe Baby* and *Bridget Jones's Diary* from his list of London 'fairy-tales' on the strength of Bruno Bettleheim's claim that fairy tales must include a suffering protagonist whereas the protagonists in these three films do not suffer. See Murphy, p. 292.
3. Comaroff and Comaroff, *Millennial Capitalism*, pp. 1–56.
4. Ibid., p. 44.
5. Ibid., pp. 14–15.
6. Ibid., p. 15.
7. Ibid., p. 12.
8. See M.M. Bakhtin, 'Forms of Time and of the Chronotope in the Novel', in *The Dialogic Imagination: Four Essays by M.M. Bakhtin*, (ed.) Michael Holquist (Austin: University of Texas Press, 1981), pp. 84–258. For Bakhtin, the pastoral is one aspect of the idyllic chronotope. See Bakhtin, pp. 224–6.
9. Robert Stam, *Film Theory: An Introduction* (Oxford: Blackwell, 2000), pp. 204–5.
10. Bakhtin, 'Forms of Time', p. 217.
11. Ibid., p. 217.
12. Ibid., p. 225.
13. Ibid., p. 225.
14. Ibid., pp. 231–3.
15. Ibid., p. 232.
16. Ibid., p. 232.
17. Ibid., p. 232.
18. Franco Moretti, *The Way of the World: The Bildungsroman in European Culture* (London: Verso, 1987), p. 204.
19. Note how this reading is compatible with Wood's understanding of the function of English ideologies of class.

20. Moretti, *The Way of the World*, pp. 202–3.
21. Ibid., p. 205.
22. Bakhtin, 'Forms of Time', p. 232.
23. Ibid., p. 234.
24. Ibid., p. 234. See also Moretti, *The Way of the World*, passim.
25. See Wood, *The Pristine Culture of Capitalism*, pp. 81–93.
26. Bakhtin, 'Forms of Time', p. 91.
27. As Moretti argues, it is the social 'middle' to which the hero of the English novel belongs and it is English middle classes who are represented as projecting a 'peculiarly innocent' view of the world and presentation of themselves. See Moretti, *The Way of the World*, p. 200. For an application of Moretti's interpretation of the 'niaf' hero of the English novel to *Four Weddings and a Funeral*, see Dave, 'Heritage Cinema', pp. 114–17.
28. Bakhtin, 'Forms of Time', p. 226.
29. Stam, *Film Theory*, p. 204.
30. Church Gibson, 'Imaginary Landscapes', p. 368.
31. Bakhtin, 'Forms of Time', p. 225.
32. Ibid., p. 225.
33. Angus Fletcher, *The Prophetic Moment: An Essay on Spenser* (Chicago: University of Chicago Press, 1971) p. 14.
34. Ibid., p. 15.
35. Ibid., pp. 14–17.
36. Ibid., p. 22.
37. See Murphy, 'Citylife', p. 296, and Monk and Sargeant, 'The Past in British Cinema', in Monk and Sargeant (eds), *British Historical Cinema*, p. 8.
38. Bakhtin, 'Forms of Time', p. 225.
39. Ibid., pp. 206–10.
40. Ibid., p. 213.
41. Ibid., p. 213.
42. Ibid., p. 214.
43. Ibid., p. 234.
44. Ibid., p. 232.
45. Ibid., p. 233.
46. Philip French, in The *Observer*, 14 November 2004.
47. Moretti, *The Way of the World*, pp. 63–4.
48. Roger Bromley, 'The Theme That Dare Not Speak Its Name: Class and Recent British Film', in Sally R. Munt (ed.), *Cultural Studies and the Working Class: Subject to Change* (London: Cassell, 2000), p. 53.
49. Ibid., p. 53.
50. Fellner quoted in Mike Wayne, 'Working Title Mark II: A Critique of the Atlanticist Paradigm for British Cinema', unpublished manuscript.
51. Tim Bevan, quoted in Wayne, Ibid..
52. Ibid.

53. Ibid.

54. Ibid.

55. Ibid.

56. Ibid.

57. Alex Callinicos, 'The "New Middle Class" and socialist politics', in Alex Callinicos and Chris Harman (eds), *The Changing Working Class: Essays on Class Structure Today* (London: Bookmarks, 1989), p. 35.

58. To take a contemporary example, in *Groundhog Day* (1993), as Kristin Thompson argues, there is a sense that it is the central character's moral state that ultimately motivates the temporal anomaly. See Kristin Thompson *Storytelling in the New Hollywood: Understanding Classical Narrative Technique* (Cambridge, Massachusetts: Harvard University Press, 1999), p. 132.

59. Ibid., pp. 378-9.

60. Marshall Berman, *All That Is Solid Melts Into Air: The Experience of Modernity* (London: Verso, 1983).

61. Ibid., pp. 134-42.

62. Ibid., pp. 153-4.

63. See Callinicos, 'The "New Middle Class"', pp. 35-6.

64. Murphy, 'Citylife', p. 298.

65. I have been influenced by Fredric Jameson's approach to textual interpretation here, in particular by his elaboration of the 'political unconscious' of cultural texts. See Fredric Jameson, *The Political Unconscious: Narrative as a Socially Symbolic Act* (London: Methuen, 1981), pp. 17-102. As Adam Roberts puts it, this approach holds that 'the surface narration usefully mediates the unconscious reality of the text's relationship with history'. See Adam Roberts, *Fredric Jameson* (London: Routledge, 2000), p. 76.

66. Luckett, 'Image and Nation', p. 98.

67. Berman, *All That Is Solid*, p. 135.

68. Gerry's pub confessions to his friend Russell establish this aspect of his character.

CHAPTER 3
THE WORKING CLASS: ELEGIES

1. See Claire Monk, 'Underbelly UK: The 1990s Underclass Film, Masculinity and the Ideologies of "New" Britain', in Ashby and Higson (eds), *British Cinema* pp. 274-87, and Claire Monk, 'Men in the 90s', in Murphy (ed.), *British Cinema in the 90s*, pp. 156-66. See also, Hill, 'Failure and Utopianism', p. 178; Bromley, 'The Theme', pp. 64-7, and Lay, *British Social Realism*, pp. 104-5.

2. See John Hill, 'From New Wave to "Brit-Grit": Continuity and Difference in Working-Class Realism', in Ashby and Higson (eds), *British Cinema*, pp. 252-3.

3. Kaplan, 'The Death of the Working-Class Hero', pp. 94–110; Monk, 'Underbelly UK', pp. 283–6, and Luckett, 'Image and Nation', pp. 88–99.

4. Luckett, 'Image and Nation', pp. 96–7.

5. Kaplan, 'The Death of the Working-Class Hero', p. 101.

6. Ibid., p. 107. Kaplan's reference to Blairite 'conservative modernity' is drawn from the work of Stuart Hall. See Kaplan, ibid., p. 97.

7. Hill, 'Failure and Utopianism', p. 184.

8. Huw Beynon 'Images of Labour/Images of Class', in Huw Beynon and Sheila Rowbotham (eds), *Looking at Class: Film, Television and the Working Class in Britain* (Rivers Oram Press: London, 2001), p. 38. See also, pp. 30–40.

9. Karen Lury discusses 'youth' in contemporary cinema and its relationship to commodity culture. See Lury, 'Here and Then: Space, Place and Nostalgia in British Youth Cinema', in Murphy (ed.), *British Cinema in the 90s*, pp. 100–8.

10. Department of Employment Training advertisement, 1988. It is interesting to note that this slogan re-appears in New Labour political rhetoric in the 1990s. See transcripts of the following speeches by Gordon Brown: Pre-budget report 1999 http://news.bbc.co.uk/1/hi/uk_politics/512484.stm and Urban Summit Birmingham, 1 November 2002 http://www.hm-treasury.gov.uk/newsroom_and_speeches/speeches/chancellorexchequer/speech_chex_011102.cfm

11. Karen Lury, *British Youth Television: Cynicism and Enchantment* (Oxford, Oxford University Press, 2001), p. 4. The origin of the term 'McJob' is to be found in Douglas Coupland's, *Generation X: Tales for an Accelerated Culture* (London: Abacus, 1991).

12. See Georges Bataille, *Visions of Excess: Selected Writings, 1927–1939*, ed., Allan Stoekl (Manchester: Manchester University Press, 1985), pp. 116–29.

13. See Seumas Milne, *The Enemy Within: The Secret War Against the Miners* (London: Verso, 2004), p. x.

14. Ibid., p. 9.

15. Ibid., pp. 10–13.

16. Ibid., p. 28.

17. Ibid., p. x.

18. Ibid., p. 28.

19. Kaplan, 'The Death of the Working-Class Hero', p. 104.

20. Beynon, 'Images of Labour', p. 34.

21. See Judith Williamson, 'Judith Williamson in Conversation with Huw Beynon and Sheila Rowbotham', in Beynon and Rowbotham (eds), *Looking at Class* pp. 105–6.

22. Patrick Keiller, *Robinson in Space* (London: Reaktion, 1999), p. 214. As the narrator in *Robinson in Space* matter-of-factly informs us: 'Not long after our visit, they sacked 329 dock workers for refusing to cross a picket-line.'

23. Jimmy McGovern interviewed in *Writing the Wrongs*, Channel 4, transmitted on 11 July 1999.

24. Slavoj Žižek, 'Risk Society and its Discontents', *Historical Materialism*, 2 (Summer 1998), p. 162. Žižek borrows the phrase 'post-political' from Jacques Rancière. See Žižek, p. 146.

25. On Lacan's three orders of the 'Imaginary', 'Real' and 'Symbolic', see Malcolm Bowie, *Lacan* (London: Fontana, 1991), pp. 88–121.

26. Žižek, 'Risk Society', p. 147.

27. Ibid., p. 146.

28. Ibid., p. 147.

29. Ibid., p. 147.

30. Ibid., p. 148.

31. Ibid., p. 148.

32. Ibid., pp. 147–8.

33. See Andrew Higson, 'Space, Place, Spectacle: Landscape and Townscape in the "Kitchen Sink" Film', in Higson (ed.), *Dissolving Views*, p. 138.

34. See Hill, *Sex, Class and Realism*, p. 12.

35. Isaac Julien points out that *The Full Monty* was originally the idea of black London club-organiser Paul Bucknor. Bucknor, however, lost creative control of the film. The character of Horse is a remnant of his original idea. See Isaac Julien, 'Revealing Desires', in Beynon and Rowbotham (eds), *Looking at Class*, pp. 179–80.

36. Hill, 'Failure and Utopianism', p. 184.

37. Luckett, 'Image and Nation', p. 96.

38. Ibid., p. 96.

39. Kaplan, 'The Death of the Working-Class Hero', p. 107.

40. Ibid., p. 101.

41. Ibid., p. 99.

42. Monk, 'Underbelly UK', p. 285.

43. Luckett, 'Image and Nation', p. 96.

44. Kaplan, 'The Death of the Working-Class Hero', p. 108.

45. Milne, *The Enemy Within*, pp. 1–36.

46. For a fictional account of the strike which places emphasis on the use of the secret State see David Peace, *GB84* (London: Faber & Faber, 2004). See also Milne, *The Enemy Within*, passim.

47. Kaplan, 'The Death of the Working-Class Hero', p. 109.

48. Ibid., p. 109.

49. Saul Metzstein, 'Cast and Crew Interviews', *Late Night Shopping*, DVD Film Four Video, 2003.

50. Lury, 'Here and Then', p. 101.

51. See Monk, 'Men in the 90s', pp. 160–5.

52. Paul Virilio, *Speed and Politics: An Essay on Dromology* (New York: Semiotext(e), 1981), p. 99.

53. Sleeve notes, *Late Night Shopping*, DVD.

54. Lury, *British Youth Television*, p. 4.

55. Ibid., p. 4.

56. Metzstein, 'Cast and Crew Interviews'.

57. Saul Metzstein, 'Grit and Polish', *Sight and Sound* (May 2001), p. 13–14.

CHAPTER 4
THE UNDERCLASS: FANTASY AND REALISM

1. Robert Murphy, 'Introduction: British Cinema Saved – British Cinema Doomed', in Murphy (ed.), *The British Cinema Book*, p. 3.

2. See Joe Brooker, 'England's Screening', http://www.film-philosophy.com/vol3-1999/n10brooker

3. See Martin McLoone, 'Internal Decolonisation? British Cinema in the Celtic Fringe', in Murphy (ed.), *The British Cinema Book*, pp. 184–90.

4. Murray Smith, *Trainspotting* (London: BFI, 2002), p. 75.

5. Charles Murray, 'The Emerging British Underclass', in Ruth Lister (ed.), *Charles Murray and the Underclass: The Developing Debate* (London: IEA Health and Welfare Unit, in association with the *Sunday Times*, 1996), p. 25. See also Mark Cowling, 'Marx's Lumpenproletariat and Murray's Underclass', in Mark Cowling and James Martin (eds), *Marx's 'Eighteenth Brumaire': (Post) modern Interpretations* (London: Pluto, 2002), pp. 228–42.

6. Murray, 'The Emerging British Underclass', pp. 108–17. See also Lydia Morris, *Dangerous Classes: The Underclass and Social Citizenship* (London: Routledge, 1994).

7. Monk, 'Underbelly UK', p. 276.

8. Stallabrass, *High Art Lite*, p. 253.

9. Paul Quinn, 'Britain Projected', *Tate*, Issue 20 (Spring 2000), p. 36.

10. Stallabrass, *High Art Lite*, p. 254.

11. Ibid., p. 254.

12. Iain Sinclair, 'Heartsnatch Hotel', in *Sight and Sound* (December 2002), p. 32.

13. Chris Haylett, '"This is About Us, This is Our Film!": Personal and Popular Discourses of the "Underclass"', in Munt (ed.), *Cultural Studies and the Working Class*, p. 80.

14. Monk, 'Men in the 90s', pp. 163–5.

15. Glen Creeber, '"Can't Help Lovin' Dat Man": Social Class and the Female Voice in *Nil by Mouth*', in Munt (ed.), *Cultural Studies and the Working Class*, p. 200.

16. Ibid., p. 197.

17. Moretti, *The Way of the World*, pp. 194–5.

18. Ibid., p. 195.

19. Ibid., p. 195.

20. Ibid., p. 195.

21. Creeber, 'Can't Help', p. 199.

22. Chibnall, 'Travels', p. 283.
23. Kerry William Purcell, 'Reimagining the Working Class: From *Riff-Raff* to *Nil by Mouth*', in Beynon and Rowbotham (eds), *Looking at Class*, pp. 127–8. It interesting to note that Purcell does not use the term 'underclass' in his article on the film.
24. Ibid., pp. 125–8.
25. Ibid., p. 126.
26. D. Hevey quoted in Purcell, ibid., p. 128.
27. Ibid., pp. 125–6.
28. Ibid., p. 125.
29. Ibid., p. 125.
30. Duncan Petrie, *Screening Scotland* (London: BFI, 2000), p. 196.
31. Michael O'Pray, '"New Romanticism" and British Avant Garde Film in the Early 80s', in Murphy (ed.), *The British Cinema Book*, pp. 256–7. O'Pray is referring to film-makers such as Cerith Wynn Evans, John Maybury, Holly Warburton and Michael Kostiff.
32. Ibid., p. 257.
33. Matthew Collin, 'Preface' to Steve Beard, *Logic Bomb: Transmissions from the Edge of Style Culture* (London: Serpent's Tail, 1998), p. xi.
34. See Robin Murray, 'Fordism and Post-Fordism', in Stuart Hall and Martin Jacques (eds), *New Times: The Changing Face of Politics in the 1990s* (London: Lawrence & Wishart, 1989), pp. 38–53, and John Godfrey (ed.), *A Decade of i-Deas: The Encyclopaedia of the 80's* (London: Penguin, 1990), p. 206.
35. See Dick Hebdige, 'A Report on the Western Front: Postmodernism and the "Politics" of Style', *Block* 12 (1986/7), p. 23.
36. Ibid., p 19.
37. Hebdige, 'After the Masses', in Hall and Jacques (eds), *New Times*, p. 90.
38. Ibid., p. 91.
39. Ibid., p. 90.
40. Dick Hebdige, 'Digging for Britain: An Excavation in Seven Parts', in Dominic Strinati and Steve Wagg (eds), *Come on Down: Popular Media Culture in Post-War Britain* (London: Routledge, 1992), pp. 351–3.
41. Ibid., p. 339.
42. See Hebdige, 'A Report on the Western Front', pp. 22–4.
43. Rosalind Coward, 'Whipping Boys', *Guardian Weekend* (3 September 1994), p. 32.
44. Tony Parsons, 'The Tattooed Jungle: Tony Parsons on the Decline of the Working Class', *Arena*, 27 (Autumn 1989), pp. 26–7.
45. Ibid., p. 26.
46. See Hill, *British Cinema in the 1980s*, pp. 162–4.
47. Parsons, 'The Tattooed Jungle', p. 26.
48. Ibid., p. 27.

49. Smith, *Trainspotting*, p. 75.
50. Ibid., p. 75.
51. Ibid., p. 79.
52. Ibid., pp. 32–3.
53. Ibid., p. 33.
54. Ibid., p. 35.
55. Ibid., p. 30.
56. Ibid., p. 29.
57. Ibid., p. 29.
58. Ibid., p. 29.
59. Ibid., p. 29.
60. Ibid., p. 46.
61. Ibid., p. 46.
62. Ibid., p. 45. Seeing a touchstone of value in the overlooked and lowly, is, as Stallabrass points out in his reading of Britart, a typically 'pastoral' move. See Stallabrass, *High Art Lite*, p. 256.
63. Smith, *Trainspotting*, p. 11. See also Stephen Frears's film adaptation of Hornby's book, *High Fidelity* (2000).
64. Smith, *Trainspotting*, p. 18.
65. Note that Stallabrass refers to the development, in 1990s Britain, of what he calls 'an art of pure consumer choice'. See Stallabrass, *High Art Lite*, p. 266.
66. Smith, *Trainspotting*, p. 26.
67. Perry Anderson, *The Origins of Postmodernity* (London: Verso, 1998), pp. 84–6.
68. Ibid., p. 85.
69. Smith, *Trainspotting*, p. 45.
70. Anderson, *The Origins*, p. 85.
71. Ibid., p. 86.
72. Ibid., p. 86.
73. Terry Eagleton, *After Theory* (London: Allen Lane, 2003), p. 17.
74. Smith, *Trainspotting*, p. 50.
75. Ibid., p. 50.
76. Ibid., p. 45. See also Moretti, *The Way of the World*, passim.
77. Smith, *Trainspotting*, p. 50.
78. See Terry Eagleton, 'Capitalism and Form', *New Left Review*, 14 (March/April 2002), p. 127.
79. Smith, *Trainspotting*, p. 51.
80. Ibid., p. 35.
81. Ibid., p. 86.
82. Brooker, 'England's Screening'. See also Alan Lovell, 'The British Cinema: The Known Cinema?', in Murphy (ed.), *The British Cinema Book*, pp. 200–5; Charles Barr 'Introduction: Amnesia and Schizophrenia', in Charles Barr (ed.), *All Our Yesterdays: 90 Years of British Cinema* (London: BFI,

1986) pp. 1–29, and John Ellis, 'The Quality Film Adventure: British Critics and the Cinema 1942–1948', in Higson (ed.), *Dissolving Views*, pp. 66–93.

83. Brooker, 'England's Screening'.
84. Ibid.
85. Ibid.
86. Ibid.
87. Smith, *Trainspotting*, p. 35.
88. Ibid., p. 75.
89. Leonard Quart, 'The Politics of Irony: The Frears–Kureishi Films', in W.W. Dixon (ed.), *Re-Viewing British Cinema, 1900–1992: Essays and Interviews* (New York: State University of New York Press, 1994), p. 242.
90. Ibid., pp. 246–8.
91. Hill, *British Cinema in the 1980s*, p. 217, and Smith, *Trainspotting*, pp. 75–6.
92. Hill, *British Cinema in the 1980s,* p. 217.
93. Smith, *Trainspotting*, p. 75.
94. Ibid., p. 77.
95. Ibid., p. 76.
96. Ibid., p. 75.
97. Ibid., p. 47.
98. Ibid., p. 48.
99. Quart, 'The Politics', p. 246.
100. Hill, *British Cinema in the 1980s*, p. 218.
101. Quart, 'The Politics', p. 249.
102. Ibid., p. 248.
103. Ibid., p. 243.
104. See Hill, *British Cinema in the 1980s*, p. 211.
105. Smith, *Trainspotting*, p. 15.
106. Stallabrass, *High Art Lite*, p. 141.
107. Ibid., p. 215.
108. Ibid., p. 123.
109. Ibid., p. 168.
110. Ibid., p. 121.
111. Ibid., p. 152.
112. Ibid., p. 153.
113. Ibid., p. 139.
114. Ibid., p. 153.
115. Ibid., p. 154.
116. Smith, *Trainspotting*, p. 51.
117. Hirst quoted in Stallabrass, *High Art Lite*, p. 152.
118. See Stallabrass, *High Art Lite*, p. 139.
119. Ibid., p. 251.

CHAPTER 5
THE LUMPENPROLETARIAT: COUNTERCULTURAL PERFORMANCES

1. Colin MacCabe, 'Is this the Best British Film ever Made', *Evening Standard*, 6 May 2004, p. 30.
2. The influence of *Performance* can be seen in *Gangster No.1* (2000), *Sexy Beast* (2001) and *Lock, Stock and Two Smoking Barrels*.
3. Colin MacCabe, *Performance* (London: BFI, 1998), p. 81.
4. Ibid., p. 9.
5. Ibid., pp. 9–10. The phrase 'bastard foreign female' is uttered by one of Chas's gang and is directed not at Lucy or Pherber but an unseen motorist.
6. Ibid., p. 79.
7. Ibid., p. 78.
8. Andrew Hill, '*Performance*: La Bohème, the Garden and the Ending of the Sixties', *Visual Cultures*, 3, (1) (2002), pp. 25–6.
9. MacCabe, *Performance*, p. 55.
10. Ibid., p. 79.
11. Ibid., p. 31.
12. Ibid., p. 41.
13. See Hill, '*Performance*: La Bohème', p. 28. The concept of 'heterotopia' is taken from Michel Foucault. Hill defines it as a space which is 'distinct and separate from the rest of society' offering what Foucault calls an 'effectively enacted utopia'. Michel Foucault quoted in Hill, ibid., p. 28.
14. MacCabe, *Performance*, p. 79.
15. Ibid., p. 15.
16. Ibid., p. 15.
17. Ibid., p. 17.
18. Ibid., p. 9.
19. Ibid., p. 15.
20. Ibid., p. 81.
21. Hill, '*Performance*: La Bohème', p. 25.
22. MacCabe, *Performance*, p. 17.
23. Nik Cohn quoted in MacCabe, ibid., p. 14. The mythology of *Performance* is explored in Iain Sinclair and Chris Petit's film *The Cardinal and the Corpse* (1993) which contains references to David Litvinoff and his role on the film, along with interviews with ex-Kray gang member Tony Lambrianou and Robin Cook whose book, *The Crust on its Uppers* (1962), describes the coming together, in 1960s London, of a Chelsea bohemia with a criminal underworld.
24. See also Jon Savage, 'Tuning into Wonders', *Sight and Sound* (September 1995), pp. 24–5.
25. MacCabe, *Performance*, p. 15.
26. See Hill, '*Performance*: La Bohème', p. 25.

27. MacCabe, *Performance*, p. 40.
28. Ibid., p. 39.
29. Savage, 'Tuning', p. 24.
30. Gareth Stedman Jones, *Languages of Class: Studies in English Working Class History: 1832-1982* (Cambridge: Cambridge University Press, 1993), p. 228.
31. Hill, '*Performance*: La Bohème', p. 25.
32. Karl Marx, *The Eighteenth Brumaire of Louis Bonaparte*, translated by Terrell Carver, in Cowling and Martin (eds), *Marx's 'Eighteenth Brumaire'*, p. 63.
33. Karl Marx quoted in Tom Bottomore (ed.), *A Dictionary of Marxist Thought*, 2nd Edition (Oxford: Blackwell, 1991), p. 327.
34. Peter Stallybrass, 'Marx and Heterogeneity: Thinking the Lumpenproletariat', in Bob Jessop and Russell Wheatley (eds), *Karl Marx's Social and Political Thought: Critical Assessments: Second Series*, Vol 6, *Modes of Production, The World System, Classes and Class Struggle* (London: Routledge, 1999), p. 329.
35. MacCabe, *Performance*, p. 32.
36. Ibid., p. 75.
37. Ibid., p. 81.
38. Stallybrass, 'Marx', p. 349 and p. 355.
39. MacCabe, *Performance*, p. 82.
40. See Terry Eagleton, 'Defending the Free World', in Ralph Miliband and Leo Panitch (eds), *Socialist Register 1990: Retreat of the Intellectuals* (London: Merlin Press, 1990), p. 90.
41. Terry Eagleton, *Ideology: An Introduction* (London: Verso, 1991), p. 217.
42. Wood, *Democracy Against Capitalism*, p. 259.
43. Ibid., p. 259.
44. Peter Wollen, 'Possession', *Sight and Sound* (September 1995), p. 23.
45. MacCabe, *Performance*, p. 64.
46. Hill, '*Performance*: La Bohème', p. 26.
47. Ibid., p. 28.
48. Wollen, 'Possession', p. 23.
49. Ibid., p. 23
50. MacCabe notes that the location for Turner's house was Lowndes Square. See MacCabe, *Performance*, p. 51.
51. *Withnail and I* is situated further east than Notting Hill in the Camden/ Regents Park area; however, there is an excursion into Chelsea to visit Uncle Monty.
52. Wollen's identification with *Performance* makes an impression similar to the one conveyed in MacCabe's book. As the former puts it: 'It was our film—London, '68, the counterculture'. See Wollen, 'Possession', p. 23.
53. Hill, '*Performance*: La Bohème', pp. 28-9.
54. Wollen, 'Possession', p. 23.

55. Hill, '*Performance*: La Bohème', p. 33.

56. Ibid., p. 33.

57. Ibid., p. 31.

58. Ibid., pp. 30–1.

59. Ibid., p. 30.

60. Christopher Hill, *Puritanism and Revolution: Studies in Interpretation of the English Revolution of the 17th Century* (London: Penguin, 1990), p. 347.

61. Hill, '*Performance*: La Bohème', p. 32.

62. Ibid., p. 32.

63. Ibid., p. 32. See also Edward W. Said, *Culture and Imperialism*, (London: Chatto & Windus, 1993), pp. 95–116.

64. Franco Moretti, *Atlas of the European novel: 1800–1900* (London: Verso, 1998), pp. 24–6.

65. Ibid., p. 27.

66. On the history of British 'capitalist imperialism' see Wood, *Empire of Capital*, pp. 73–117.

67. MacCabe relates Cammell's unfulfilled desire to have the final shot of the film show Chas/Turner arriving in America, the 'Promised Land'. The white Rolls Royce was to enter Central Park and then, after a while, it would disappear into the New York horizon. MacCabe's comment on this unrealised end is to observe that its 'final moment of liberation breaks national boundaries'. See MacCabe, *Performance*, p. 80.

68. See Vladimir Propp, *The Morphology of the Folktale* (Austin: University of Texas Press, 1998).

69. MacCabe comments on this world when he notes how in the 1960s music inspired by 'African-American rhythms' 'burst out of the pubs and clubs of Liverpool, London and Newcastle'. See MacCabe, *Performance*, p. 17. The references to the 'black Atlantic' in MacCabe's study remain contextual rather than textual – they do not lead to a consideration of the role of Noel in the narrative or of his 'gig' in Liverpool. For more on the 'black Atlantic' see Paul Gilroy, *The Black Atlantic: Modernity and Double Consciousness* (London: Verso, 1993).

70. I was first alerted to the systematic nature of these looks by Peter Playdon's paper, 'Bastard Foreign Female' given at 'Cultural Studies and the Working Class Reconsidered', a conference held at the University of East London in January 2000.

71. MacCabe, *Performance*, pp. 78–9.

72. Hill, '*Performance*: La Bohème', p. 29.

73. Moretti, *Atlas*, p. 15n.

74. Wollen, 'Possession', p. 23.

75. See Kevin Jackson, *Withnail and I* (London: BFI, 2004).

76. See Martin Green, *Children of the Sun: A Narrative of 'Decadence' in England after 1918* (London: Pimlico, 2001). The same interwar cultural formation discussed in Green's book is on display in *Another Country*.

77. For a similar effect see the comic play around the name 'St. John' in the Rowan Atkinson cameo in *Four Weddings and a Funeral*.

78. On the tradition of the anonymous hero in English nineteenth-century literature see Moretti, *The Way of the World*, p. 191.

79. See the scenes in the Lake District pub, in particular the exchanges between the ex-army – officer class – landlord, the General (Noel Johnson) and the Poacher (Michael Elphick).

80. Bruce Robinson, *Withnail and I: The Original Screenplay* (London: Bloomsbury, 1995), p. 5.

81. Ibid., p. 18.

82. Prior to this scene Danny is ordered out of Marwood's bed. Beds in the film represent sexual fear and physical exhaustion. Marwood refuses, repeatedly, to share his bed.

83. This dilemma is summed up by Eagleton in his foreword to Kristin Ross's study of Rimbaud and the Paris Commune of 1871 in which he argues that the split between two necessary but apparently irreconcilable aspects of revolutionary insurrectionism – libertarian and Marxist – underlines the fact that there remains 'as yet no adequate political model to articulate these two vital moments in some persuasive way'. See Terry Eagleton, 'Foreword', in Kristin Ross, *The Emergence of Social Space: Rimbaud and the Paris Commune* (London and Minneapolis: Macmillan and the University of Minnesota Press, 1988), p. vii.

84. Sinfield quoted in Ellen Meiksins Wood, 'Capitalist Change and Generational Shifts', http://www.monthlyreview.org/1098wood.htm

85. Ibid.

86. Ibid.

87. Ibid.

88. J.K. Huysmans's *À Rebours* was first published in 1884 and was an important text for the Decadence movement in France and England. Robert Baldick describes the novel's hero Des Esseintes as an aesthete who yearns for 'solitude'. See Robert Baldick, 'Introduction', in J.K. Huysmans's *Against Nature* (London: Penguin, 1979), p. 11.

89. Jackson, *Withnail and I*, p. 78.

90. Alex Callinicos, *Against Postmodernism: A Marxist Critique* (Cambridge: Polity, 1989), p. 169.

91. Ibid., p. 171.

92. Ibid., p. 169. As Kevin Jackson notes, *Withnail and I* is an example of a '*Bildungsfilm*' – Dickens's *David Copperfield* follows Huysmans into Marwood's suitcase. We might add that Marwood's immaculate detachment fits with Moretti's reading of the English *bildungsroman*'s 'innocent' culture of capitalism. Marwood is destined for an idyll – maybe in a location further west than Camden, possibly even Notting Hill. See Jackson, *Withnail and I*, p. 11.

CHAPTER 6
THE PROBLEM OF ENGLAND: AESTHETICS OF
THE EVERYDAY

1. Keiller's earlier 16mm shorts include: *Stonebridge Park* (1981), *Norwood* (1983), *The End* (1986), *Valtos* (1987) and *The Clouds* (1989).
2. An interview with Robinson, *Time Out*, 8–15 January 1997, p. 69.
3. See Alex Callinicos, 'Tony Blair and the British Left', in Abigail B. Bakan and Eleanor Macdonald (eds), *Critical Political Studies: Debates and Dialogues from the Left*, (Montreal: McGill-Queen's University Press, 2002), p. 72.
4. See Nairn, *The Enchanted Glass*, pp. vii–xi.
5. See Keiller, *Robinson in Space*, p. 207.
6. Ibid., p. 211.
7. Ibid., p. 211.
8. Ibid., p. 229.
9. See Wood, *The Origin of Capitalism*, pp. 105–8.
10. Ellen Meiksins Wood and Neal Wood, *A Trumpet of Sedition: Political Theory and the Rise of Capitalism* (London: Pluto, 1997), p. 133.
11. Wood, *The Origin of Capitalism*, p. 106. See also Williams, *Keywords*, pp. 242–3.
12. Keiller, *Robinson in Space*, p. 228.
13. On the Tolpuddle Martyrs see Bill Douglas's *Comrades* (1987).
14. Martin J. Wiener, *English Culture and the Decline of the Industrial Spirit 1850–1980*, (Harmondsworth: Pelican, 1987) p. 52.
15. See Rubinstein, *Capitalism, Culture and Decline*, pp. 1–3.
16. Keiller, *Robinson in Space*, p. 233. See also Stallabrass, *High Art Lite*, p. 247.
17. Wood, *The Pristine Culture of Capitalism*, p. 11.
18. Charles Murray, 'Underclass: The Crisis Deepens', in Lister (ed.), *Charles Murray and the Underclass*, p. 109. See also Cowling, 'The Lumpenproletariat and Murray's Underclass', pp. 236–7.
19. Keiller, *Robinson in Space*, pp. 219–20.
20. In his written reflections on the film Keiller reminds us that during the time of the post-1979 Tory governments the UK economy remained the fifth largest in the world. See Patrick Keiller, *Robinson in Space*, p. 220. See also Patrick Keiller, 'Port Statistics', in Iain Borden and Joe Kerr (eds), *The Unknown City* (Cambridge, Massachusetts: MIT Press, 2000), p. 444.
21. The cataloguing of prisons and detention centres forms a motif in the film – see references to Campsfield House, Blakenhurst and the three prisons at Doncaster.
22. The narrator quotes the spokesman (George Monbiot): 'We are challenging the government's whole philosophy about the pre-eminence of property rights.'
23. See Iain Sinclair, *London Orbital: A Walk around the M25* (London: Granta, 2002), pp. 248–55.

24. See Brian Manning, *1649: The Crisis of the English Revolution* (London: Bookmarks, 1992) pp. 79–134.

25. See Hill, *Sex, Class and Realism*, pp. 60–1.

26. Higson, *Waving the Flag:* pp. 51–8. See also, Higson, 'Re-presenting the National Past', p. 115.

27. Higson, 'Re-presenting the National Past', p. 117.

28. Ibid., p. 119.

29. See Hewison, *The Heritage Industry*, p. 72.

30. On the heritage style see also Hill, *British Cinema in 1980s*, p. 81.

31. Hewison sees the column at West Green as an 'architectural emblem' of the process whereby the obsession with the past in heritage culture threatens to 'take over the present'. Hewison, *The Heritage Industry*, p. 79.

32. Ibid., pp. 141–2.

33. Ibid., p. 78.

34. Williams, *The Country and the City*, pp. 132–4.

35. Ibid., p. 132. See also Williams's comments on the 'values of the rural capitalist order' in *Politics and Letters: Interviews with New Left Review* (London: Verso, 1981), p. 312.

36. Williams, *The Country and the City*, p. 132.

37. Ibid., p. 132.

38. Ibid., pp. 132–3.

39. Ibid., p. 133.

40. Ibid., p. 133.

41. Ibid., p. 133.

42. Robert B. Ray, *How a Film Theory Got Lost and Other Mysteries in Cultural Studies* (Bloomington: Indiana University Press, 2001), p. 5.

43. Louis Aragon, in Patrick Keiller, 'Architectural Cinematography', in Kester Rattenbury (ed.), *This is not Architecture* (London: Routledge, 2002), p. 37.

44. Patrick Keiller, Interviewed by Anna Price, *Artifice* 1 (1994), University College London, p. 34. Keiller also describes this subjectivity in terms of the 'state of mind' implied in Walter Benjamin's description of Marseilles. See Keiller, 'Architectural Cinematography', p. 39.

45. Claire Barwell, 'Flaneur of London/Interview with Patrick Keiller', *Pix* (January 1997), p. 165. Note that there is an unattributed reference to Tom Nairn's book on the English monarchy here. The phrase 'the glamour of backwardness' is the title for the third section of Nairn's *The Enchanted Glass*, pp. 213–324.

46. Keiller, 'Architectural Cinematography', p. 38.

47. Ibid., p. 38.

48. Ibid., p. 38.

49. Ibid., p. 41.

50. Bill Nichols, *Blurred Boundaries: Questions of Meaning in Contemporary Culture* (Bloomington: Indiana University Press, 1994), pp. 92–106.

51. Ibid., pp. 92–5.

52. Ibid., pp. 100–3.

53. Ibid., p. 104.

54. Nichols's five modes of documentary representation are: expository, observational, interactive, reflexive and performative. See Nichols, ibid., pp. 92–106.

55. Ibid., p. 102. In an interview with David Martin Jones, Keiller comments that he is 'fairly sceptical' about the 'redemptive potential' of 'subjective transformation'. See Patrick Keiller, Interviewed by David Martin Jones, *Journal of Popular British Cinema*, 5 (2002), p. 127.

56. Patrick Keiller, 'The Poetic Experience of Townscape and Landscape, and Some Ways of Depicting It', *Undercut*, 3/4 (March 1982), pp. 42–8.

57. Ibid., p. 45. In 'A Short History of Photography', Walter Benjamin argued that Atget was a precursor to the surrealists. See Walter Benjamin, *One Way Street and Other Writings* (London: NLB, 1979), pp. 249–51.

58. Keiller, 'The Poetic', p. 45.

59. Ibid., p. 45.

60. See Rodney Mace, *Trafalgar: Emblem of Empire* (London: Lawrence & Wishart, 1976).

61. Ian Christie, *A Matter of Life and Death* (London: BFI, 2000), p. 78.

62. Interview with the author, 18 April 2002.

63. See Michael E. Gardiner, *Critiques of Everyday Life* (London: Routledge, 2000).

64. A. Kaplan and K. Ross, 'Introduction', *Yale French Studies*, 73 (1987), p. 3.

65. Patrick Keiller, 'Photogenie', *Cambridge Architecture Journal*, 8 (1996/7), pp. 44–5.

66. Jakobson, quoted in Keiller, ibid., p. 44.

67. As the narrator in *Robinson in Space* puts it in the opening statement of the film quoting from the situationist Raoul Vaneigem's *The Revolution of Everyday Life* (Seattle: Left Bank Books, 1983). See Keiller, *Robinson in Space*, p. 1.

68. Keiller, *Robinson in Space*, pp. 250–3.

69. Michael Tarantino, 'Richard Billingham: A Short, By No Means Exhaustive Glossary', in *Richard Billingham* (Birmingham: Ikon Gallery, 2000), p. 85.

70. Stallabrass, *High Art Lite* p. 253.

71. Ibid., pp. 251–2.

72. Ibid., p. 252.

73. Tarantino, 'Richard Billingham', p. 87

74. Stallabrass, *High Art Lite*, pp. 127–69.

75. Charles Murray, 'Rejoinder', in Lister (ed.), *Charles Murray and the Underclass*, p. 82.

76. Kristin Ross, 'French Quotidian', in Lynn Gumpert (ed.), *The Art of the Everyday: The Quotidian in French Post-War Culture* (New York: New York University Press, 1997), p. 25.

77. Keiller, Interviewed by David Martin Jones, p. 127.

78. See Kristin Ross, *Fast Cars, Clean Bodies: Decolonisation and the Re-ordering of French Culture* (Cambridge, Massachusetts: MIT Press, 1996).

79. As the narrator puts it in *Robinson in Space*: 'Everything is changed into something else in my imagination, then the dead weight of things changes it back into what it was in the first place. A bridge between the imagination and reality must be built...'

80. Gardiner, *Critiques of Everyday Life*, pp. 157–79. See also, Michel de Certeau, *The Practice of Everyday Life* (Berkeley: University of California Press, 1988), pp. 29–42, and Keiller, *Robinson in Space*, p. 2.

81. Wood, *The Origin of Capitalism*, p. 183.

82. Gardiner, *Critiques of Everyday Life*, p. 15.

83. Anthony Easthope, *Englishness and National Culture* (London: Routledge, 1999).

84. Ibid., p. 107.

85. Ibid., p. 107.

86. See for instance N. Andrews, *Financial Times*, 9 January 1997, p. 21.

87. Easthope, *Englishness*, pp. 109–10.

88. Gardiner, *Critiques of Everyday Life*, p. 22.

89. Interview with the author, 18 April 2002.

90. Patrick Keiller, 'Popular Science', in *Landscape* (British Council Catalogue, 2000), p. 64.

91. Keiller, Interviewed by David Martin Jones, p. 127. Keiller finds Certeau 'more sympathetic' because he relies less on 'the idea of radical subjectivity'.

92. Ibid., p. 128.

93. Robinson is a member of NATFHE; however, the union seems unable to prevent him losing his job. As an academic part-timer, Robinson's relationship to the union is likely to have been tenuous. It has only been since the late 1990s that unions such as NATFHE have attempted to catch up with the changes brought about by the casualisation of much teaching in the expanded British Higher Education sector.

94. Keiller, 'Popular Science', p. 61.

95. Ibid., p. 62.

96. Ibid., p. 63.

97. Keiller, 'Port Statistics', pp. 453–4.

98. Keiller, 'Popular Science', p. 66.

99. Keiller, 'Port Statistics', p. 456.

100. *The Dilapidated Dwelling* has not yet been transmitted by its commissioning television station, Channel 4.

101. Keiller, Interviewed by David Martin Jones, p. 130.

102. Partrick Keiller, 'The Dilapidated Dwelling', *Architectural Design*, 68 (7–8) (1998), p. 22.

103. Ibid., p. 22.
104. Ibid., p. 27.
105. Keiller, Interviewed by David Martin Jones, p. 128.
106. Patrick Keiller, 'London in the Early 90s', in Kerr and Gibson (eds), *London*, pp. 353–61.
107. Ibid., p. 355.
108. Ibid., p. 357.
109. Dave, 'Heritage Cinema', p. 122.
110. Keiller, 'London in the Early 90s', p. 359.
111. See Wood, *The Pristine Culture of Capitalism*, p. 108.
112. Wood, quoted in Keiller, 'London', p. 359.
113. Ibid., p. 359.
114. Ibid., p. 360.
115. Ibid., p. 360.
116. Ibid., p. 360.
117. Ibid., p. 360.
118. Wayne, 'Working Title Mark II'
119. Ibid.

CHAPTER 7
PECULIAR CAPITALISM: OCCULT HERITAGE

1. On the 'terminus films' of the 90s see Bromley, 'The Theme', p. 64.
2. Tony Peake, *Derek Jarman* (London: Abacus, 1999), p. 249.
3. Michael O'Pray, *Derek Jarman: Dreams of England* (London: BFI, 1996), p. 108.
4. Fredric Jameson, 'Postmodernism, or the Cultural Logic of Late Capital', *New Left Review*, 146 (July/August), 1984, p. 53.
5. O'Pray, *Derek Jarman*, p. 104.
6. Phil Baker, 'Secret City: Psychogeography and the End of London', in Kerr and Gibson (eds), *London*, p. 330.
7. Iain Sinclair in *The Verbals: Kevin Jackson in Conversation with Iain Sinclair* (Tonbridge: Worple Press, 2003), p. 135.
8. See Walter Benjamin, *The Arcades Project*, translated by Howard Eiland and Kevin McLaughlin (Cambridge, Massachusetts: The Belknap Press of Harvard University, 1999), p. 462.
9. Walter Benjamin, *Illuminations*, translated by Harry Zohn (ed.) Hanah Arendt (London: Fontana/Collins, 1982), p. 257.
10. Iain Sinclair, *Downriver: (Or the Vessels of Wrath) A Narrative in Twelve Tales* (London: Paladin, 1992), p. 265.
11. Baker, 'Secret City', p. 325.

12. Ibid., p. 328.

13. See Iain Sinclair, *Lud Heat and Suicide Bridge* (London: Vintage, 1995) and Patrick Wright, *A Journey Through Ruins: The Last Days of London* (London: Radius, 1991), pp. 164–5.

14. Wright, *A Journey*, p. 165.

15. Ibid., p. 164.

16. Sinclair, *London Orbital*, p. 404.

17. Originally transmitted by London Weekend Television, 19 December, 1993. The text is included in Peter Ackroyd, *The Collection* (Chatto & Windus: London, 2001), pp. 341–51.

18. Ibid., p. 350.

19. Peter Ackroyd, *Albion: The Origins of The English Imagination* (London: Chatto & Windus, 2002), p. 307.

20. Ackroyd, *The Collection*, p. 342.

21. Peter Ackroyd, *London: The Biography* (London: Chatto & Windus, 2000) pp. 11–13.

22. Ibid., pp. 18–19. Sinclair discusses the London Stone in *Lights Out for the Territory*, see p. 102 and p. 116.

23. Ackroyd, *London*, p. 19

24. Steve Beard gives the London Stone twenty-four descriptions in his novel *Digital Leatherette* (Hove: Codex, 1999). See Beard, pp. 97–8.

25. Wood points out that in the 'commercialisation model' the profit generated in pre-capitalist trading practices from the activity of the merchant's mediatory role between separate markets – 'profit on alienation' or buying cheap here, selling dear there – is superimposed upon a very different kind of profit-making in capitalism which is dependent on historically unique social relations of production. See Wood, *The Origin of Capitalism*, p. 79.

26. Sinclair, *Lights Out*, p. 301.

27. Iain Sinclair, *Sorry Meniscus: Excursions to the Millennium Dome* (London: Profile Books, 1999), p. 47.

28. Ibid., p. 47.

29. Alan Moore and Eddie Campbell, *From Hell: Being a Melodrama in Sixteen Parts* (London: Knockabout Comics, 1989). In particular see Chapter 4, 'What doth the Lord Require of Thee?'. See also Iain Sinclair, *White Chappell: Scarlet Tracings* (London: Paladin, 1988); E.O. Gordon, *Prehistoric London: Its Mounds and Circles* (London: Covenant, 1925); Stewart Home, 'Smash the Occult Establishment', *The London Psychogeographical Association Newsletter*, Issue 6; and John Michell, *The New View Over Atlantis* (London: Thames and Hudson, 1983).

30. Iain Sinclair, 'Jack the Rip-Off', *Observer Review*, 27 January 2002, p. 8. Judy Dench's Queen Victoria is to be found in *Mrs. Brown* (1997).

31. On Home see Sinclair, *Lights Out*, pp. 220–31.

32. Sinclair, *Lights Out*, p. 26.

33. See Ellen Meiksins Wood, 'The non-history of capitalism', *Historical Materialism*, 1 (1997), pp. 5-19. The 'commercialisation model' of capitalism is an example of such 'non-history'.
34. Nairn, *The Enchanted Glass*, pp. 260-8.
35. Sinclair, *London Orbital*, p. 134.
36. Roger Luckhurst, 'Occult London', in Kerr and Gibson, *London*, pp. 335-40.
37. Ibid., p. 335-6.
38. For Luckhurst, Thatcher's act of abolishing municipal socialism has hardly been reversed by New Labour's changes to the capital's governance.
39. See Iain Sinclair in conversation with Kevin Jackson, *The Verbals*, p. 67.
40. It does need to be recognised that the Jarman home movies evoke a sense of painful nostalgia for the familial past and at the same time offer a critique of the national past – catching as they do evidence of the late imperial moment. Equally, however, in contrast to the vision of urban destruction and decay in the film, these images speak of Jarman's sense of the sacrifices of his parents' generation and his identification of that generation with the promise of the post-war welfare state which, he argued, was being destroyed by the 'gangsters' of the New Right. See Lawrence Driscoll, 'The Rose Revived: Derek Jarman and the British Tradition', in C. Lippard (ed.), *By Angels Driven: The Films of Derek Jarman* (Trowbridge: Flicks Books, 1996), p. 71.
41. Sinclair, 'Paperback writer', *Guardian Review* 25 October 2003, p. 31.
42. See Esther Leslie, 'Documents of Revolution, Incompetence and Resistance', *Film International*, 10 (2004), pp. 26-37.
43. Ackroyd, *London*, p. xvi.
44. Franco Moretti, *Signs Taken for Wonders* (London: Verso, 1988), pp. 90-91.
45. Marx quoted in Moretti, ibid., p. 91.
46. Moretti, ibid., pp. 91-2.
47. Ackroyd, *London*, p. 779.
48. A book which was later to become the film *Essex Boys* (2000).
49. Wood, *The Retreat from Class*, p. 113.
50. Sinclair, *London Orbital*, p. 413.
51. O'Pray, *Derek Jarman*, p. 104.
52. Ibid., p. 12.
53. See Paulin, *The Faber Book of Political Verse*, p. 16.
54. Jon Mee argues that this tradition remained available to Blake in the popular culture of the eighteenth century. See Jon Mee, 'Is there an Antinomion in the House? William Blake and the After-Life of a Heresy', in Steve Clark and David Worrall (eds), *Historicising Blake* (London: St. Martin's Press, 1994), p. 55. See also, A.L. Morton, *The Everlasting Gospel: A Study in the Sources of William Blake* (London: Lawrence & Wishart, 1958); E.P. Thompson, *Witness Against the Beast: William Blake and the Moral Law* (Cambridge: Cambridge University Press, 1993); Christopher Hill, *The English Bible and the Seventeenth-Century Revolution* (London: Penguin, 1993), p. 444, and

Christopher Hill, 'Radical Pirates?', in Margaret C. Jacob and James R. Jacob (eds), *The Origins of Anglo-American Radicalism* (New Jersey: Humanities Press, 1991), pp. 19–34.

55. Cromwell quoted in O'Pray, *Derek Jarman*, p. 159.

56. Ibid., p. 96.

57. Driscoll, 'The Rose', p. 77.

58. Jon Mee, *Dangerous Enthusiasm: William Blake and the Culture of Radicalism in the 1790s* (Oxford: The Clarendon Press, 1992), p. 27.

59. Robert Lowth quoted in Mee, ibid., p. 24.

60. See Hill, *British Cinema in the 1980s*, p. 161.

61. Mee, *Dangerous Enthusiasm*, pp. 37–8.

62. Ibid., p. 30.

63. Ibid., pp. 31–2.

64. Driscoll, 'The Rose', pp. 65–7.

65. Alan Sinfield, *Literature, Politics and Culture in Postwar Britain* (Oxford: Blackwell, 1993) p. 40.

66. Steven Dillon, *Derek Jarman and Lyric Film:The Mirror and the Sea* (Austin: Texas University Press, 2004), p. 164.

67. Cannadine, 'The Context, Performance and Meaning of Ritual', pp. 101–64.

68. Peter Linebaugh, 'A Little Jubilee? The Literacy of Robert Wedderburn in 1817', in John Rule and Robert Malcolmson (eds), *Protest and Survival: The Historical Experience* (London:The Merlin Press, 1993), p. 212. See also Linebaugh and Rediker, *The Many-Headed Hydra*, pp. 287–326.

69. Linebaugh, 'A Little Jubilee', p. 212.

70. Linebaugh and Rediker, *The Many-Headed Hydra*, pp. 287–326.

71. Driscoll, 'The Rose', p. 78.

72. Mee, *Dangerous Enthusiasm*, p. 72.

73. Mee is referring here to Dissenters such as Richard Price and Joseph Priestley. See Mee, ibid., p. 20.

74. Ibid., p. 28. Thus for Mee, Blake is closer to figures such as Richard Brothers and Thomas Spence whose visionary prophetical enthusiasm and plebeian audiences distinguished them from 'respectable' Dissent. See Mee, p. 20.

75. Linebaugh and Rediker, *The Many-Headed Hydra*, p. 351.

76. See Driscoll, *Dangerous Enthusiasm*, pp. 74–5.

77. See Wood and Wood, *A Trumpet of Sedition*, pp. 131–4.

78. Patricia Seed, *Ceremonies of Possession in Europe's Conquest of the New World, 1492–1640* (Cambridge: Cambridge University Press, 1995), p. 27.

79. The subtitle of Tom Vague's account of the English situationist movement (known as King Mob) is 'From Gordon Riots to Situationists and Sex Pistols'. See Tom Vague, *King Mob Echo* (London: Dark Star, 2000). See also Tom Vague, 'London Calling', *Dazed and Confused*, 42 (May 1998), pp. 99–103. For an account dismissing the situationist/punk link see Stewart Home, *Cranked-Up Really High* (Hove: Codex, 1995).

80. At this time the film was entitled *History of Oxford Street*. See Jon Savage, *England's Dreaming: Sex Pistols and Punk Rock* (London: Faber & Faber, 1991), pp. 37–44.

81. See Vague, *King Mob Echo*, p. 53.

82. McLaren and Reid, in Vague, ibid., p. 53.

83. See George Rudé, *Paris and London in the Eighteenth Century: Studies in Popular Protest* (London: Fontana/Collins, 1974), pp. 268–92.

84. McLaren and Reid, in Vague, *King Mob Echo*, p. 56. Vague dates the treatment April 1971.

85. See Douglas Hay, Peter Linebaugh, John G. Rule, E.P. Thompson and Cal Winslow (eds), *Albion's Fatal Tree: Crime and Society in Eighteenth-Century England* (London: Penguin, 1975), pp. 65–117. See also Peter Linebaugh, *The London Hanged: Crime and Civil Society in the Eighteenth Century* (London: Penguin, 1991).

86. See David V. Erdman, *Prophet Against Empire* (New York: Dover Publications, 1977), pp. 462–7.

87. Ibid., p. 464.

88. Ibid., p. 464.

89. In 1781 Lord George Gordon was charged with inciting the rioters of June 1780. Tried for high treason in 1781 he was, however, acquitted.

90. Gordon is described as defending 'Newgate prisoners, Botany Bay convicts, and vagabond blacks' in *The Times*. See Douglas Hay, 'The Laws of God and the Laws of Man: Lord George Gordon and the Death Penalty', in Rule and Malcolmson, *Protest and Survival*, p. 72.

91. Hay indicates that the source for Spence was Leviticus 25. See Hay, ibid., p. 85.

92. Vague, *King Mob Echo*, p. 57.

93. Driscoll, 'The Rose', p. 70

94. Isaac Julien and Colin MacCabe, *Diary of a Young Soul Rebel* (London: BFI, 1991), p. 1.

95. Ibid., p. 1.

96. Ibid., p. 136.

97. Ibid., p. 2.

98. Ibid., pp. 1–2.

99. Ibid., p. 2. Clio Barnard's evocative short film *Lambeth Marsh* (2000) opens up Brixton, London to a migrant Atlantic through the work of Blake.

100. See Peter Ackroyd, *Blake* (London: Sinclair-Stevenson, 1995), pp. 74–5.

101. Linebaugh, *The London Hanged*, p. 368.

102. Erdman argues that Albion's dance is a Blakean reversal of Edmund Burke's judgement on the Gordon Riots and the French Revolution. Burke saw both as a kind of 'death-dance of democratic revolution'. In Blake's transvaluation of Burke, the Riots represent a 'dance of insurrection (apocalyptic self-sacrifice) to save the Nations'. See Erdman, *Prophet*, pp. 10–11.

EPILOGUE
'AND THEN WHAT?'

1. Comaroff and Comaroff, *Millennial Capitalism*, p. 5.
2. Andy Medhurst, 'Mike Leigh: Beyond Embarrassment', *Sight and Sound* (November 1993), p. 11.
3. Judith Williamson, 'Changing Images', in Beynon and Rowbothan, *Looking at Class*, p. 99.
4. Baker, 'Secret City', p. 332.
5. Brooker, 'England's Screening'.

Index